Routledge Guides to the Great Books

The Routledge Guidebook to Kierkegaard's *Fear and Trembling*

Søren Kierkegaard is one of the key figures of nineteenth-century thought, whose influence on subsequent philosophy, theology and literature is both extensive and profound. *Fear and Trembling*, which investigates the nature of faith through an exploration of the story of Abraham and Isaac, is one of Kierkegaard's most compelling and widely read works. It combines an arresting narrative, an unorthodox literary structure and a fascinating account of faith and its relation to 'the ethical'.

The Routledge Guidebook to Kierkegaard's *Fear and Trembling* introduces and assesses:

- Kierkegaard's life and the background to *Fear and Trembling*, including aspects of its philosophical and theological context;
- the text and key ideas of *Fear and Trembling*, including the details of its account of faith and its connection to trust and hope;
- the book's reception history, the diversity of interpretations it has been given and its continuing interest and importance.

This Guidebook assumes no previous knowledge of Kierkegaard's work and will be essential reading for anyone studying the most famous text of this important thinker.

John Lippitt is Professor of Ethics and Philosophy of Religion at the University of Hertfordshire in the UK and Honorary Professor of Philosophy at Deakin University, Australia. He is the author of *Kierkegaard and the Problem of Self-Love* (2013) and *Humour and Irony in Kierkegaard's Thought* (2000) as well as co-editor of *Narrative, Identity and the Kierkegaardian Self* (2015) and *The Oxford Handbook of Kierkegaard* (2013).

THE ROUTLEDGE GUIDES TO THE GREAT BOOKS
Series Editor: Anthony Gottlieb

The Routledge Guides to the Great Books provide ideal introductions to the work of the most brilliant thinkers of all time, from Aristotle to Marx and Newton to Wollstonecraft. At the core of each Guidebook is a detailed examination of the central ideas and arguments expounded in the great book. This is bookended by an opening discussion of the context within which the work was written and a closing look at the lasting significance of the text. *The Routledge Guides to the Great Books* therefore provide students everywhere with complete introductions to the most important, influential and innovative books of all time.

Available:

Einstein's Relativity James Trefil
Gramsci's Prison Notebooks John Schwarzmantel
Thoreau's Civil Disobedience Bob Pepperman Taylor
Descartes' Meditations Gary Hatfield
Hobbes' Leviathan Glen Newey
Galileo's Dialogue Maurice A. Finocchiaro
Wittgenstein's Philosophical Investigations Marie McGinn
Aristotle's Nicomachean Ethics Gerard J. Hughes
Heidegger's Being and Time Stephen Mulhall
Hegel's Phenomenology of Spirit Robert Stern
Locke's Essay Concerning Human Understanding E. J. Lowe
Plato's Republic Nickolas Pappas
Wollstonecraft's A Vindication of the Rights of Woman Sandrine Bergès
Kierkegaard's Fear and Trembling John Lippitt

Forthcoming:

De Beauvoir's The Second Sex Nancy Bauer
Paine's Rights of Man Frances Chiu
Aquinas' Summa Theologiae Jason Eberl
Machiavelli's The Prince John Scott
Gibbon's History of the Decline and Fall of the Roman Empire David Womersley

Foucault's History of Sexuality Chloe Taylor
Fanon's Wretched of the Earth Jean Khalfa
Jacobs' Death and Life of Great American Cities Peter Laurence
Weber's Protestant Ethic and the Spirit of Capitalism David Chalcraft
Augustine's Confessions Catherine Conybeare

Routledge Guides to the Great Books

The Routledge Guidebook to Kierkegaard's *Fear and Trembling*

John Lippitt

LONDON AND NEW YORK

First published as *The Routledge Philosophy Guidebook to
Kierkegaard and Fear and Trembling*, 2003
This edition published as *The Routledge Guidebook to Kierkegaard's
Fear and Trembling*, 2016
by Routledge
2 Park Square, Milton Park, Abingdon, OX14 4RN

and by Routledge
711 Third Avenue, New York, NY 10017

Routledge is an imprint of the Taylor & Francis Group, an informa business

© 2003, 2016 John Lippitt

The right of John Lippitt to be identified as the author of this work has been
asserted by him in accordance with sections 77 and 78 of the Copyright, Designs and
Patents Act 1988.

All rights reserved. No part of this book may be reprinted or
reproduced or utilised in any form or by any electronic, mechanical, or other means, now
known or hereafter invented, including photocopying and recording, or in any information
storage or retrieval system,
without permission in writing from the publishers.

Trademark notice: Product or corporate names may be trademarks or registered
trademarks, and are used only for identification and
explanation without intent to infringe.

British Library Cataloguing in Publication Data
A catalogue record for this book is available from the British Library

Library of Congress Cataloging in Publication Data
Lippitt, John.
[Routledge philosophy guidebook to Kierkegaard and Fear and Trembling]
The Routledge guidebook to Kierkegaard's Fear and Trembling /
John Lippitt. -- 1 [edition].
pages cm. -- (The Routledge guides to the great books)
Rev. ed. of: Routledge philosophy guidebook to Kierkegaard and Fear and
Trembling. 2003.
Includes bibliographical references and index.
1. Kierkegaard, Søren, 1813-1855. Frygt og bæven. 2. Christianity--Philosophy. I. Title.
B4373.F793K54 2015
198'.9--dc23
2015014092

ISBN: 978-0-415-70718-3 (hbk)
ISBN: 978-0-415-70720-6 (pbk)
ISBN: 978-1-315-67369-1 (ebk)

Typeset in Garamond
by Taylor & Francis Books

For Sylvie, in shared hope

Contents

Series editor's preface	xii
Preface to the second edition	xiii
Acknowledgements	xvi
Reference key to Kierkegaard's texts	xviii
Key to commonly used editions of *Fear and Trembling*	xxii

1 Introduction — 1
Kierkegaard's life and works — 2
Søren and Regine — 5
Kierkegaard's methodology: indirect communication and the pseudonyms — 8
Abraham and Isaac — 11
Plan of the book — 15

2 Tuning up: 'Preface', 'Attunement' and 'Speech in Praise of Abraham' — **20**
Preface — 20
Attunement — 24
Speech in Praise of Abraham — 32

3 Infinite resignation and faith: the 'Preamble from the Heart'	**40**
Tragic heroism and infinite resignation: a preamble	45
Infinite resignation and faith	47
The lad and his princess	50
What is the connection between faith and infinite resignation?	57
What does Abraham believe at the point of drawing the knife?	73
4 Suspending the ethical: Problemata I and II	**88**
Problema I: is there a teleological suspension of the ethical?	88
Problema II: is there an absolute duty to God?	110
Summary	114
5 The sound of silence: Problema III	**119**
Four poetic personages	124
Returning to Abraham	138
Epilogue	142
6 What is *Fear and Trembling* really about?	**146**
Introducing its reception history	147
Lévinas: against Kierkegaard's 'violence'	150
Tarquin's poppies	152
A message to Regine?	153
A call to commitment: theological shock treatment	155
The psychology of faith	156
Norms in the Christian life	156
Mooney: ethics, dilemma and subjectivity	164
Derrida: sacrificing ethics	171
'It's not about ethics!' A dissenting voice	173
Faith, 'eschatological' trust and 'radical' hope	175
Fear and Trembling's hidden Christianity?	196
Conclusion	206

7	**How reliable is Johannes de silentio?**	**220**
	Daniel Conway and Andrew Cross: Johannes' evasion	221
	Stephen Mulhall: Johannes and the literal	237
	Conclusion	249
	Bibliography	255
	Index	265

SERIES EDITOR'S PREFACE

'The past is a foreign country', wrote a British novelist, L. P. Hartley, 'they do things differently there.' The greatest books in the canon of the humanities and sciences can be foreign territory, too. This series of guidebooks is a set of excursions written by expert guides who know how to make such places become more familiar.

All the books covered in this series, however long ago they were written, have much to say to us now, or help to explain the ways in which we have come to think about the world. Each volume is designed not only to describe a set of ideas, and how they developed, but also to evaluate them. This requires what one might call a bifocal approach. To engage fully with an author, one has to pretend that he or she is speaking to us, but to understand a text's meaning, it is often necessary to remember its original audience too. It is all too easy to mistake the intentions of an old argument by treating it as a contemporary one.

The Routledge Guides to the Great Books are aimed at students in the broadest sense, not only those engaged in formal study. The intended audience of the series is all those who want to understand the books that have had the largest effects.

AJG, October 2012

PREFACE TO THE SECOND EDITION

It is a strange experience to return to a book written over twelve years ago to work on a second edition. And a decidedly mixed one: I have found a combination of things I still think I got more or less right and things that seem obvious to me now that did not seem so then. I have taken seriously the idea that this is a revised edition of an existing book rather than an entirely new book. Thus, I have sought to update and expand the first edition rather than asking myself how I might have approached this job if I were starting, from scratch, to write a first edition now.

The five readers' reports on the first edition solicited by Routledge were all useful, some of them enormously so, and have helped considerably in shaping the rewriting. Their judgements about the first edition were positive and encouraging, and they were unanimous that the basic structure and layout of the book worked well and should not be altered. I have taken this advice, sticking to the same chapter structure as before but making various alterations to each chapter. The readers made various suggestions about what sections might be added, though adopting all of these would have led to a book at least twice as long as the original: hardly desirable for a Guidebook. I have therefore adopted some but not all of these suggestions. The changes I have made are mostly of two kinds.

There is, throughout the book, reworked material which I have aimed to bring into dialogue with some key developments in the secondary literature (and various other thoughts) since the first edition was published in 2003. Second, there are several portions of entirely new material. The most substantial of these latter are to be found in Chapter 3 (to account for the fact that my view of the relationship between 'faith' and 'infinite resignation' has changed) and, especially and relatedly, in the greatly expanded Chapter 6, where I have added a new section on faith as 'eschatological trust' (John Davenport's phrase) and 'radical hope' (where I draw on Jonathan Lear's use of that phrase, connecting this with Kierkegaard's 1843 'upbuilding' discourse 'The Expectancy of Faith', published five months before *Fear and Trembling*). In Chapter 6, I have also added an updated section on 'divine command ethics' in relation to *Fear and Trembling* and a brief section near the start giving something of the 'reception history' of the text, saying a little about figures as diverse as Kafka, Sartre and Lukács, to underline the sheer diversity of ways in which it has been read. Finally, I have shifted my position somewhat on part of the debate in Chapter 7, in a way that will be apparent at the appropriate point.

In total, this new edition is over a quarter as long again as the first edition. Nevertheless, the upper word limit wisely set by Routledge has led to some tough choices. I would have liked to engage with more of the recent secondary literature than space has allowed (though I do think there are limits to how much of this is desirable in a book of this sort, which seeks to orient readers new to the text as well as hopefully having something of interest for more experienced scholars). Some of the notes aim to point the reader in the direction of potentially helpful further reading. And although I have not axed substantial sections of the first edition, I have cut (from the original Chapter 6) some material on virtue ethics which several readers of the first edition report having liked. However, I have replaced this relatively general discussion of virtue ethics with more specific discussion of virtue-terms such as trust and hope in the life of faith, which I hope more than makes up for it.

Given the recommendation to keep the basic structure intact, I considered that it would be artificial to add a further section on 'the lasting significance of the book' at the very end. This significance is, in my view, best inferred from the discussion throughout (though perhaps especially from Chapter 6). Indeed, it is characteristic of my approach that, while I hope not unmindful of Kierkegaard's historical context where significant, I am predominantly interested in 'past thought as living argument'.

For comments on translations see the Reference Key to Kierkegaard's Texts on p. xviii.

Acknowledgements

Looking back at the Acknowledgements page in the first edition, I am struck by how many of those people I thanked for their help then have now been dialogue partners over many years. So I have special pleasure in thanking once again Brendan Larvor, Hugh Pyper and Anthony Rudd. Over the intervening years, more new interlocutors on Kierkegaardian matters have emerged than I can name here – including the many students who, over two decades now, have served as a regular reminder of *Fear and Trembling*'s ability to impact on the imagination. But I must also make special mention of Niels Jørgen Cappelørn, Clare Carlisle, Dan Conway, John Davenport, Steve and Jan Evans, Jamie Ferreira, Rick Furtak, Sharon Krishek, Ed Mooney, Paul Muench, Jack Mulder, George Pattison, Kyle Roberts, Steve Shakespeare and Patrick Stokes. I would also like to thank Alastair Hannay and Sylvia Walsh for their valuable help with my niggling questions about various choices each of them made in their respective translations.

Thanks to all at Routledge who helped to shepherd this book, in both versions, through to publication and to the five reviewers whose helpful comments on the first edition I remark upon in the Preface. (Officially all were anonymous, but often one can guess ...)

I am also grateful to the University of Hertfordshire for the period of research leave that has enabled me to work on revising this manuscript, and to the Community of Mary and Martha at Sheldon, Devon, the inspiring setting in which some of the final stages were completed.

In the first edition, I thanked Gordon Marino and Cynthia Lund of the Hong Kierkegaard Library at St Olaf College (Northfield, Minnesota) for the fabulous support that institution makes available to visiting Kierkegaard scholars. This book is scheduled to appear in the year that Cynthia takes a well-earned retirement. Like many others, I can't quite imagine the world of Kierkegaard scholarship without her.

Some of the material in Chapter 6 is developed from my essay 'Learning to Hope: The Role of Hope in *Fear and Trembling*', in Daniel Conway (ed.), *Kierkegaard's Fear and Trembling: A Critical Guide* (Cambridge University Press, 2015). I am grateful to the editor and publisher for kind permission to include this material here. I am also grateful to Dan for sharing with me the proofs of this collection before its publication so that I could incorporate into my discussion here mention of several of the articles in that valuable volume.

As noted in the first edition, some of the material in Chapter 3 was developed from part of my 'Nietzsche, Kierkegaard and the Narratives of Faith', in John Lippitt and Jim Urpeth (eds), *Nietzsche and the Divine* (Manchester: Clinamen, 2000) – again, used with kind permission.

Finally, my thanks once again to my parents, Pat and Ken, and to the ever-supportive Sylvie, who, by the time this book appears in print, will be my wife, and who really has enabled hope to triumph over experience.

REFERENCE KEY TO KIERKEGAARD'S TEXTS

The standard edition of Kierkegaard's works in Danish is now the series *Søren Kierkegaards Skrifter* (SKS) [*Søren Kierkegaard's Writings*] (vols. I–XXVIII and K1–28, edited by Niels Jørgen Cappelørn et al., Copenhagen: Gads Forlag, 1997–2014). *Fear and Trembling* [*Frygt og Bæven*] is part of vol. IV. The series is also available online at www.sks.dk.

Several English translations of *Fear and Trembling* are now in common use. In this book, I have quoted primarily (though not exclusively) from Alastair Hannay's widely available Penguin Classics translation (Harmondsworth: Penguin, 1985), still probably the edition most commonly used for classroom purposes. Page numbers of quotations refer to this edition. However, since the first edition of this Guidebook came out, another fine translation has been published, by Sylvia Walsh (Cambridge: Cambridge University Press, 2006), with a useful introduction by C. Stephen Evans, which gives a helpful overview of the text. Walsh's translation also has very good footnotes, especially useful for readers likely to miss Johannes' many *en passant* biblical allusions. I have also extensively consulted this translation, along with SKS. I have occasionally amended Hannay's translation, and sometimes commented in the endnotes where issues of translation seem to me particularly significant (or just interesting for some reason).

Probably the other most commonly used English translation is that by Howard V. Hong and Edna H. Hong, in a volume containing both *Fear and Trembling* and *Repetition* (Princeton, NJ: Princeton University Press, 1983). Matters are further complicated by the fact that Hannay's translation has also been reissued in Penguin Books' 'Great Ideas' series, though without the translator's helpful introduction, and, thus, with different pagination. Although it is the norm in contemporary Kierkegaard scholarship to give page numbers to SKS as well as the translation being used, I have – given the nature of this series – respected the wishes of the publisher to refer only to page numbers of the English translation. However, since several translations are in widespread use, I have included a 'Key to Commonly Used Editions' in which can be found the different ways the sections of the text are translated (along with the original Danish) and the page numbers of SKS and the different translations compared. Since most of *Fear and Trembling*'s sections are relatively short (with the notable exception of the third Problema), I hope this will help readers wishing to locate particular pieces of text in a different translation to do so.

Fear and Trembling is cited as FT. Otherwise, the English translations I have used are mostly from the *Kierkegaard's Writings* series. Numerical references in relation to Kierkegaard's texts are to page numbers. Texts from which I explicitly quote, and the sigla used, are detailed below:

CUP   *Concluding Unscientific Postscript*, trans. Howard V. Hong and Edna H. Hong, 2 vols., Princeton, NJ: Princeton University Press, 1992. All references are to the first volume unless otherwise stated.
EO   *Either/Or*, trans. Alastair Hannay, Harmondsworth: Penguin, 1992.
EUD   *Eighteen Upbuilding Discourses*, trans. Howard V. Hong and Edna H. Hong, Princeton, NJ: Princeton University Press, 1990.
FSE   *For Self-Examination*, trans. Howard V. Hong and Edna H. Hong, Princeton, NJ: Princeton University Press, 1987.

PC   *Practice in Christianity*, trans. Howard V. Hong and Edna H. Hong, Princeton, NJ: Princeton University Press, 1991.

PF/JC *Philosophical Fragments* and *Johannes Climacus*, trans. Howard V. Hong and Edna H. Hong, Princeton, NJ: Princeton University Press, 1985.

PV   *The Point of View*, trans. Howard V. Hong and Edna H. Hong, Princeton, NJ: Princeton University Press, 1998.

R   *Repetition*, trans. Howard V. Hong and Edna H. Hong, Princeton, NJ: Princeton University Press, 1983.

SUD   *The Sickness unto Death*, trans. Howard V. Hong and Edna H. Hong, Princeton, NJ: Princeton University Press, 1980.

TA   *Two Ages*, trans. Howard V. Hong and Edna H. Hong, Princeton, NJ: Princeton University Press, 1978.

TDIO   *Three Discourses on Imagined Occasions*, trans. Howard V. Hong and Edna H. Hong, Princeton, NJ: Princeton University Press, 1993.

UDVS   *Upbuilding Discourses in Various Spirits*, trans. Howard V. Hong and Edna H. Hong, Princeton, NJ: Princeton University Press, 1993.

WA   *Without Authority*, trans. Howard V. Hong and Edna H. Hong, Princeton, NJ: Princeton University Press, 1997.

WL   *Works of Love*, trans. Howard V. Hong and Edna H. Hong, Princeton, NJ: Princeton University Press, 1995.

For references to Kierkegaard's journals and notebooks, I have cited where possible from the following ongoing translation in eleven volumes:

KJN   *Kierkegaard's Journals and Notebooks*, Princeton, NJ: Princeton University Press, 2007–.

I have also cited from the edition in seven volumes known for many years to readers of Kierkegaard in English:

JP *Søren Kierkegaard's Journals and Papers*, ed. and trans. Howard V. Hong and Edna H. Hong, Bloomington, Ind.: Indiana University Press, 1967–78.

Here I have given both volume and entry number (e.g., JP 6: 6491).

All biblical quotations are taken from the King James Version. The specific edition used is *The King James Study Bible*, Nashville, Tenn.: Thomas Nelson, 1988.

Key to commonly used editions of *Fear and Trembling*

SKS 4	Pages	Hannay	Pages (Penguin Classics)	Pages (Penguin 'Great Ideas')	Walsh (Cambridge)	Pages	Hong and Hong (Princeton)	Pages
Forord	101–4	Preface	41–3	3–7	Preface	3–6	Preface	5–8
Stemning	105–11	Attunement	44–8	8–13	Tuning Up	7–11	Exordium	9–14
Lovtale over Abraham	112–19	Speech in Praise of Abraham	49–56	14–24	A Tribute to Abraham	12–20	Eulogy on Abraham	15–23
Foreløbig Expectoration	123–47	Preamble from the Heart	57–82	27–61	A Preliminary Outpouring from the Heart	21–46	Preliminary Expectoration	27–53
Problema I	148–59	Problema I	83–95	62–79	Problem I	46–59	Problema I	54–67
Problema II	160–71	Problema II	96–108	80–97	Problem II	59–71	Problema II	68–81
Problema III	172–207	Problema III	109–44	98–148	Problem III	71–106	Problema III	82–120
Epilog	208–10	Epilogue	145–7	149–52	Epilogue	107–9	Epilogue	121–3

1

INTRODUCTION

Fear and Trembling [*Frygt og Bæven*] is probably Kierkegaard's best known and most commonly read work, and Kierkegaard himself seems to have seen this coming. In an entry in the journal that he kept for most of his adult life, he claimed that 'once I am dead, *Fear and Trembling* alone will be enough for an imperishable name as an author. Then it will be read, translated into foreign languages as well. The reader will almost shrink from the frightful pathos in the book' (JP 6: 6491).[1] Yet the book's fame has been a mixed blessing. Robert L. Perkins is probably still right in his claim that *Fear and Trembling* is 'the most studied of Kierkegaard's works in the undergraduate curriculum', but this comes at a price.[2] Sometimes, it is the only text in a course in which Kierkegaard appears as one amongst several thinkers, a situation that brings with it twin dangers. First, the apparent argument of *Fear and Trembling* is often attributed to 'Kierkegaard'. Yet, like many of Kierkegaard's works, *Fear and Trembling* was not written under his own name but under that of a pseudonym, in this case the mysterious Johannes de silentio, signalling the importance of 'silence' to the text. This fact should not be forgotten, and we shall consider its significance shortly. Second, *Fear and Trembling* is sometimes mistakenly taken to be 'Kierkegaard's' definitive view of the nature of faith and the relation between ethics and religion. It is not, as an acquaintance with such later texts as *Concluding Unscientific Postscript*, *The Sickness unto Death* and *Works of Love*, to name but three, will show any curious reader. But this second issue is not merely a function of the first. That is, as well as the fact that the text is the work of a pseudonym, there is a rather more obvious problem in attributing *Fear and Trembling*'s message to Kierkegaard. This is that it is far from obvious what actually *is* '*Fear and Trembling*'s message'. While it may be true that *Fear and Trembling* has immortalised Kierkegaard's name, it is a text which is at least as likely to be greeted by puzzlement or downright exasperation as admiration. Often the book has been read as a strident demand for obedience to God even when divine commands override ethical requirements. But we shall see in due course that the story it has to tell is rather more complex and nuanced than that. Moreover, if the sheer range of interpretations of a text is in any way testimony to its richness, *Fear and Trembling* is a rich text indeed.

KIERKEGAARD'S LIFE AND WORKS

Before considering what the book is about, we should turn to consider its author – or, more precisely, since its author is a pseudonym, its author's inventor. It is quite common in books in this series to start with a brief biography of the thinker concerned. But there is a peculiar problem with doing so in the case of Kierkegaard. With considerable plausibility, Howard V. Hong and Edna H. Hong claim: 'No thinker and writer ever tried as Kierkegaard did to leave the reader alone with the work.'[3] That is, Kierkegaard was concerned to an extraordinary degree with attempting to drive a wedge between his life and his thought so that the latter would not be interpreted solely in the light of the former. (As we shall see, this was part of the purpose behind writing pseudonymously.) This was a far from unalloyed success: there have been no shortage of attempts to 'explain' the work in terms of the life. For instance, Kierkegaard's broken engagement to a young girl, Regine Olsen, has been thought by some to be the key needed to 'explain' the 'secret message' of *Fear and Trembling*, and we shall need to discuss this matter later (though without accepting this conclusion). So it is with a warning about the dangers of a merely 'biographical' reading in mind that the following brief account of Kierkegaard's life should be read.

Søren Aabye Kierkegaard was born on 5 May 1813 in Copenhagen, Denmark, a city in which he lived for virtually his whole life. Søren was the youngest of seven children. His father, Michael Pedersen Kierkegaard, was a successful, self-made businessman, who exerted a great influence on the young Søren. An important part of this influence consisted of bringing up his children in an atmosphere of intense religiosity. But this was a religiosity steeped in Michael's personal melancholy. Søren seems to have been convinced that he would die at an early age, but this ostensibly strange fixation was not without foundation. By the end of 1834 his mother and no fewer than five of his siblings had died. Moreover, no sibling had lived to be older than thirty-four, and Kierkegaard's father seems to have passed on to the surviving sons, Peter and Søren, his belief that his tragedy would be that he would outlive all his children. However, this turned out to be incorrect, and when the old man died in 1838, Søren, as one of only two surviving children, inherited a considerable amount of money. Though nominally a student of theology at the University of Copenhagen since 1830, he had been living a fairly bohemian life, reading more in the way of literature and philosophy than studying hard for his theology exams.[4] His father's death seems to have galvanised Søren into re-dedicating his efforts to formal study as a mark of respect to his father. (As an intelligent but entirely self-educated man, the formal education of his sons had been a matter of great importance to Michael.) Søren finally took his theology exams in 1840, shortly after having become engaged to Regine (more of which later). Having passed with the respectable but not outstanding grade of *laudibilis* [commendable], he stayed on at the university, submitting a lengthy dissertation, now known as *The Concept of Irony*, in 1841. Following the break with Regine that same year, Kierkegaard travelled to Berlin, ostensibly to hear Schelling's lectures, and from this point on began a quite phenomenal output of work, in stark contrast to the – apparent – indolence of most of his student years.

Over the next few years some of the works for which Kierkegaard is most famous appeared: *Either/Or, Fear and Trembling* and *Repetition* in 1843 (the latter two on the same day, 16 October); *Philosophical Fragments, The Concept of Anxiety* and *Prefaces* in 1844; *Stages on Life's Way* in 1845 and *Concluding Unscientific Postscript* in 1846. All of these works are pseudonymous, but alongside them appeared various more explicitly religious 'upbuilding discourses', published under his own name, and various other short pieces. Some of the discourses were also published on the same day as the pseudonymous works: in the case of *Fear and Trembling*, there were three such discourses: two entitled 'Love Will Hide a Multitude of Sins' and one entitled 'Strengthening in the Inner Being' (all contained in EUD). One sense in which the *Postscript* was supposed to be 'concluding' is that Kierkegaard seems to have planned to cease his output there and perhaps take a post as a country pastor. However, the direction of his life was changed in part by the first of two conflicts, with a scandalous but influential Copenhagen paper, *The Corsair*. A challenge to *The Corsair* from one of the pseudonyms, Frater Taciturnus, led to Kierkegaard being ruthlessly ridiculed in print, *The Corsair* focusing on such matters as his slightly hunchbacked appearance and the uneven length of his trouser legs. Perhaps the most significant aspect of this spat was that it led to Kierkegaard's determination to keep writing. So began what has become known as his 'second authorship', including such important works as *Works of Love* in 1847, *The Sickness unto Death* (published in 1849) and *Practice in Christianity* (published in 1850). Being the victim of public ridicule must also have contributed to the hardening of Kierkegaard's view, evident from *A Literary Review* (1846), of the dangers of 'the crowd' or 'the public'.[5]

The second great conflict came with the established Lutheran state church. Kierkegaard had long been concerned with the incongruity he saw between 'genuine' Christianity and what he heard preached from pulpits, which he saw as an evasion of the radical teaching of the New Testament. This came to a head in the 1850s. In *Practice in Christianity, For Self-Examination* and *Judge for Yourself!*, Kierkegaard contrasts his view of New Testament Christianity with the establishment religiosity he labels

'Christendom', famously proclaiming the need to 're-introduce Christianity into Christendom'.[6] In the last two years of his life, this 'attack upon Christendom' became venomous. In a series of articles, he accused the Church of rank hypocrisy in betraying the message of the gospel, a particular target being Jakob Peter Mynster, Bishop of Zealand and Primate of the Danish State (later Danish People's) Church. In the midst of this furore, Kierkegaard collapsed in the street, dying in hospital some weeks later, on 11 November 1855, at the age of forty-two. At his funeral, there was a disturbance led by his nephew Henrik Lund, a student, who protested that it was hypocritical to bury his uncle as if he was a member of a church the hypocrisy of which he had spent his last years trying to expose. One suspects that Kierkegaard would have approved of this. According to the recollections of his friend Emil Boesen (the only priest Kierkegaard would allow to visit him in hospital), when Kierkegaard was asked whether he wanted to receive the last rites, he said yes, but from a layman rather than a priest, as 'the priests are royal functionaries [who] have nothing to do with Christianity'.[7] Though most of his money had run out by the time of his death, Kierkegaard's will, believed to have been written in 1849, left everything to Regine. However, possibly owing to the intervention of Fritz Schlegel, the man whom she had by then married, she declined, asking only that her letters to Søren and a few personal items be returned.[8]

SØREN AND REGINE

In the above, I have skated over one of the most famous elements of Kierkegaard's biography, and which some have thought to be crucial to *Fear and Trembling*: the story of his broken engagement to Regine. Here, then, are the basic details. Søren and Regine were engaged for thirteen months before the former broke off the engagement in 1841. Why? According to Kierkegaard's journal, he had wrestled with the possibility of marriage and a conventional bourgeois life and reached the conclusion that his 'melancholy and sadness' would make married life impossible. Writing retrospectively, Kierkegaard says:

> In the course of half a year or less she would have gone to pieces. There is – and this is both the good and bad in me – something spectral about me, something that makes it impossible for people to put up with me every day and have a real relationship to me. Yes, in the light-weight cloak in which I usually appear, it is another matter. But at home it will be evident that basically I live in a spirit world, I had been engaged to her for one year and yet she really did not know me.[9]

Kierkegaard claims that Regine failed to see that his melancholy was no mere personality quirk: beneath it was a 'religious collision'. Alastair Hannay suggests that this term, used by Hegel to describe motivational conflicts that are the stuff of tragedy, is significant. According to Hannay, 'Kierkegaard looked at his own situation, at least in retrospect, as a tragic one.'[10] This makes it difficult to disentangle Kierkegaard's thoughts at the time from retrospective self-justification, and there may well be some truth in Hannay's further suspicion that Kierkegaard is writing himself 'into a real-life drama'.[11]

Indeed, there seems something almost *melodramatic* about the way in which Kierkegaard broke off the engagement. The letter with which he returned Regine's ring contained the following: 'Above all forget the one who writes this: forgive someone who whatever else he was capable of could not make a girl happy.'[12] (Kierkegaard later used this letter as part of *Stages on Life's Way*, the book the longest section of which, 'Quidam's Diary', possibly tells us most in the published works about his perspective on the broken engagement.[13]) But if his hope had been to inspire Regine to a stoic acceptance of the fact that this marriage was not to be, Kierkegaard was to be disappointed. With a determination and tenacity that he later compared to that of a lioness, Regine fought to try to persuade him to change his mind. According to his post-hoc justifications (if that is what they are), Kierkegaard recognised the need to change tactics. For two months prior to the final break, he attempted to act so indifferently to Regine that *she* would make the final break, or at least accept the dissolution of the engagement as a lesser evil than spending the rest of her life with such a man. Kierkegaard's claimed reasoning here seems to have been that it was better for her to want to be rid of him than to feel that he had rejected her. After two months of this, in October 1841, Kierkegaard went to Regine to break things off once and for all. His later journal description of this seems even more melodramatic. (Hannay's wry judgement of it is as 'sadly reminiscent of television soap-opera'.[14]) According to this description, immediately after his visit to Regine, Kierkegaard went to the theatre:

> where I was to meet Emil Boesen (this is the basis of the story around town that I was supposed to have told the family, as I took out my watch, that if they had anything more to say they had better hurry, for I was going to the theatre). The act was over. As I was leaving the back stalls, the Counsellor [Regine's father] came to me from the front stalls and said: May I speak with you? I accompanied him home. She is in despair, he said, it will be the death of her, she is in utter despair. I said: I will try to calm her but the matter is settled. He said: I am a proud man, this is hard, but I beg you not to break with her. He was truly magnanimous; he jolted me. But I stuck to my guns. I ate supper with the family, spoke with her when I left. The next morning I received a letter from him saying that she had not slept that night, that I must come and see her. I went and made her see reason. She asked me: Will you never marry? I answered: Yes, in ten years' time, when I have had my fling, I will need a lusty girl to rejuvenate me. It was a necessary cruelty. Then she said to me: Forgive me for what I have done to you. I answered: I'm the one, after all, who should be asking that. She said: Promise to think of me. I did. She said: Kiss me. I did – but without passion – Merciful God![15]

After such behaviour, it is easy to sympathise with Regine's brother, who wrote to Kierkegaard saying that what had happened 'had taught him to hate as no one had hated before'.[16] But while it is no part of this study to pass judgement on Kierkegaard's character in relation to the broken engagement, it is certainly possible that he might have been right about his inability to make Regine happy. What is important for our purposes about the tactics Kierkegaard used to 'wean' Regine of him is that secrecy, concealment, and the desire to protect someone from the worst – as well as the possibility that something might transcend 'ethical' requirements – are all significant themes in *Fear and Trembling*.

KIERKEGAARD'S METHODOLOGY: INDIRECT COMMUNICATION AND THE PSEUDONYMS

Before turning to the content of the book, however, we should return to the fact that it is a pseudonymous text. Why did Kierkegaard publish such a substantial proportion of his work under pseudonyms?

Pseudonymity is an important strand of a methodology Kierkegaard labelled 'indirect communication'. We have space here to give this only the briefest of treatments. The basic contrast between 'direct' and 'indirect' communication relates to a distinction between two possible ways of relating oneself to an idea. To certain ideas – a mathematical proof, for instance – I can relate myself, entirely appropriately, in a disengaged, impersonal manner. But to certain other ideas – such as what kind of person I ought to become, or the fact that I will shortly die – such a disengaged reaction would be entirely inappropriate. Indeed, to turn the fact of my own mortality into the occasion for disinterested reflection on how death was conceived by this philosopher as opposed to that one is a way of *evading* the significance my impending death has for me. Similarly, if my ethical reflections never go any further than learning how utilitarianism differs from Kantianism so that I can pass my 'Theories of Ethics' exam, then I am doing what Kierkegaard calls relating 'unethically to the ethical' (JP 1: 649, §10). To relate oneself appropriately to certain ideas means to relate to them *in the first person*. Ethical and religious concerns, Kierkegaard insists, fall into this latter category. And for communication to be successful in such cases, a subtle 'art' of communication is necessary.

Part of Kierkegaard's reason for thinking this is his view that people exist in various states of confusion or 'illusion'. Moreover, he thinks that such illusions can only be 'dispelled' by bringing people round to recognise, from their own inner experience, their perhaps unconscious reasons for adopting a particular view of the world and way of living. This in turn can only be done by entering imaginatively into their point of view, showing empathy with the emotional foundations on which it rests. In the posthumously published *The Point of View for My Work as an Author*, Kierkegaard, speaking in his own voice, claims that 'an illusion can never be removed directly, and basically only indirectly ... one who is under an illusion must be approached from behind' (PV 43). One must begin 'by taking the other's delusion at face value' (PV 54). This is, at least in part, what Kierkegaard tried to do by writing pseudonymously. In the case of at least some of the pseudonyms, then, the reader is supposed to enter into the minds of the characters involved. As Edward F. Mooney puts it,

> The use of pseudonyms is a pedagogical strategy. It works by first drawing readers one by one into a life-view. The view is meant to appeal inwardly, as if in fact it could be one's own. Having established a sympathetic bond with the reader, the pseudonym can then expose, from within that intimate relationship, its limitations and inadequacies.[17]

Kierkegaard talks of indirect communication as a 'maieutic art', key to which is the *withdrawal* of the communicator. There is a huge danger of the personality of or facts about the communicator getting in the way: we have already alluded to one example of this in our mention of the tendency of some commentators to try and 'explain' *Fear and Trembling* in terms of Kierkegaard's own biography. But here is where pseudonymity, if taken seriously, can help, for we know nothing about the Kierkegaardian pseudonyms other than what the texts themselves choose to reveal about them. Pseudonymity, then, is one way of a communicator *withdrawing*.

So as well as understanding *what* it is he is trying to communicate, the indirect communicator must also pay close attention to the *form* in which he aims to communicate (the 'how', as opposed to the 'what'). Most importantly, he must make clear that this communication is not to be understood in an abstract or impersonal fashion. This is an insight Johannes de silentio seems to have learned: as we shall see, in telling the story of Abraham, he puts great emphasis on the 'anguish', and on his own strenuous efforts to try to understand Abraham. In this latter sense, like some of the other pseudonyms (such as Johannes Climacus in the *Postscript*), Johannes is a character in his own narrative.

Thus we can begin to see that pseudonymity, and other aspects of the ways in which Kierkegaard wrote, are not mere stylistic or biographical quirks. I propose that we should take seriously Kierkegaard's 'wish' and 'prayer' as to how he should be read. In 'A First and Last Explanation', a short but important piece of text added to the end of the *Postscript* under Kierkegaard's own name, he makes the following plea:

> My pseudonymity or polyonymity has not had an *accidental* basis in my *person* ... but an *essential* basis in the *production* itself ... I am impersonally or personally in the third person a *souffleur* [prompter] who has poetically produced the *authors*, whose *prefaces* in turn are their productions, as their *names* are also ... what and how I am are matters of indifference ... Therefore, if it should occur to anyone to want to quote a particular passage from the books, it is my wish, my prayer, that he will do me the kindness of citing the respective pseudonymous author's name, not mine.
>
> (CUP 625–6)

In this study, I shall respect Kierkegaard's wish. Rather than attributing *Fear and Trembling* to him, which brings with it the danger that we might look upon the text as Kierkegaard's (definitive) word on the nature of 'faith', I shall attribute its words to Johannes de silentio. As C. Stephen Evans puts it, 'taking the pseudonym seriously safeguards several significant possibilities for the reader while foreclosing none'.[18] By doing so, we leave open the possibility that Johannes is a less than fully reliable guide to the subject on which he addresses us. (We shall return to this matter in Chapter 7.) That is, the fact that he denies that he understands faith does not imply that this denial is Kierkegaard's own. Moreover, note in the above quote that Kierkegaard draws attention to the pseudonyms' *names*. What are we to make of Johannes' name: 'de silentio'? Some commentators have rushed to the conclusion that there is something obviously invalid about someone with such a name writing or speaking to us at all. For example, Jerry Gill claims the fact that an author with such a name writes a whole book embodies 'Kierkegaard's favourite conceptual device ... irony'.[19] However, such a conclusion is far too hasty. Gill overlooks the simple possibility that Johannes has such a name because the book is, to a considerable extent, *about* silence. As we shall see, the third and longest of its 'problemata' explores aesthetic and religious forms of silence and concealment. But keeping Johannes de silentio centre-stage will have the added advantage of reminding us of his name, and the possibility – for which I shall argue in Chapter 7 – that this focus on silence is even more important than we are yet in a position to realise.[20]

What, then, is *Fear and Trembling* about? The simple answer, already alluded to, is 'faith'.[21] Johannes aims to understand the nature of faith by an engagement with an individual he considers to be its paradigm exemplar: the biblical patriarch Abraham, whose story is told in the book of Genesis.[22] But Johannes' focus is on one particular episode in Abraham's life: the occasion on which God tests his faith by demanding that he sacrifice Isaac, his long awaited and beloved son and heir. For those readers unfamiliar with this story, we should give a brief summary of it and its background as it appears in Genesis.

ABRAHAM AND ISAAC

Abraham's significance in the book of Genesis is hard to underestimate. The last thirty-nine of the fifty chapters of this first book of the Bible are concerned with Abraham and his family.[23] In Chapter 12, God promises Abram that he will 'make of [him] a great nation'.[24] (Abram is Abraham's original name: the former means 'high (or exalted) father'; the latter 'father of a great multitude'.) But Abram and his wife Sarai endure a long period of childlessness, until Sarai suggests (in accordance with the legal codes and marital contracts of the time) that Abram have a child with her maid, the Egyptian slave-girl Hagar. Thus, Abram takes Hagar as an additional wife, and, when Abram is eighty-six, Ishmael is born.[25] When Abram is ninety-nine, God tells him that henceforth his name shall be Abraham, 'for a father of many nations have I made thee',[26] and establishes with him the following covenant:

> I will establish my covenant between me and thee and thy seed after thee in their generations for an everlasting covenant, to be a God unto thee, and to thy seed after thee. And I will give unto thee, and to

thy seed after thee, the land wherein thou art a stranger, all the land of Canaan, for an everlasting possession; and I will be their God.[27]

As an outward sign of their dedication to him, God demands in return male circumcision of Abraham and his kin. God also renames Sarai Sarah ('princess') and again promises that she will provide Abraham with a son. Abraham laughs, 'and said in his heart, Shall a child be born unto him that is a hundred years old? and shall Sarah, that is ninety years old, bear?'[28] God instructs that the child should be called Isaac ('he laughs'),[29] perhaps to remind Abraham of his incredulous reaction. (However, God also promises that 'a great nation' should come through Ishmael too, and, indeed, according to Muslim tradition, Ishmael is the forefather of the Arabs.[30]) Despite his initial reaction, Abraham shows his faith by having himself, Ishmael and 'all the men of his house'[31] circumcised, a sign of the covenant between God and Abraham.[32] Sarah also laughs when she hears the news,[33] God's reaction being 'Is any thing too hard for the Lord?'[34] God's next action is to destroy the cities of Sodom and Gomorrah ('because their sin is very grievous'[35]), and Abraham's privileged status is shown by that fact that God reveals his intention to him.[36] Abraham attempts to intercede on behalf of the cities, questioning whether a God of justice would destroy the innocent along with the guilty.[37] Ultimately, Abraham's intercessory attempt fails, though God does spare Abraham's nephew, Lot (but not the latter's wife, who is famously turned into a pillar of salt).[38]

In fulfilment of God's promise, Sarah gives birth to Isaac when she is ninety, and Abraham one hundred. When Isaac is old enough to be weaned, Abraham throws a great feast,[39] at which Ishmael, whose hopes for an inheritance now appear to be dashed,[40] is seen mocking. As a result of this, Sarah asks Abraham to 'cast out' Hagar and Ishmael, which Abraham does (apparently with God's approval).[41] But to Abraham now[42] and to Hagar later in the wilderness of Beer-sheba, God renews his promise concerning Ishmael, telling Hagar that he will make Ishmael 'a great nation'.[43]

Now we come to the part of the story that so fascinates Johannes de silentio. Some unspecified time later, God now 'tests' Abraham in an event that has become known as the *akedah* ('the binding').[44] Amazingly, given that Isaac is the fulfilment of God's promise that Abraham and Sarah shall have a son, God now issues to Abraham the following command: 'Take now thy son, thine only [sic] son Isaac, whom thou lovest, and get thee into the land of Moriah; and offer him there for a burnt offering upon one of the mountains which I will tell thee of.'[45] This is the test of faith that so fascinates Johannes. Having waited so long to have a son by his wife, Abraham now faces a situation in which it looks as if God is demanding that he sacrifice – put to death – this long-awaited, beloved son. Yet, according to the Genesis narrative, Abraham's reaction is obedience: 'Abraham rose up early in the morning, and saddled his ass, and took two of his young men with him, and Isaac his son, and clave the wood for the burnt offering, and rose up and went unto the place of which God had told him.'[46]

On the third day of the journey to Moriah, Abraham says to the young men (presumably household servants): 'Abide ye here with the ass; and I and the lad will go yonder and worship, and come again to you.'[47] This apparent deception is part of what Johannes will refer to as Abraham's 'silence': as Problema III will put it, he 'conceals his purpose' (FT 109). Isaac, apparently oblivious to what is about to happen, himself carries the wood,[48] and asks 'where is the lamb for a burnt offering?'[49] Abraham's response is – significantly, I shall later argue – ambiguous: 'My son, God will provide himself a lamb for the burnt offering'.[50] Thus they go to the appointed place, Abraham builds an altar upon which he lays the wood and binds Isaac ready for sacrifice. He takes out the knife and, just as he is about to slay Isaac, hears the voice of 'the angel of the Lord' calling his name. 'Here am I',[51] Abraham answers. He then hears these words: 'Lay not thine hand upon the lad, neither do thou any thing unto him: for now I know that thou fearest God, seeing thou hast not withheld thy son, thine only son from me.'[52] Abraham then sees a ram caught in a thicket, which he sacrifices in Isaac's place. He has passed the test of faith, and God therefore reconfirms his promise:

> because thou hast done this thing, and hast not withheld thy son, thine only son: That in blessing I will bless thee, and in multiplying I will multiply thy seed as the stars of the heaven, and as the sand

which is upon the seashore; and thy seed shall possess the gate of his enemies; And in thy seed shall all the nations of the earth be blessed; because thou hast obeyed my voice.[53]

These, then, are the events in which Johannes is interested. Traditionally, Abraham has been praised for the faith in God that his willingness to obey this command demonstrates. It is this that Johannes is desperate to understand. On one level, *Fear and Trembling* seems to be one long attempt to get inside the head of someone who, it appears, was prepared to go through with such a thing. If Abraham represents faith, is this really what faith is about?

Johannes de silentio is hardly the first writer whose attention has been captured by the story of the *akedah*. As already noted, this dramatic narrative (and the less dramatic counterpart recounted in sura 37 of the Qur'an) has played a range of significant roles in the Jewish, Christian and Islamic traditions, as well as appearing in various ways in popular culture.[54] To summarise these roles is way beyond the scope of a book such as this, but, given Kierkegaard's being part of the Christian tradition, it is worth noting some key New Testament passages. On Abraham in general, Paul's letter to the Romans (especially Chapter 4) is key. Citing Genesis 15:6 ('he believed in the Lord, and he counted it to him for righteousness'), Paul presents Abraham as righteous on the grounds of his trusting faith in God, rather than on the grounds of his being circumcised.[55] Here there is no specific mention of the *akedah*, but in the letters to the Hebrews and of James, Abraham's willingness to sacrifice Isaac plays a more central role in his exemplarity. Here we see a potential tension between 'faith' and 'works': compare the focus on Abraham's faith (e.g., Galatians 3:6–9) with what Abraham *did* (e.g., John 8:39). But perhaps this is a false dichotomy: in the letter of James (a biblical text much liked by Kierkegaard), Abraham's willingness to sacrifice is provided as evidence for justification not just by 'faith alone' but also by 'works': Abraham's willingness to offer Isaac on the altar shows his faith and his actions working together.[56] In Chapter 11 of the Letter to the Hebrews, several figures from the Hebrew Bible are lined up to demonstrate faith in action. Amongst them is Abraham, and amongst the evidence for Abraham's faith is, again explicitly, the *akedah*: 'By faith Abraham, when he was tried, offered up Isaac: and he that had received the promises offered up his only begotten son ... Accounting that God was able to raise him up, even from the dead.'[57]

So here we get the possibility that Abraham believed God could raise people from the dead, thus establishing a link with the Christian focus on the resurrection of Christ. Allegorical or anagogical readings of the *akedah* (in which Abraham's willingness to sacrifice Isaac is seen to foreshadow God the Father being willing to sacrifice God the Son) have been important within the Christian tradition and have been significant as a strand of interpretation of *Fear and Trembling* – as we shall see in Chapters 6 and 7.

There is one more aspect of background to which we should draw attention. It is significant that Johannes' approach to the nature of faith is by considering an *individual*, someone held up as an *exemplar* of faith. This method is in stark contrast to the Hegelianism with which Kierkegaard's philosophical views are so often contrasted, in the following sense. Central to Hegel's philosophy of religion was the idea that religion, for all its insights, needed to be superseded in philosophy: that a key task of philosophy was to render the content of faith into *conceptual* form. For Kierkegaard, such a view is fundamentally wrongheaded. We shall see in more detail in Chapter 4 what is at stake in this disagreement, but it is worth mentioning this fundamental difference at the outset. It is such a disagreement that Johannes has in mind when he says that 'faith begins precisely where thinking leaves off' (FT 82).

PLAN OF THE BOOK

In what follows, we shall go through the text of *Fear and Trembling* section by section. There are eight such sections, and, as several commentators have noted, the first four of them look like different kinds of beginning. We are given a 'Preface', an 'Attunement' and a 'Speech in Praise of Abraham' before Johannes gets to the three 'Problemata' often thought to be the dialectical heart of the text.[58] But even then, before beginning on Problema I, he gives us yet another preamble: a 'Preamble from the Heart'. Then come the three problemata, followed by a brief epilogue. We shall resist the temptation to skim the various beginnings in our hurry to get on to the problemata, and we shall not automatically assume that the problemata amount to the real 'meat' of the text. Though most attention has traditionally been given to the notorious question of Problema I ('Is there a teleological suspension of the ethical?'), we shall see that it would be a grave mistake to hurry past the early sections: they introduce aspects of Johannes' concern that we overlook at our peril.

Chapter 2, then, investigates the 'Preface', 'Attunement' and 'Speech in Praise of Abraham' and Chapter 3 the 'Preamble from the Heart'. In the 'Preamble', Johannes makes an important distinction between 'faith' and 'infinite resignation'. How are these two modes of existence related? And, given Johannes' confusing claims, what are we supposed to think that Abraham actually believes at the point of being willing to sacrifice Isaac? Does he think that he will have to kill Isaac or not? In this chapter, as well as offering a close reading of the primary text, I discuss some important recent contributions to the secondary literature in an attempt to answer these questions. Chapter 4 deals with Problemata I and II: the notorious issue of the 'teleological suspension of the ethical' and the related question of whether there is an absolute duty to God. Chapter 5 addresses Problema III's concerns about Abraham's 'silence' and whether he was ethically justified in concealing his purpose. It also briefly discusses the Epilogue. Having thus worked our way through the whole text, Chapter 6 takes stock, sketching something of the reception history of *Fear and Trembling* and asking what the real message of this mysterious text really is. Is it, as so often supposed, the claim that a divine command means that we should always suspend our ethical obligations and commitments – even if this amounts to being prepared to kill? Or is there some rather more subtle, perhaps 'hidden' or 'secret', message? We tackle these questions via a review of some of the key secondary literature, on the way noting the sheer range of ways in which *Fear and Trembling* has been read. Finally, in Chapter 7, we consider the possible critical distance between Kierkegaard and his pseudonym, and what degree of confidence we are entitled to have in Johannes de silentio. Here

I offer a partial defence of Johannes against various commentators' charges that he represents a form of ethical and religious confusion and evasion.

No commentary or secondary text should ever be taken as a substitute for the primary text. With that in mind, the way I suggest using this book is as follows. For each of the exegetical chapters (Chapters 2–5), I suggest first reading the relevant sections of *Fear and Trembling*. Then – and only then – should the relevant chapter of this book be read.

Let us turn, then, to the first of *Fear and Trembling*'s many beginnings.

NOTES

1 Indeed, as Kierkegaard's work has been translated into many of the world's languages, *Fear and Trembling* is often one of the first – sometimes *the* first – to be translated. See, for just two examples, Qi 2009: 105 and Töpfer-Stoyanova 2009: 285 on the cases of China and Bulgaria respectively.
2 Perkins 1993: 3.
3 In the Foreword to Malantschuk 1971: viii.
4 The following journal entry gives a flavour of the young Kierkegaard's personality and attitude to his studies: 'As far as little irritations are concerned, I will remark only that I am embarked on studies for the theological degree, an occupation that does not interest me in the least and which therefore is not going particularly quickly. I have always preferred free, perhaps therefore also rather indefinite, studies to the offerings at private dining clubs where one knows beforehand who the guests will be and what food will be served each day of the week' (KJN 1 AA: 12/JP 5: 5092). Nevertheless, he resolves to knuckle down and study, in part to please his father, who 'thinks that the real Canaan lies on the other side of the theological degree' (KJN 1 AA: 12/JP 5: 5092).
5 This text is perhaps better known as *Two Ages*, the title of the novel of which it purports to be a review.
6 For a good brief overview of Kierkegaard's critique of what passed for Christianity amongst his contemporaries, see Walsh 2009: Chapter 7.
7 See Hannay 2001: 416.
8 See Hannay 2001: 419.
9 Cited in Hannay 2001: 157 in his own translation; see also KJN 6 NB 12: 138.
10 Hannay 2001: 157.
11 Hannay 2001: 157.
12 Cited in Hannay 2001: 155.
13 More light is shed by various entries in Kierkegaard's journals and notebooks: see especially KJN 3 Not. 15.

14 Hannay 2001: 158.
15 Cited in Hannay 2001: 158, in his own translation. See also KJN 3 Not. 15: 4 (p. 434) and Kirmmse 1996: 46.
16 Cited in Hannay 2001: 158. However, in seeking to set the record straight some decades later, Regine seems to have wanted to deny that Kierkegaard ever 'misused' his love to 'torment' her or to 'carry out spiritual experiments' on her, as was rumoured (see Kirmmse 1996: 33–54, especially pp. 33, 53). Compare also the brother's remark with the very different reaction of Regine's sister Cornelia (KJN 3 Not. 15: 12; Kirmmse 1996: 46).
17 Mooney 1991: 6.
18 Evans 1992: 7.
19 Gill 2000: 64.
20 Commentators have disagreed on whether we should see something suspicious about Johannes' alleged garrulousness. On this point, see, for instance, the very different perspectives of Conway 2008 and Hannay 2008: 238–40.
21 The Danish term *tro* can mean either 'faith' or 'belief'. Thus *Abraham troede* could be – and has been – translated either as 'Abraham had faith' or 'Abraham believed'. In general, Hannay prefers the former, Walsh the latter.
22 For an illuminating account of the paradigmatic but very different aspects of Abraham stressed in each of Judaism, Christianity and Islam, see Levenson 2012: especially Chapters 5 and 6.
23 The reader approaching *Fear and Trembling* who could do with a refresher on the book of Genesis should first read all that first book of the Bible, up to and including Chapter 25, especially Chapters 12–22 inclusive. Chapter 22 contains the part of Abraham's story on which Johannes concentrates.
24 Genesis 12:2.
25 Genesis 16:16.
26 Genesis 17:5.
27 Genesis 17:7–8.
28 Genesis 17:17.
29 Isaac's Hebrew name, *Yitshak*, derives from the verb *tsahak*, to laugh.
30 Genesis 17:20. In the significantly different and much briefer Qur'anic account, the son is unnamed throughout. Early Muslim exegetes thus disagreed on whether the son whom Abraham was called upon to sacrifice was Isaac or Ishmael. By about the tenth century, the consensus was that it was Ishmael. For more on this, see Levenson 2012: 104–6.
31 Genesis 17:27.
32 Genesis 17:9–14.
33 Genesis 18:12.
34 Genesis 18:14.
35 Genesis 18:20.
36 Genesis 18:17–21.
37 Genesis 18:22–32. Levenson argues that this is to be read as Abraham recognising the gravity of sin and yet pleading for mercy for the sinners (2012: 62–3).

38 Genesis 19:26. According to Christian tradition, her inability to escape was owing to her turning back and looking longingly after her material possessions: see Luke 17:29–31.
39 Genesis 21:8. Weaning becomes significant in the 'Attunement', which we shall discuss in Chapter 2.
40 This is the third shift in who is likely to inherit from Abraham. Prior to the birth of Ishmael, there is a suggestion (Genesis 15:1–4) that his steward Eleazer might have been in line to inherit Abraham's estate, perhaps in exchange for taking care of Abraham and Sarah in their old age.
41 Genesis 21:12.
42 Genesis 21:13.
43 Genesis 21:18.
44 For an account of various interpretations of this within Jewish tradition, see Jacobs 1981; Gellman 2003; and Levenson 2012: especially Chapter 3. The fact that the timescale is unspecified leads to a lack of clarity about Isaac's age at the time of this event. According to some parts of the traditions that have grown up around them in Judaism, Christianity and Islam, Isaac was an adult, in other parts thereof, a child.
45 Genesis 22:2.
46 Genesis 22:3.
47 Genesis 22:5.
48 Genesis 22:6.
49 Genesis 22:7.
50 Genesis 22:7.
51 Genesis 22:11. Levenson suggests that this utterance (one word, *hinneni*, in Hebrew) denotes 'readiness, attentiveness, responsiveness' (2012: 67, 79).
52 Genesis 22:12. According to Levenson, fear ['*yere*'] here connotes not fright but covenantal service (2012: 80).
53 Genesis 22:16–18.
54 Bob Dylan's song 'Highway 61' is perhaps the most famous example of the latter.
55 Romans 4:3, 9–13. Levenson also finds Romans 8:28–32 important for the Christian tradition (2012: 101–2).
56 James 2:20–6. Levenson notes that this combination is also found in the Jewish tradition (2012: 171).
57 Hebrews 11:17, 19.
58 For details of the different titles used for each section by different translators (as well as the Danish originals), see the 'Key to Commonly Used Editions'.

2

TUNING UP
'PREFACE', 'ATTUNEMENT' AND 'SPEECH IN PRAISE OF ABRAHAM'

PREFACE

Fear and Trembling is framed by a Preface and an Epilogue, two very short pieces of text, each of only a few pages, both of which open with economic imagery. The point of both these images is relatively clear, and important to the overall theme of the book. In the 'world of ideas', Johannes complains, 'our age is putting on a veritable clearance sale. Everything can be had so dirt cheap that one begins to wonder whether in the end anyone will want to make a bid' (FT 41). Amongst the items on sale at a knock-down price is faith. This opening thus trails one of the central ostensible motivating forces behind the book: to get its audience to realise the true 'value' of faith. Johannes then connects faith with its apparent opposite, the philosophically fashionable topic of doubt, and Descartes, typically presented as the champion of systematic doubt. He notes two things about Descartes. First, that he 'was no doubter in matters of faith' (FT 41). Although Descartes offers arguments for the existence of God, he appears elsewhere in the *Meditations* to *assume* God's existence as a ground of certainty. For instance, in part of the passage that Johannes quotes, Descartes insists that 'we should impress on our memory as an infallible rule that what God has revealed to us is incomparably more certain than anything else'.[1] It is this latter aspect – Descartes' own undoubting faith or trust in God – that Johannes stresses here. (Whether Descartes' faith would meet the standard of the model of faith that *Fear and Trembling* will present us with is another matter.) Second, Johannes notes the essentially *first person* nature of Descartes' meditations. The second lengthy quote from Descartes is intended to show that he is not recommending a universal method 'which everyone should follow in order to promote the good conduct of Reason' (cited at FT 42), but rather how *he himself* has conducted his enquiry. As we noted in Chapter 1, the importance of approaching ethical and religious issues in the first person – that is, as questions which must be asked by a human being for himself and about himself – is central to Kierkegaard's authorship. This is perhaps most clearly expressed by Johannes Climacus in the *Concluding Unscientific Postscript* where, amongst other examples, he stresses the importance of your asking questions about death not in the abstract – that is, relating to death impersonally, as something which happens to human beings in general – but in the first person – that is, relating to *your* death as something that will happen *to you*.[2] One way in which the importance of the first person approach manifests itself in *Fear and Trembling* is in the emphasis, already alluded to, on Abraham's 'anguish' and the *passionate* dimension of faith. This is the dimension of his concern that Johannes is trailing in the Preface when he unfavourably compares his contemporaries – 'every speculative score-keeper who conscientiously marks up the momentous march of modern philosophy, every lecturer, crammer, student, everyone on the outskirts of philosophy or at its centre' (FT 41) – with the much more profound Ancient Greeks. Where the Greeks score in this respect is that they recognised doubt as 'the task of a whole lifetime, doubt not being a skill one acquires in days and weeks' (FT 42). Yet, Johannes complains, the academics of his day – later described as those who 'doubt for an hour every term at the lectern but can otherwise do anything' (FT 134) – have made genuine doubt out to be much easier than it really is. It is a place 'where nowadays everybody begins' (FT 42): this 'everybody', remember, includes beginning 'crammers' and students. If we note how often Cartesian doubt is taught as a staple ingredient of 'Introduction to Philosophy' courses, we might wonder whether anything much has changed. Yet there is a more specific context that we should note.

Jon Stewart has argued that (contrary to the common picture of Kierkegaard as straightforwardly an opponent of Hegel), his primary target is in fact a number of contemporary Danish Hegelians, prominent amongst them being Hans Lassen Martensen.[3] Martensen, an influential theological thinker in the Copenhagen of Kierkegaard's day, was one of Kierkegaard's university tutors. He later succeeded Jakob Peter Mynster (another of Kierkegaard's later foes, as we noted in Chapter 1) as Bishop of Zealand, Martensen's funeral eulogy for Mynster being crucial to the final stages of Kierkegaard's venomous attack on the Danish Church in the last years of his life. Stewart suggests that both the references to Descartes and the jibe at Kierkegaard's contemporaries ('[e]very speculative score-keeper') (FT 41) are digs at Martensen and his students. On the latter point, the target is Martensen's popular lectures, which Stewart suggests Kierkegaard saw as mere reports from the philosophical front lines in Germany, with nothing new or original added.[4] Doubt is a central topic in this dispute, Martensen being well known for his claim 'to have doubted everything and to have surpassed the standpoint of skepticism'.[5] Kierkegaard satirised this in an unpublished text called *Johannes Climacus*, or *De omnibus dubitandum est* ['Everything Is to Be Doubted'], in which he presents universal scepticism as absurdly impractical as a view of life.[6] On this view, the contemporary 'speculative score-keeper' or lecturer, who is 'unwilling to stop with doubting everything' but who instead must 'go further' (FT 41) is Martensen. Descartes, by contrast, was no simple precursor of the slogan associated with Martensen (that 'everything must be doubted'), and thus Johannes' objection is to the presentation of 'a descriptive account of a certain method employed by a specific thinker in the history of philosophy' as a 'prescriptive maxim'.[7]

What is most important about the introduction of doubt at this early part of the text is that there is a structural analogy here with faith. Just as the Ancient Greeks recognised genuine doubt as a real existential challenge, so faith too was also once recognised as 'a task for a whole lifetime' (FT 42) rather than being 'where nowadays everybody begins'. In other words, Johannes' contemporaries think of themselves as having faith, of being Christians, in virtue of being baptised members of the state church. Thus, they need, to distinguish themselves, to 'go further' than this faith that everyone has. On the view that Kierkegaard associates with Martensen, this involves applying the method of speculative philosophy to Christian dogmatics. But Johannes wants to get us to see that to think this is to misunderstand and undervalue the kind of challenge and difficulty in which genuinely having faith consists.

Thus, we must understand the spirit in which Johannes' assertion that he 'is no philosopher, he has not understood the [Hegelian] System' (FT 42–3) should be taken. This is not the intellectual modesty that it may strike the unsuspecting reader as being. As the apparent conflation of being a philosopher with understanding the System shows, Johannes is here pretty much equating the term 'philosopher' with 'Hegelian' (though not, perhaps, with Hegel himself).[8] And Johannes thinks that Hegelians such as Martensen are just those who have failed properly to grasp what it means to have faith.[9] His scepticism (indeed, is it sarcasm?) about the System is palpable, not knowing 'if there really is one, or if it has been completed' (FT 43). But what really matters here is the following claim: 'Even if one were able to render the whole of the content of faith into conceptual form, it would not follow that one had grasped faith, grasped how one came to it, or how it came to one' (FT 43).

Understanding faith conceptually is not at all the same thing as grasping (still less embodying) faith as lived experience. Thus, when Johannes signs off his Preface with the insistence that 'this is not the System, it hasn't the slightest thing to do with the System' (FT 43), we can take him at his word. The book that follows is no contribution to 'philosophy' in the sense that his Danish Hegelian contemporaries would have tended to understand the term. This does not, of course, mean that it is no contribution to philosophy at all: Kierkegaard's model of philosophy has far more in common with Ancient Greek thinkers, especially Socrates, with their focus on human existence, than it does with 'philosophy' in a more 'speculative' sense. But if *Fear and Trembling* 'hasn't the slightest thing to do with the System' (FT 43), this is because neither, according to Johannes, has faith.

ATTUNEMENT

We noted earlier the significance of the fact that Johannes' approach to faith does not take the form of a purely conceptual enquiry. No doubt this is partly to distance himself from 'the System'. But the approach that he chooses is presented in a particularly stark fashion at the opening of the 'Attunement' [*Stemning*].[10] 'There was once a man', Johannes begins (FT 44). This is not quite 'Once upon a time', but it is not far off. What follows is a series of interrelated narratives, each requiring some kind of imaginative identification. Pivotal to all of them is the book's central narrative, that of Abraham (named here for the first time in the text) and Isaac. In the Attunement, we get five other narratives, all parasitic on this central one. First, right from the start, we get a story about a man haunted and intrigued by the narrative of how Abraham faced and withstood his trial. Second, we get no fewer than four further variations on this Abraham narrative. These four versions all portray what I shall call a 'sub-Abraham': that is, a plausible possible response from someone faced with Abraham's situation. We shall look at these four sub-Abrahams shortly. Note, though, to begin with, that what all four have in common is that, psychologically comprehensible though their actions may be, none is held by Johannes to be as admirable as 'the' Abraham. We shall soon see why.

Before turning to these four narratives, however, let us focus on the first: the story of the man haunted by the story of Abraham. There is good reason to suppose that this man is Johannes himself. Impressed as a child by this 'beautiful tale', as he grows older he reads the story 'with even greater admiration' (FT 44). Yet the more he dwells on and admires the story, the less can he understand it. Moreover, of the whole Abraham narrative in Genesis, one feature more than any other comes to obsess him: the events on Mount

Moriah. His only wish and longing is to 'witness these events' (FT 44): 'He wanted to be there at that moment when Abraham raised his eyes and saw in the distance the mountain in Moriah, the moment he left the asses behind and went on up the mountain alone with Isaac' (FT 44). There are at least two reasons to think that this man might be Johannes himself. First, just as Johannes has described himself as 'no philosopher', so this man is described as 'no thinker': 'he felt no need to go further than faith. To be remembered as its father seemed to him to be surely the greatest glory of all' (FT 44). Second, exactly that dimension of the whole narrative of Abraham which obsesses this man is that on which Johannes' book concentrates.

FOUR 'SUB-ABRAHAMS'

The four remaining narratives offer pictures of possible responses Abraham could conceivably have made to his spiritual trial.[11] Each represents an Abraham whom Johannes considers not to be worthy of the title 'knight of faith', each an Abraham who is not *the* Abraham, owing to a breach of trust or loss of faith.[12] Each narrative ends with the use of a weaning metaphor that has met with relative silence from commentators.[13]

Let us consider how each of these narratives differs from the portrait of the Abraham whom Johannes valorises. In the first narrative, contrary to the theme of silence and concealment which (as we shall see in our discussion of Problema III in particular) Johannes sees as of central importance, Abraham does not 'conceal from Isaac where this way is leading him' (FT 45). Abraham makes obvious to Isaac that he intends to sacrifice him, though he attempts to sweeten the pill with 'encouraging' words 'full of comfort and exhortation' (FT 45). Unsurprisingly, Isaac pleads for his life, reminding Abraham of the 'sorrow and loneliness' that he had known when he and Sarah were childless. Again unsurprisingly, Isaac's 'soul could not be uplifted' by the prospect of his impending death! Abraham's original tactic, of levelling with Isaac, presumably explaining (in a way that Johannes will later argue is impossible) that the sacrifice is a divine command, has apparently failed. There thus occurs a crucial shift in Abraham's approach:

when Isaac saw his face a second time it was changed, his gaze was wild, his mien one of horror. He caught Isaac by the chest, threw him to the ground and said: 'Foolish boy, do you believe I am your father? I am an idolator. Do you believe this is God's command? No, it is my own desire.' Then Isaac trembled and in his anguish cried: 'God in heaven have mercy upon me, God of Abraham have mercy upon me; if I have no father on earth, then be Thou my father!' But below his breath Abraham said to himself: 'Lord in heaven I thank Thee; it is after all better that he believe I am a monster than that he lose faith in Thee.'
(FT 45–6)

Abraham's last utterance – the sentence with which this first narrative closes – can, I think, be taken as this sub-Abraham's genuine motivation for the change in tactic. This first sub-Abraham genuinely does love his son as well as his God and, though he feels obliged to obey the divine command, he also feels strongly the need to shelter Isaac's faith. (The piece of dialogue given to Isaac suggests that this works.) But notice something else about this narrative, not explicitly stated but clearly implied. In order for the above course of action to make sense, Abraham must, at least from the moment of his change of tactic onwards, believe that he will indeed have to go through with the sacrifice. Unlike Johannes' 'real' Abraham – who as we shall see believes paradoxically, 'on the strength of the absurd', that he will 'get Isaac back', and in *this* life, not merely in an afterlife – the Abraham of this first narrative seems *unequivocally* resigned to having to kill Isaac. The matter for him, therefore, becomes one of how he can do so with the least damage possible to Isaac's 'soul'. His answer is to act in such a way that on the point of death Isaac's faith in God is unharmed – even if his faith in his father has been utterly destroyed. But this raises a further question. At first glance, it looks as if this solution preserves the faith of both Abraham (in so far as he obeys God's command) and Isaac (in the way outlined above). But things are not so simple. The God in whom the dying Isaac has faith is presumably a God who would *not* demand such a sacrifice. (Aiming to explain to Isaac the necessity of the sacrifice, in the first part of the narrative, has, recall, got Abraham nowhere.) And this fact impacts upon Abraham's faith as well, in so far as the God who would demand such a sacrifice is precisely the kind of God against whom Abraham feels the need to protect Isaac's faith. In feeling the need to protect Isaac from the terrible truth, therefore, can Abraham genuinely be said to have been 'faithful' to his God?

Each of the four 'sub-Abraham' narratives closes with a brief paragraph on a mother weaning her child.[14] These stories are clearly connected with the Abraham story at least in so far as they are about a parent's relationship to a child. In the first, the weaning mother blackens her breast to make it look unappealing to the child. Johannes remarks: 'Lucky the one that needed no more terrible means to wean the child!' (FT 46). The point of this is presumably to contrast the tactics of such a mother with the more desperate tactics that this first sub-Abraham needed to employ. Though the mother needs to make her breast unattractive to the child, she herself appears just the same as before, 'her look loving and tender as ever' (FT 46). Thus 'the child believes that the breast has changed but the mother is still the same'. This stands in stark contrast to the last thing this imagined Isaac would see before he dies: a father who has changed, terribly and horribly, beyond recognition.[15]

There is another reason why this first sub-Abraham cannot be *the* Abraham. As Linda Williams points out, we can *understand* his 'madman act to not let Isaac lose his faith as well as his life. That the act is understandable is the failing of the Abraham retelling'.[16]

The second narrative — notably shorter and less dramatic — presents basically the same events as the privileged Abraham narrative, but in a minor key. (The events are also told entirely from Abraham's — and, to a very limited extent, Sarah's — perspective: unlike the first narrative, where the reader is encouraged to enter into Isaac's point of view, Isaac here remains object and never subject.) The events are all here: the journey to the mountain, the binding of Isaac, the drawing of the knife, Abraham's seeing the ram and sacrificing it instead of Isaac. But, crucially, this sub-Abraham is joyless: 'From that day on, Abraham became old' (FT 46). An excessively literal-minded reader might think that Abraham, already 100 at the time of Isaac's birth, was old already. But the use of 'old' here is surely a metaphor. The 'real' Abraham, despite his great age, is kept spiritually 'young' by his love of God and the joy he and Sarah take in Isaac. ('Youth' is also used metaphorically in the next narrative, in which Sarah is described as the 'young mother' [FT 46], and the following 'Speech in Praise of Abraham', in which Abraham and Sarah are described as 'young enough to wish' [FT 52], against all the odds, for parenthood.) Not so this sub-Abraham, who has become *disillusioned* by his spiritual trial: 'he could not forget that God had demanded this of him. Isaac throve as before; but Abraham's eye was darkened, he saw joy no more' (FT 46).

In the weaning metaphor here, the mother covers her breast 'so the child no more has a mother'. But this transitional stage is no *real* loss: 'Lucky the child that lost its mother in no other way!' What this emphasis seems to suggest is that, by contrast, in the second narrative, the child – Isaac – *has* lost his parent. How so? Abraham, we have seen, has become a shadow of his former self. So perhaps the claim that 'Isaac throve as before' is simply the situation *as the diminished Abraham sees it*. Amongst the things that this Abraham has lost, therefore, is the capacity genuinely to understand and empathise with the cares, concerns and losses of his son. Isaac recedes from the narrative of Abraham's life as a disillusioned self-absorption takes over. This narrative's low-key telling of the tale, and its omission of Isaac's perspective altogether (save for this possibly inaccurate claim that 'Isaac throve as before'), would seem to square with such a reading. This sub-Abraham, while remaining *obedient* to God, does not manifest the joy and trust that true faith demands.

The third narrative, while also focusing upon Abraham's perspective alone, nevertheless returns to something of the pathos and drama of the first. Although initially prepared to carry out the sacrifice ('he drew the knife' [FT 47]), he later appears to make a separate journey, this time alone, in which 'he threw himself on his face, he begged God to forgive his sin at having been willing to sacrifice Isaac, at the father's having *forgotten his duty to his son*' (FT 47, my emphasis).[17]

What this sub-Abraham is unable to come to terms with ('he found no peace' [FT 47]) is that he could have even contemplated violating what he takes to be his most sacred duty. But he is confused: 'He could not comprehend that it was a sin to have been willing to sacrifice to God the best he owned' (FT 47). In other words, why is it a sin to be prepared to sacrifice that which one loves most? If a life of commitment to God means being prepared to make sacrifices, why isn't willingness to part with one's most treasured possession the logical consequence of such a life of religiously motivated self-denial? (Talk of 'possession' here is no exaggeration: as we have just seen, Isaac is 'the best he *owned*' [my emphasis].) On the other hand, if it is a sin, then how could such a sin be forgiven: 'for what sin was more terrible' (FT 47)? Part of this sub-Abraham's emotional turmoil and inability to find peace, therefore, would seem to inhere in his confusion.

There may be more than one way of interpreting this confusing third narrative, but in the light of themes that later become central to *Fear and Trembling*, I suggest the following. This sub-Abraham, at least at the point of begging God's forgiveness, clearly holds his duty to his son as of ultimate importance. There seems every reason to suppose that this is an *ethical* duty – and, moreover, there seems no reason why such a duty cannot be expressed in 'universal' terms. That is, we can state as a universalisable moral rule, in language comprehensible to all, that which Abraham is horrified at having been prepared to violate. 'One ought not to kill an innocent person', say, or, more specifically, 'One ought not to kill one's own innocent offspring.' All this can be *understood*: it is publicly comprehensible. (The importance of this point will become clear when we get to the problemata, and in particular the contrast Johannes attempts to draw between Abraham and the 'tragic hero'.) What this sub-Abraham's 'sin' amounts to, on this understanding, is the violation of such a universalisable moral rule. What he sees as his 'temptation', therefore, is having been prepared to contemplate that he, a particular individual, could possibly have thought that his relationship to God enabled him to override such an ethical duty. In his remorse, this sub-Abraham would perhaps agree with Kant's sentiments:

Abraham should have replied to this supposedly divine voice: 'That I ought not to kill my good son is quite certain. But that you, this apparition, are God – of that I am not certain, and never can be, not even if this voice rings down to me from (visible) heaven.'[18]

(More on this later.) And yet this sub-Abraham is confused (emotionally and intellectually): he also struggles to understand why being prepared to sacrifice his most treasured possession really is a sin, rather than the highest manifestation of a life of self-denial. What can we make of this?

The relevance to the above of the corresponding weaning passage here is at first obscure. Johannes stresses that a mother, as well as a child, suffers 'sorrow' in the process of weaning, 'that she and the child grow more and more apart; that the child which first lay beneath her heart, yet later rested at her breast, should no longer be so close … [yet] Lucky the one who kept the child so close and had no need to sorrow more!' (FT 47). I suggest that the significance of this passage lies in the contrast it effectively draws between the feelings of love and care that a mother has for her child (crucially, *this particular* child) and the level of generalised abstraction required by an approach to ethics which aims to trade exclusively in terms of 'duties' stemming from 'universal' ethical laws. If I am right, the idea is that to claim that what ought to motivate our moral action is nothing more than a rule such as 'One ought not to kill an innocent human being' is inhuman. From this perspective, there is something inhuman about that part of the third sub-Abraham who is prepared to overlook his 'human' commitment to his son, instead viewing him (inhumanly?) under the aspect of 'the best he owned', as a possession. This aspect of our confused sub-Abraham overlooks his *love* for his son: the paternal equivalent of the feelings of the mother outlined in the quote above. The mother's keeping the child close – the suffering of the separation of weaning is only temporary (a '*brief* sorrow' [FT 47, my emphasis]) – is thereby contrasted with this sub-Abraham who, in so far as he valorises a duty, has lost sight of the particularity of *his* love for *his* son, *this* person Isaac. This theme of the relation between the universal and the particular is central to *Fear and Trembling*, as we shall see.[19]

The fourth narrative shifts the perspective predominantly to that of Isaac. At the point of sacrifice, 'Isaac saw that Abraham's left hand was clenched in anguish [*Fortvivlelse*],[20] that a shudder went through his body – but Abraham drew the knife' (FT 47). In this version, on returning home – the replacement of Isaac by the ram is by now taken as read – we learn that '*Isaac* had lost his faith' (FT 47, my emphasis). The idea of silence is introduced, though here is it Isaac, not Abraham, who lives in silence and concealment: 'Never a word in the whole world is spoken of this, and Isaac told no one what he had seen, and Abraham never suspected that anyone had seen it' (FT 47–8).

The weaning passage here reads, in full, as follows: 'When the child is to be weaned the mother has more solid food at hand, so that the child will not perish. Lucky the one who has more solid food at hand!' (FT 48). The significance of this, I suggest, is that this sub-Abraham lacks such 'solid food', such spiritual sustenance for his son. Though prepared to go through with the sacrifice, this sub-Abraham does so in despair: he has no sense of joy or hope (more of this later) in what he is prepared to do. Moreover, Isaac suddenly realises this. In other words, Isaac's life is profoundly changed by an insight into his father's despair; his hopelessness.[21]

Notwithstanding the differences between these 'sub-Abrahams', they all have two crucial features in common. First, each and every one of them is prepared to go through with the sacrifice. Second, none of them, Johannes insists, is as 'great' as 'the' Abraham. These twin facts are of crucial significance. *Fear and Trembling* has often been read, superficially, as sponsoring the message that when what appears to be an ethical duty contradicts the will of God, one ought always to obey the will of God. But if that and that alone were the message, then there would be no reason why each and every one of the sub-Abrahams could not be lauded as 'father of faith'. All are prepared to obey God and sacrifice Isaac. The fact that Johannes clearly considers them all to be inferior to 'the' Abraham shows that mere willingness to obey the will of God no matter how outrageous the ostensible demand cannot be what is being commended. (At the very least, *how* that will is obeyed is clearly a crucial factor.) The message, even at this early stage of the book, should be clear: simple willingness to obey God's command is no guarantee of what Johannes means by 'faith'. For Johannes, therefore, the message is not about simple obedience.[22] Yet things may be even more complicated than this. After attempting to identify himself imaginatively with Abraham – a feat achievable, it would appear from the foregoing, in the case of each of the sub-Abrahams – Johannes (assuming that he is indeed the man) despairs of having got much closer to understanding the true Abraham. To these four narratives, we are told, could be added others (FT 48). Yet any such imaginative identification leaves Johannes' man weary, and he invariably ends up exclaiming that 'no one was as great as Abraham; who is able to understand him?' (FT 48). The difficulty of an observer's *understanding* Abraham now becomes a major theme of the book.

SPEECH IN PRAISE OF ABRAHAM

It is important to bear in mind, in this third of the preliminary sections, the theme of an observer's admiration for an exemplar whom he nevertheless professes to find incomprehensible. Johannes talks of a poet's admiration for a hero, and this is what the 'Speech in Praise' appears to be. Utilising some poetic licence, Johannes makes a series of *prima facie* bizarre claims. Let us start right at the beginning. The passage with which Johannes' speech begins has struck many readers as recognising the threat of nihilism:

> If there were no eternal consciousness in a person, if at the bottom of everything there were only a wild ferment, a power that twisting in dark passions produced everything great or inconsequential; if an unfathomable, insatiable emptiness lay hid beneath everything, what would life be then but despair? If it were thus, if there were no sacred bond uniting mankind, if one generation rose up after another like the leaves of the forest, if one generation succeeded the other as the songs of the birds in the woods, if the human race passed through the world as a ship through the sea or the wind through the desert, a thoughtless and fruitless whim, if an eternal oblivion always lurked hungrily for its prey and there were no power strong enough to wrest it from its clutches – how empty and devoid of comfort would life be!
> (FT 49, translation slightly adjusted)

John D. Caputo reports having written 'Nietzsche!' in the margin of his copy at this point.[23] And yet there follows what Caputo describes as the 'thud' of a 'terrible disappointment',[24] as

Johannes simply asserts: 'But for that reason it is not so' (FT 49). Is this anything other than a *non sequitur*?[25]

Similarly odd, on the face of it, is the list of Johannes' claims that start with the claim that the greatness of a person is a function of 'the greatness of what *he loved*' (FT 50). This and what follows seems to have been specifically selected in order to valorise Abraham. In short, the claim is that the great shall be remembered in proportion to: the greatness of what they love; their 'expectancy'; and 'the magnitude of what [they] struggled with [*stred med*]' (FT 50).[26] By these criteria, Abraham is 'greater than all' (FT 50). Loving God, the greatest possible being, makes Abraham, by this strange reasoning, great himself. Abraham also scores well on expectancy, since what he expected – that Isaac would be returned to him – is 'the impossible' (FT 50). (Here is trailed what will be a central theme of *Fear and Trembling* – and we shall see the importance of expectancy [*Forventning*] in Chapter 6.) Again, since that which he 'struggled with' was God, this again is supposed to make Abraham 'greater than all'. This greatness takes the form of a series of ostensible contradictions: Abraham is 'great with that power whose strength is powerlessness, great in that wisdom whose secret is folly, great in that hope whose outward form is insanity, great in that love which is hatred of self' (FT 50).[27]

What is going on here? If this is a 'speech in praise' of Abraham by a poet, then perhaps we should not expect rigour of argument to be high on the agenda. It certainly isn't. (Consider an example. If my greatness is in part a function of the difficulty of what I expect, culminating in 'the impossible', am I somehow made 'greater' if, all other things being equal, I expect to win the lottery *without* having bought a ticket than if I actually go out and buy one?) Are passages such as this intended to cast doubt on Johannes' reliability? Just how seriously should we worry about this poetic excess? We shall return to this issue in Chapter 7, but let me make a preliminary suggestion, relevant to an interpretation I shall endorse in Chapter 6. *Fear and Trembling*'s subtitle calls it a 'dialectical lyric', and Johannes' utterances in this part of the text seem to have far more 'lyric' than 'dialectic' about them. We should read them – especially the *non sequitur* that so disappointed Caputo – not as bad arguments, but as an expression of a *trust* which relates to what, in Chapter 6, I shall outline as 'radical hope'. It is in his role as an exemplar of such trust and hope that Abraham can count as a 'guiding star that saves the anguished' [*en ledende Stjerne, der frelse den Ængstede*] (FT 54). Thus the picture that is being set up here is faith as a radical alternative to nihilism.[28]

Johannes continues his eulogy with a series of reminders of the wider story of which the sacrifice of Isaac is a part (see FT 50–1). The purpose of these reminders is to show that Abraham keeps faith in God's promise that he would become the father of nations in spite of its increasing unlikelihood.[29] This seems dependent upon Abraham's leaving behind his 'worldly understanding [*jordiske Forstand*]' (FT 50). Here is an important clue to what Johannes counts as faith: whatever it is, 'worldly understanding' cannot deal with it. Indeed, faith and worldly understanding seem to be presented as opposites: Abraham 'left behind his worldly understanding and took with him his faith' (FT 50). In the light of this, the previous set of contrasts can be seen to draw attention to crucial features of faith: its power, wisdom and hope appear to worldly understanding as powerlessness, folly and insanity. Perhaps this is why the ostensible reasoning of the previous paragraph seems easy to mock.

There is a perspective open to Abraham in which he could just renounce God's promise, reasoning to himself that – as he and Sarah grow still older and remained childless – perhaps this, after all, was not God's will. Johannes argues that someone capable of making such a sacrifice could quite reasonably be greatly admired, he could even have 'saved many by his example' (FT 52). Yet he would *not* be the paradigm exemplar of faith that Abraham is, according to Johannes. At this point, then, what is being introduced – though not yet named as such – is a crucial distinction between the 'knight of infinite resignation' and the 'knight of faith'. We shall unpack this crucial distinction between infinite resignation and faith in more detail in the next chapter, when the contrast is formally introduced for the first time via a discussion of another narrative, of a young lad's love for an unattainable princess.

What Johannes tries to do here is to show just how much more 'reasonable' (to 'worldly understanding') and comprehensible what he will later label 'infinite resignation' is than 'faith'. Again, he tries to do this by an attempted imaginative identification with Abraham. Abraham's trial is set against the background of the length of time he and Sarah had to wait for Isaac, their joy at God's having fulfilled his promise to give them a son, and the concomitant horror of God's later demand that he should sacrifice Isaac. In lyrical terms as befitting a 'poet', Johannes contrasts Abraham's faith with alternative possible reactions, more readily comprehensible and reasonable to our 'worldly understanding'. ('So all was lost, more terrible than if it had never been! So the Lord was only making sport of Abraham! Through a miracle he had made the preposterous come true, now he would see it again brought to nothing' [FT 53].)

A crucial dimension of Abraham's faith is now introduced, namely that it is 'faith for *this* life' (FT 53). This is a vital point. Johannes suggests that 'had his faith only been for a future life it would indeed have been easier to cast everything aside in order to hasten out of this world to which he did not belong' (FT 54). In other words, Johannes suggests, first, that Abraham could have used the thought of being 'reunited' with Isaac in an afterlife as some kind of crutch to support himself against the horror of what he had been commanded to do. Second, he implies that the process of doing this brings with it a devaluing of *this* life, *this* world – a world which has become one to which Abraham feels that 'he did not belong' (FT 54). (We can compare such an attitude with Nietzsche's idea that by attaching beliefs and hopes to 'afterworlds' – life after death; or, indeed, a belief in any 'transcendental' world – one thereby devalues *this* life and world.) Such a 'faith', Johannes insists, is not faith at all. It is crucial to understand that Abraham's faith is in an important sense immanent to this world: 'it was for this life that Abraham believed, he believed he would become old in this land, honoured among his people, blessed in his kin, eternally remembered in Isaac' (FT 54).

Another possible response available to Abraham, also arguably more understandable than being willing to sacrifice his son, would be to offer *himself* in sacrifice. (One can certainly imagine this possibility being movingly portrayed in a tragedy – and as we shall see, the 'tragic hero' is another figure who, like the knight of infinite resignation, Johannes goes on to contrast with the knight of faith.) Johannes considers this possibility but insists that Abraham would have been less great had he done this. The reason is less than entirely clear. In this imagined possibility, Johannes has Abraham implore God not to 'scorn this sacrifice', despite the fact that 'it is not the best I possess ... for what is an old man compared with the child of promise' (FT 54). But it also seems possible that the reason Johannes views this as less admirable is that it amounts to attempting to *negotiate* with God (which, as we noted in Chapter 1, didn't go too well in the case of Sodom and Gomorrah): God demands Isaac, but gets Abraham. In other words, rather than obeying the divine command, Abraham offers a substitute product. We could consider this as an extension of the mercantile imagery which both opens and closes *Fear and Trembling*. Online or mail-order companies sometimes reserve the right to substitute for an out-of-stock product a replacement product of 'equal or greater value'. This is effectively what Abraham does – with the crucial difference that, if his own admission is to be believed, the replacement product is of *less* value! For some such reason, then, Johannes insists that such a sub-Abraham could be admired – much in the way that one can admire a self-sacrificing 'tragic hero' – 'but it is one thing to be admired, another to be a guiding star that saves the anguished' (FT 54).

Abraham, we are told, is the latter. Johannes praises his courage, favourably contrasting Abraham's resolute 'here I am' in response to God's 'Abraham, where are you?' with the likely response of a less courageous person.[30] Here Johannes addresses the reader directly: 'was that the case with you? When you saw, far off, the heavy fate approaching, did you not say to the mountains, "hide me", to the hills, "fall on me"? Or if you were stronger, did your feet nevertheless not drag along the way?' (FT 55). Abraham's resoluteness is also shown in the fact that 'he did not doubt, he did not look in anguish to left or right, he did not challenge heaven with his prayers ... he ... knew that no sacrifice was too hard when God demanded it' (FT 55). Such factors need to be recognised in any competent telling of the Abraham story. In a precursor to his criticism of the preacher in the 'Preamble from the Heart', of whom more in Chapter 3, Johannes criticises any cheapening of the story that says 'it was only a trial' (FT 55).

(Recall here that Johannes has been concerned from the outset with the true 'value' of faith.) Centre-stage, then, are Abraham's courage and his lack of doubt. The 'Speech' closes with a valedictory paragraph which, while claiming to be superfluous ('When you journeyed home from the mountain in Moriah you needed no speech in praise to console you for what was lost; for in fact you gained everything and kept Isaac' [FT 56]) is at least fitting in so far as it is neither lukewarm nor unappreciative of Abraham's greatness. Again trailing the preacher of the 'Preamble', Johannes asks Abraham to 'forgive him who would speak in your praise if he did not do it correctly' (FT 56). The 'Speech' closes by stressing the importance of remembering that Abraham 'needed a hundred years to get the son of [his] old age, against every expectation, that [he] had to draw the knife before keeping Isaac' (FT 56). And, perhaps most important of all, it offers a dig at those of Kierkegaard's contemporaries concerned with 'going further' and for whom faith and religion were in an important sense 'lower' stages that needed to be superseded in philosophy. To these, Johannes points out 'that in one hundred and thirty years [Abraham] got no further than faith' (FT 56).

These, then, are the first three 'beginnings' of *Fear and Trembling*. It might seem odd that after three such beginnings, the next section should sound like yet another: the 'Preamble [or Preliminary Outpouring] from the Heart'. (This time, it is a 'preamble' to the three 'problemata'.) But, as we shall now see, this section contains some of the text's most important material.

NOTES

1 Johannes quotes from Descartes's *Principles of Philosophy*: Descartes 1973: I, 252.
2 See also the discourse 'At a Graveside' in TDIO. This theme is taken up later by Heidegger in his discussion of being-towards-death in *Being and Time* (Heidegger 1962).
3 See Stewart 2003.
4 Stewart 2003: 307.
5 Stewart 2003: 307.
6 Stewart 2003: 307. See also Chapter 5, this volume.
7 Stewart 2003: 308.

8 Stewart 2003 offers a nuanced account, rich in historical detail, of the ways in which Kierkegaard opposes Hegel and the ways in which he is indebted to him.

9 Note, though, Stewart's claim that Martensen had himself brought against Hegel the same objection that Johannes here raises (2003: 309).

10 I prefer Hannay's translation 'Attunement' (or Walsh's 'Tuning Up') to the Hongs' 'Exordium'. As Edward Mooney puts it, 'Attunement', with its musical resonance, suggests 'tuning an instrument and ear for what is to follow' (1991: 25).

11 For a treatment of the 'Attunement' as akin to rabbinic midrash, see Howland 2015: 29, who notes its 'freewheeling and imaginative nature' and use of storytelling as a means of interpretation. See also Loungina 2009: 273.

12 Cf. Rumble 2015: 254.

13 The exceptions to this rule are increasing in number. See Mooney 1991: 30–1; Williams 1998; and, more recently, Conway 2015b; Mooney and Lloyd 2015; and Rumble 2015. There has also been some attempt to treat these passages on a purely autobiographical level, as Kierkegaard's attempt to 'wean' Regine of him following his breaking off their engagement. For a clear account of this, see, for instance, Williams 1998: 310–11.

14 Howland notes how the child's growing up and being weaned would dramatically increase that child's chances of survival, and is thus to be celebrated (2015: 37).

15 In a journal entry that is presumably a draft of what became the first sub-Abraham narrative, Kierkegaard talks of Abraham blackening *himself*, needing 'to travel to Hell in order to learn what the Devil looks like' (KJN 2 JJ 87).

16 Williams 1998: 313.

17 That this is a separate journey is a point missed by Mooney, in whose exegesis Abraham 'at the last moment throws himself down before God' (Mooney 1991: 27). But Johannes explicitly says that Abraham 'rode out alone' on a 'tranquil evening', whereas when he sets out with Isaac, it was 'early morning' (FT 43–4).

18 Kant 1996a: 283.

19 For a reading of the 'sub-Abrahams' as failing because of their 'improper or skewed emotional comportment', see Furtak 2015 (especially pp. 153–7; above quote at p. 153). Commenting on the first edition of the present book, Furtak claims that my focus on the third sub-Abraham's confusion does not 'take into account his emotional feelings or his passionate disposition' (2015: 155n58). I am not sure why he thinks that, given the way in which I introduce the third narrative, my references to the pathos of the situation and the emphasis on Abraham's inability to 'find peace'. Perhaps Furtak takes 'confusion' to refer only to *intellectual* confusion, but that was not my intention. I don't agree with Furtak that only the third sub-Abraham gives us a 'revealing glimpse' into the subjectivity of a human being (2015: 156). It seems to me that all do this in different ways, the difference being in the *way* in which subjectivity is displayed, some being more 'filmic' – and thus leaving more for the reader to infer – than others. On a related point, Clare Carlisle notes, in stark contrast to Johannes' account, the absence of 'signs of interiority' in the Abraham of the

original Genesis narrative, which she describes as 'a detached narrative described as if by an invisible spectator, which makes no mention of the protagonists' thoughts, feelings, gestures and body language' (2010: 48).
20 *Fortvivlelse* is translated by Hannay as 'anguish', by the Hongs and by Walsh as 'despair'. This is the term translated as 'despair' throughout *The Sickness unto Death*, Kierkegaard's primary text on that important subject. Hannay has now expressed a preference for 'despair' (personal correspondence). Note, though, that most of Hannay's uses of 'anguish' are translations of *Angest*, often rendered 'anxiety'. As a translation of the latter term, I prefer Hannay's usage: 'anguish' seems, to my ear, to have a stronger emotional charge than 'anxiety'.
21 Williams wonders *why* an insight into Abraham's despair would necessarily cause Isaac to lose his faith in God, and it is true that *Fear and Trembling* gives no clear-cut answer to this (see 1998: 315–16). However, this fourth narrative seems the clearest illustration of what Vanessa Rumble suggests is the contagious, intergenerational nature of despair, which she links to *The Concept of Anxiety*: see Rumble 2015: 255–6.
22 Carlisle contrasts Johannes with Luther in this respect: see Carlisle 2010: 17–19.
23 Caputo 1993: 16.
24 Caputo 1993: 15.
25 George Pattison (2002: 198) suggests a way of reading it that sidesteps this worry.
26 Here I slightly prefer Walsh's 'struggled' to Hannay's 'strove'.
27 Note, in light of the fact that many have seen in *Fear and Trembling* a specifically Christian message, that this passage has a New Testament resonance. The reference to wisdom and folly comes in Paul's First Letter to the Corinthians: 'If any man among you seemeth to be wise in this world, let him become a fool, that he may be wise. For the wisdom of the world is foolishness [in God's sight]' (1 Corinthians 3:18–19). See also 2 Corinthians 12:9–10 (on power and weakness) and John 12:25 (on loving and hating one's worldly life). We shall consider in Chapter 6 interpretations of *Fear and Trembling* that find in it a specifically Christian message. For more on the New Testament resonances, see Westphal 2014: 87–9.
28 Carlisle (2015: 53–4) brings out this point well.
29 On the importance of promising in this section, see Malesic 2013: 219–20 and Westphal 2014: Chapter 2, especially p. 27.
30 Recall here Levenson's point, in Chapter 1, about *hinneni* connoting readiness, attentiveness and responsiveness.

3

INFINITE RESIGNATION AND FAITH

THE 'PREAMBLE FROM THE HEART'

As pointed out in the previous chapter, Johannes has trailed in the 'Speech in Praise' what will turn out to be one of the main themes of the book: the contrast between 'faith' and 'infinite resignation'. It is in this section that this contrast is both named for the first time, and discussed in more detail – again, by the use of a narrative, this time of a young lad and his love for an unattainable princess.

But let us not get ahead of ourselves. So far, we have already come across various ways of (mis)telling the Abraham story, and it is to that theme that Johannes returns near the start of the 'Preamble'. (Recall his claim, towards the end of the 'Speech in Praise', that it is rare indeed to find 'he who can tell the story and give it its due' [FT 55].) But a different emphasis is placed on the form that such a mistelling could take. 'What is left out of the Abraham story', Johannes complains, 'is the anguish [*Angesten*]' (FT 58).[1] This signals the importance of the 'passionate' (cf. FT 71n) nature of faith. The focus now is on how it is commonplace to make the Abraham story too easy on the hearer. Too many of those who want to understand the story are not prepared to 'labour and be heavy laden' (FT 58) in relation to it. What is true of the hearers, moreover, is true of the tellers of the tale. Johannes tells a memorable story of a preacher who lauds Abraham to the skies without really thinking through what he is saying. Abraham becomes the topic for just another sermon. But, Johannes wonders, what if someone in the congregation were to take to heart the preacher's valorisation of Abraham? Suppose, accordingly, that he goes home and plans to sacrifice his own son. On hearing of this, the preacher's response would be outrage: '"Loathsome man, dregs of society, what devil has so possessed you that you wanted to murder your own son?"' He would fail to anticipate the reply: '"It was in fact what you yourself preached on Sunday"' (FT 59).

There seems real plausibility to Johannes' point here. How many preachers have indeed praised Abraham as a paradigm exemplar of faith, as a 'righteous' man,[2] while being scandalised by any number of leaders of 'cults' who have justified outrageous acts on the grounds that 'God told me to do it' or terrorist acts claimed to be done in God's name? If I claim that God has told me to sacrifice my offspring and the only reason I can give for this is, 'It is a trial', it seems quite likely that local religious leaders will be amongst those calling for my incarceration. I am, it will be said, a danger both to others and myself. Johannes, then, is trying to make absolutely clear what is involved in praising Abraham for his action. He claims to have 'the courage to think a thought whole' (FT 60) – precisely what the above discussed preacher allegedly lacks. This preacher and his ilk are, for Johannes, evading the enormity of what praising Abraham amounts to: what is, perhaps unconsciously, motivating their 'leaving out the anguish' is the fact that 'anguish is a dangerous affair for the squeamish' (FT 58). One way of evading the issue here is by hiding behind subtle shifts in language. This can happen either by calling Abraham great (as if 'Abraham has acquired proprietary rights to the title of great man, so that whatever he does is great' [FT 60][3]) or by calling his action a 'sacrifice' rather than a murder. ('The ethical expression for what Abraham did is that he was willing to murder Isaac; the religious expression is that he was willing to sacrifice

Isaac' [FT 60].) The key issue, then, as Johannes sees it, is that faith somehow makes a difference: 'For if you simply remove faith as a nix and a nought there remains only the raw fact that Abraham was prepared to murder Isaac' (FT 60).

All this leads Johannes to wonder about the very nature of his own project: 'Can one speak unreservedly of Abraham, then, without risking that someone will go off the rails and do likewise?' (FT 60). His conclusion is 'Yes', but only because he assumes that '[t]he great can never do harm when grasped in their greatness' (FT 61). Johannes insists on the need to stress Abraham's 'devout and God-fearing [*gudfrygtig*]' nature (FT 61) and the strength of his love for Isaac. This is presumably to make clear the difference between Abraham and a heartless murderer. But how far has this really come from the preacher's sermon, which Johannes has condemned? The answer is not clear from the text itself at this point but must rather be gleaned from the wider strategy of *Fear and Trembling*. Any adequate such speech – and we might think of the whole of *Fear and Trembling* as such a speech – must make clear, in a way in which the preacher does not, how Abraham differs from an ethical – that is 'tragic' – hero (a theme which will be the concern of a later part of the Preamble and Problema I) and also from various forms of 'aesthetic' hero (as will be outlined in Problema III). These conditions must be fulfilled if Johannes is to give an adequate portrayal of Abraham *qua* 'knight of faith'. What is it that makes Abraham a 'knight of faith', as opposed to an ethical or aesthetic hero? Even if he could achieve this, of course, it would hardly be enough to justify Abraham's action – and it may turn out that the very nature of faith is such that it *cannot* be 'justified'. But trying to draw such distinctions is a vital part of Johannes' procedure throughout the book.[4]

Talk of the difficulty of 'understanding' Abraham might give the impression that this difficulty is an intellectual one. Johannes attempts to block off this misapprehension by comparing understanding Abraham with understanding Hegel. The point here seems to be that the difficulties of understanding Hegelian philosophy[5] are indeed primarily difficulties for the intellect, difficulties in conceptual understanding, whereas with Abraham this is not the case. In the Abraham case, the difficulty is more one for the *imagination*. I do not intend to imply here that 'intellect' and 'imagination' are mutually exclusive categories. The point is simply to distinguish a difficulty in understanding in which imaginative identification with a particular person is central ('understanding Abraham') and one in which it is not ('understanding Hegel'). Johannes says he is 'virtually annihilated' by attempting to think about the 'monstrous paradox' which is the content of Abraham's life (FT 62). Two aspects of what follows confirm our suspicion that Johannes' problem with Abraham is one of imaginative identification. First, his claim to be able to understand 'the hero' (and we shall shortly see the importance of 'tragic heroes' to Johannes' discussion). He asserts, 'The hero I can *think* myself *into*, but not Abraham' (FT 63). In other words, the hero's actions are comprehensible to an imaginative observer. This is not the case with Abraham. Second, this implicit contrast between imagination and intellect is behind Johannes' insistence that 'Philosophy cannot and should not give us an account of faith, but should understand itself and know just what it has indeed to offer' (FT 63).[6] Philosophy – and Johannes surely has 'Hegelian' philosophy in particular in mind – is first and foremost a rational, conceptual enterprise. For Hegel himself, both philosophy and religion are concerned with essentially the same material, but whereas religion reaches its conclusions by appeal to faith, authority and revelation, philosophy occupies a 'higher' standpoint. It is able to 'go further' than the pictorial representations and figurative, symbolic language of religion and deal with the same subject matter in the form of thoughts and concepts.[7] As we would expect, having seen his scepticism about the possibility of 'going further', Johannes denies this; denies that philosophy can occupy a 'higher' standpoint than religion. Put simply, for Hegel, one reason to consider philosophy 'higher' than religion is that whereas philosophy can reflect upon religion, religion cannot offer a conceptual account of philosophy. But part of Kierkegaard's objection to his Hegelian contemporaries is that when (Hegelian) philosophy aims to reflect upon the subject matter of faith and religion, it misunderstands and misrepresents it – often comically so.[8] Johannes' challenge to the Hegelian is to ask exactly how Hegelian philosophy understands Abraham, *qua* exemplar of faith. How does it explain him? He insists that there are no conceptual resources at our disposal that will enable us to 'understand' 'faith' *qua* the paradox that Abraham exemplifies. We shall return in more detail to Johannes' quarrel with the Hegelians in Chapter 4. For the time being, suffice it to note that Johannes is insisting that philosophy *should* not give us an account of faith because it *cannot*. Any attempted account of faith which attempts to proceed in a manner entirely accessible to 'universal' reason and expressible in publicly available language – and more of this in Chapter 4 – will give us a picture not of faith, but of something very different.

It is worth noting at this point that Johannes is pointing to the possibility of a life – exemplified in this case by Abraham – which can be *lived* but not *thought*. That is to say, the conceptual resources of philosophy might be insufficient to make sense of – to enable the outsider like Johannes to 'understand' – certain kinds of human life. But that does not prevent it from being the case that such lives are *liveable*. A significant part of Johannes' project, then, involves pointing up – by using Abraham as a sort of test case – that there are limitations to what can be achieved by a purely rational, conceptual approach to many complex aspects of human life and behaviour. Though the primary subject here is 'faith', and the test case Abraham, it is not hard to see that this general observation could well be extended to many other aspects of life.[9]

Ultimately, as we shall see more clearly in Chapter 4, the assumption that Johannes is resisting is that faith can be dismissed as something inferior, something which we have to 'go further' than, because it cannot be dealt with in 'universal' terms. So Johannes is like the 'Hegelian' in one sense, unlike him in another. What he and the Hegelian have in common is that neither of them inhabit the form of life of what the Hegelian might call 'mere' faith. Where they differ is that whereas the Hegelian thinks he has got 'beyond' faith, Johannes admits that the form of life he – Johannes – occupies is 'lower' than that of faith. 'I do not have faith; this courage I lack', he insists. Nevertheless, he goes on to add that he is not 'underhand enough to deny that faith is something far higher' (FT 63).

What, then, is the form of life that Johannes occupies? There is good reason to think that it is what he labels 'infinite resignation'.

We are now entering a very important part of the text in which Johannes introduces by name two more key forms of what faith is not. These figures are the 'tragic hero' and the 'knight of infinite resignation'.

TRAGIC HEROISM AND INFINITE RESIGNATION: A PREAMBLE

Johannes continues his exercise in imaginative identification by considering what he would have done had he been in Abraham's sandals. The best fist he could have made of it, he tells us, would have been *'in the capacity of* [*i Qualitet*] *tragic hero'* (FT 64, Johannes' emphasis, translation adjusted).[10] The tragic hero has the courage to ride to Moriah and to be willing to perform the sacrifice – but his attitude to it is very different from that of Abraham. His attitude is one of 'resignation', described as an 'infinite movement'. For the person with such an attitude, though he professes to continue to love God, 'everything is lost' (FT 64). Thus, Johannes confesses that what he would have found most difficult would have been what for Abraham was 'the easiest of all ... to find joy again in Isaac' (FT 65). And such an attitude of resignation, Johannes insists, is no adequate substitute for faith. Here we encounter a crucial theme: faith as the capacity to appreciate the finite world as a divine gift, which seems to be a key aspect of Johannes' inability to have faith.

This should raise plenty of questions in the reader's mind. What is the relation between the 'tragic hero' and the 'knight of infinite resignation' – are they identical? What exactly is 'resignation', and in what sense is it 'infinite'? And why, when the appearance of the ram renders the need to sacrifice Isaac unnecessary, is the knight of infinite resignation unable to 'find joy again' in Isaac's return? To answer these questions, we need to consider what is one of the most famous aspects of *Fear and Trembling*: its distinction between the 'knight of infinite resignation' and the 'knight of faith'.

This contrast begins with yet another return to the actions of the Abraham Johannes so admires. Johannes tells us that he himself would have mounted his ass in 'resignation'. But with Abraham it is very different:

> All along he had faith, *he believed that God would not demand Isaac of him*, while still he was willing to offer him if that was indeed what was demanded. He believed on the strength of the absurd [*Han troede i Kraft af det Absurde*], for there could be no question of human calculation, and it was indeed absurd that God who demanded this of him should in the next instant withdraw [or revoke (*tilbagekalde*)] the demand. He climbed the mountain, even in that moment when the knife gleamed he believed – that God would not demand Isaac. Certainly he was surprised by the outcome, but by means of a double movement he had come back to his original position[11] and therefore received Isaac more joyfully than the first time.
>
> (FT 65, my emphasis)

'He believed that God would not demand Isaac of him.' Johannes speculates that Abraham could believe this 'even when the knife gleamed' (FT 65). 'He believed on the strength of the absurd, for all human calculation had long since been suspended' (FT 65). We can most clearly see why 'all human calculation had ... been suspended' if we also note Johannes' later claim that Abraham 'must know at the decisive moment what he is about to do, and accordingly must know that Isaac is to be sacrificed' (FT 143). Putting all this together, it appears on the face of it to amount to the claim that Abraham both does, and doesn't, believe that Isaac is about to die. Is that right? If so, is it this apparently contradictory belief that prevents Johannes from being able to understand Abraham? What leaves him 'aghast' (FT 66) is that it amounts to losing 'one's understanding and the whole of the finite world whose stockbroker it is' (FT 65–6), while yet expecting to get it ('exactly the same finitude') back again 'on the strength of the absurd'. Johannes – unsurprisingly – cannot begin to comprehend such a mode of being. Thus, the following comment stresses both his admiration of the person of faith and that person's incomprehensibility: 'The dialectic of faith is the most refined and most remarkable of all dialectics, it has an elevation that I can form a conception of but no more' (FT 66). Johannes professes to be unable to understand either faith itself or its paradigmatic exemplar: 'Abraham I cannot understand; in a way all I can learn from him is to be amazed' (FT 66). He says he can 'describe' but not 'perform' 'the movements of faith' (FT 67). This reinforces the idea that Johannes' is an *outsider's* view of faith. We shall return to this point in the second half of this chapter. But it is important to signal here that ultimately, I think, this is *not* a matter of contradictory beliefs. Rather, it is Abraham's ability to receive Isaac back with joy, *qua* divine gift, that is beyond Johannes' imaginative capacities.

INFINITE RESIGNATION AND FAITH

Let us try to tease out in more detail exactly what the differences are between infinite resignation – said to be the 'last stage [Abraham] loses sight of' (FT 66) – and faith. The knight of infinite resignation is probably the most fully drawn illustration of what faith is not. Nevertheless, while not being identical to faith, infinite resignation is 'the last stage before faith' (FT 75) and in so far as Abraham is said to make a 'double movement', it appears that in some way 'infinite resignation' is the first part of this movement. How does this work?

The first difference between infinite resignation and faith relates to an important overall theme of what Kierkegaard elsewhere calls the 'inwardness' of faith. This is often connected with its 'hiddenness'. Johannes claims that 'knights of infinite resignation are readily recognizable, their gait is gliding, bold' (FT 67). The knight of infinite resignation has a recognisably heroic quality, which inheres in the fact that being prepared to renounce the joys and passions of finite existence for some 'higher cause' can both be recognised as requiring courage, and judged as ethically admirable. But there is a degree of concealment and mystery about the knight of faith. This could take a variety of forms: either the (allegedly) incomprehensible example of Abraham, or the far more 'mundane' knight of faith whom Johannes now imagines. In an age which, as we have said, viewed faith as something we all already possess, thus requiring us to 'go further', note in passing that Johannes *has* to *imagine* this figure since he has 'tried ... in vain for several years' (FT 67) to find a genuine knight of faith. This failure could either be because there are none – and thus the age is deceived about itself vis-à-vis faith – or that 'every other person is one' (FT 67), but that because of the 'hiddenness' of faith, Johannes cannot distinguish them from 'the *bourgeois* philistine' (FT 67). (It is clear from the overall tone of the text, and some explicit sceptical remarks – for instance, 'I wonder whether my contemporaries really are capable of making the movement of faith' (FT 64) – that Johannes suspects it is the former possibility which pertains.)

What characterises this mundane imagined knight of faith? Two things. First, precisely his 'hiddenness', in contrast to the recognisability, stemming from 'openness', of the knight of infinite resignation. The imagined knight of faith 'looks just like a tax-gatherer' (FT 68). What Johannes means by this is that there are no heroic, 'other-worldly' traits which 'give away' the knight of faith: 'One detects nothing of the strangeness and superiority that mark the knight of the infinite' (FT 68).[12] No (and this is the second point), he 'belongs altogether to finitude': 'belongs altogether to the world' (FT 68). To see what Johannes means by this, it is worth quoting at length this memorable portrait:

> This man takes pleasure, takes part, in everything, and whenever one catches him occupied with something his engagement has the persistence of the worldly person whose soul is wrapped up in such things ... He takes a holiday on Sundays. He goes to church. No heavenly glance or any other sign of the incommensurable betrays him; if one didn't know him it would be impossible to set him apart from the rest of the crowd; for at most his hearty, lusty psalm-singing proves that he has a good set of lungs. In the afternoon he takes a walk in the woods. He delights in everything he sees, in the thronging humanity, the new omnibuses ... Towards evening he goes home, his step tireless as a postman's. On the way it occurs to him that his wife will surely have some special little warm dish for his return, for example roast head of lamb with vegetables. If he were to meet a kindred spirit, he could continue as far as Østerport so as to converse with him about this dish with a passion befitting a *restaurateur*. As it happens, he hasn't a penny and yet he firmly believes his wife has that delicacy waiting for him. If she has, to see him eat it would be a sight for superior people to envy and for plain folk to be inspired by, for his appetite is greater than Esau's. If his wife doesn't have the dish, curiously enough he is exactly the same.
>
> (FT 69)

What is striking about this description is the imagined character's ability genuinely to dwell in the finite world. He takes a genuine delight in the pleasures and curiosities it offers: singing, crowds of people, new modes of transport, a good dinner. There is no reason why tax-gatherers – or, for that matter, plumbers or university students – could not have precisely the same relation to the finite. There is nothing outwardly unusual or heroic about this character. Elsewhere in the passage from which I quoted above, Johannes tells us that this knight of faith is neither a poet nor a genius – either of which might enable an observer to distinguish him from the ordinary man in the street. *Everything that makes the knight distinctive – that makes him a spiritual 'knight' as well as an ordinary tax-gatherer, plumber or student – belongs to 'inwardness'.* He is – genuinely, not just in outward appearance – 'carefree as a devil-may-care good-for-nothing, he hasn't a worry in the world' (FT 69). And yet – *qua* knight of faith – he does everything 'on the strength of the absurd':

> this man has made and is at every moment making the movement of infinity. He drains in infinite resignation the deep sorrow of existence, he knows the bliss of infinity, he has felt the pain of renouncing everything, whatever is most precious in the world, and yet to him finitude tastes just as good as to one who has never known anything higher ... the whole earthly form he presents is a new creation on the strength of the absurd. He resigned everything infinitely, and then took back everything on the strength of the absurd. He is continually making the movement of infinity, but he makes it with such accuracy and poise that he is continually getting finitude out of it.
>
> (FT 70)

What this figure recognises – the sense in which he has gone through infinite resignation to faith – is that everything – even the next moment of life, and the next[13] – is a divine gift.[14] Mark Tietjen suggests (drawing on the biblical passage which gives *Fear and Trembling* its title[15]) that references to *continually* making the movement of faith signal that 'faith is not a static trait, it is something one practices and something in which one matures',[16] because faith is here primarily understood as 'inwardness' (rather than assent to a set of doctrines).

But none of this will be obvious to an observer. (Recall that in this respect, Johannes is not an observer: this character is his imagined creation, and in this respect only does he have a privileged insight into his knight of faith's inwardness.) The main point, then, is that there is no way of telling, from his outward and public appearance or actions, what is going on inside the knight of faith's 'soul'. Consider also (as already noted) the claim that this knight is 'continually making the movement of infinity' (FT 70), a claim which complements the earlier claim that 'the movement of faith must be made continually on the strength of the absurd' (FT 67). This implies that the 'double movement' of faith is somehow a – *simultaneous?* – movement of 'infinite resignation' and 'faith'.[17] The former amounts to renouncing the finite, the latter to the paradoxical belief (that is, 'on the strength of the absurd') that one will receive the finite back – though, perhaps, we shall shortly see, in some transfigured form. We shall return to this matter later in the chapter – in particular, the matter of whether infinite resignation and faith could be *simultaneous* movements, and if so, how.

THE LAD AND HIS PRINCESS

Johannes' most vivid contrast of infinite resignation and faith occurs in the story he tells of a young lad who falls in love with a princess (FT 70ff.). It is worth noting his reasons for doing this. Johannes' concern with the importance of paying attention to the particular includes the recognition that description at a general level can achieve less than illustrating 'in a particular case ... the respective relationships to reality' (FT 70) of infinite resignation and faith. As with the Abraham case, Johannes sees the need to pay attention to the specifics of a particular narrative.[18] The lad falls in love, yet in traditional romantic terms, nothing can come of that love: it cannot 'be translated from ideality into reality' (FT 70–1).

Recall that Johannes' primary question is how the attitude of a lad who was a knight of faith would differ from one who was a mere knight of infinite resignation. However, we need first to understand the difference between the attitude of infinite resignation and that represented by characters Johannes describes as the 'slaves of misery, the frogs in life's swamp' (FT 71). The latter are 'realists',

INFINITE RESIGNATION AND FAITH 51

in the sense that they try to persuade the lad that nothing can come of such a love. Why not, they urge, settle for someone of his own station in life?[19]

The lad considers such an attitude beneath contempt ('Let them croak away undisturbed in life's swamp' [FT 71]), relying as it does on a mode of valuation which thinks in terms of minimising risk. Johannes contrasts the knight of infinite resignation with 'those capitalists who invest their capital in every kind of security so as to gain on the one what they lose on the other' (FT 72). The point of Johannes' return to economic imagery (recall the very beginning of the book) is that it appears as if life too requires us to make certain 'investments': what is worth our attention and dedication, and what is not? According to the 'slaves of misery', a humble lad's negligible chances with a princess make the lad's love a 'bad risk'. But the lad's attitude makes it clear that for him, issues of love, care and commitment should not be approached from the perspective of risk-minimisation. Instead, once he has determined that this love 'really is the content of his life' (FT 71) – that is, that it is no mere infatuation – we are told that he concentrates 'the whole of his life's content and the meaning of reality in a single wish' (FT 72).

His love for her is unconditional, and to a large extent his sense of self is determined by it; it is an identity-conferring commitment. Such an unconditional commitment is a necessary prerequisite to the movement of infinite resignation. But this is no fairy tale: our lad and his princess do not live 'happily ever after'. The lad recognises that he will not 'get the girl', and here is where the movement of infinite resignation itself enters the picture. Despite the fact that this love is central to the lad's sense of self, he renounces it in 'resignation'. In other words, he 'resigns' that which is most precious to him in the finite world. In doing so, an important change takes place, which Johannes describes as his gaining an 'eternal consciousness' (FT 72): in renouncing something finite, he gains something infinite. This *particular* love for a *particular* finite being becomes transformed. The following passage is crucial for our purposes:

> His love for the princess would take on for him the expression of an eternal love, would acquire a religious character, *be transfigured into a*

> *love for the eternal being* which, although it denied fulfilment, still reconciled him once more in the eternal consciousness of his love's validity in an eternal form that no reality can take from him.
>
> (FT 72)

In other words, the love becomes 'eternalised': transformed and channelled into love for 'the eternal being' – God. This transcendentalising move is accompanied by a certain *comfort* ('in infinite resignation there is peace and repose and consolation in the pain' [FT 74]) and an alteration in the lad's self-relation. The 'consolation' is, I suspect, a function of the lad's coming to think of the existence he has once he has 'resigned' as 'higher' – more 'spiritual' – than his pre-resignation existence. (Perhaps the lad effectively reasons thus: once you have renounced that finite thing which is most precious to you, what but the infinite could provide consolation?) Edward Mooney puts it as follows: the lad's life 'is no longer focused by concern for a finite individual. His standpoint is now *outside* the flux of petty, worldly things.'[20] Moreover, this makes him *immune from hurt*: he has 'the eternal consciousness of his love's validity in an eternal form that no reality can take from him' (FT 72). On this view, what is most important about all this is that the lad *devalues the finite* (or immanent) *in favour of the infinite* (or transcendental). We are told that: 'He pays no further finite attention to what the princess does, and just this proves that he has made the movement infinitely' (FT 73). So much so that, on Mooney's reading, Johannes implies that the lad would actually be *embarrassed* if the princess were to return to him.[21] For Mooney, if the movement of resignation is 'correctly' and 'infinitely' (FT 73) made, then the princess's marriage to a prince will be an irrelevance to the resigned lad. In an influential reading we shall examine (but ultimately resist) below, Mooney suggests that the price that the lad has paid for his diminished hurt is diminished *care*;[22] so, on this view, the knight of infinite resignation manifests *diminished care for the finite*. This is not to say that his viewpoint is indistinguishable from the kind of view that preaches total non-attachment. There is a certain kind of 'stoic hardening of the self to disappointment'[23] which would, at the outset, counsel the lad not to get attached to anything: that way he will not be disappointed when it is taken from him. As we have seen, this is *not* the attitude of the knight of infinite resignation: his attachment is central to his mode of being and self-relation. Nevertheless, he is prepared to 'resign' – renounce – that which is most important to him. And what distinguishes him from the supporters of non-attachment is that in doing so, his attachment is *transformed* – infinitised, eternalised, transcendentalised. Yet this, Johannes seems to imply, entails a kind of loss.

There are two more vital factors to note about infinite resignation. First, it involves *self-sufficiency*: from the standpoint of infinite resignation, 'even in loving another one should be sufficient unto oneself ... one who has infinitely resigned is enough unto himself' (FT 73). One dimension of this self-sufficiency is that the movement of infinite resignation is something *the self can achieve by itself*:

> Resignation does not require faith, for what I win in resignation is my eternal consciousness, and that is a purely philosophical movement, which I venture upon when necessary, and which I can discipline myself into doing ... Through resignation I renounce everything, this movement is one I do by myself, and when I do not do it that is because I am cowardly and weak[.]
>
> (FT 77)

In other words, resignation is achievable by the individual, without outside help, and is *a function of his own will*.[24] To claim the inability to make the movement of resignation would simply be to be a coward. Second, infinite resignation *can be understood*: though it is no mean achievement, requiring 'strength and energy and freedom of spirit' (FT 76), all of this can be understood as something that human beings can achieve under their own lights. Whereas, as we have already seen, the next step – that of faith – 'dumbfounds' Johannes, whose 'brain reels' (FT 76). In summary, then, we have seen that infinite resignation involves a transcendentalising transformation of the lad's love, his self-sufficiency, and is understandable to an observer. Each of these aspects, we can now see, contrasts with faith.

A crucial difference between infinite resignation and faith is that the knight of faith's ability to dwell in the finite remains undiminished. As we have seen, what amazes Johannes about

Abraham is that, faced with the divine command to sacrifice Isaac, Abraham, while prepared if need be to carry out the sacrifice, trusts in God so that 'on the strength of the absurd' he believes that he will 'get Isaac back' – and with joy (of which more shortly).[25] Not in an afterlife, but in *this* life. If Johannes' lad were a knight of faith, Johannes tells us, he would do 'exactly the same as the other knight, he infinitely renounces the claim to the love which is the content of his life; he is reconciled in pain; but then comes the marvel, he makes one more movement, more wonderful than anything else, for he says: "I nevertheless believe that I shall get her, namely on the strength of the absurd, on the strength of the fact that for God all things are possible"' (FT 75). And what Johannes judges 'wonderful' [*Vidunderligt*] is not 'repose' or 'rest' [*Hvile*] in the 'pain of resignation' but 'joy on the strength of the absurd' (FT 79).

Exactly what Johannes means by 'belief on the strength of the absurd' is a notorious question. Johannes insists that this does not merely mean 'improbable', 'unexpected' or 'unforeseen' (FT 75), but downright *impossible*, 'humanly speaking' (FT 75). Note, though, his qualifier: the knight of faith is not obliged to believe the *logically* impossible but to submit his trust to God: that God can achieve what is humanly impossible.[26] '[A]ll that can save him is the absurd; and this he grasps by faith' (FT 75–6). For present purposes, I want merely to note that the relation of the knight of faith to the finite is significantly different to that of his 'resigned' counterpart. The knight of faith's 'greatness' inheres in large part in the way in which he is able 'to stick to the temporal after having given it up' (FT 52). A full account of the meaning of this phrase would turn upon the Kierkegaardian idea of 'repetition' [*Gjentagelse*], central to which is the idea of giving something up and yet getting it back in some transformed and transfigured sense.[27] *This* is where he differs from the knight of infinite resignation, and it is *this*, Johannes insists, which makes Abraham, qua knight of faith, so 'great'. Note that his dependence on God, and willingness to submit to God in trust, contrasts significantly with the self-sufficiency of the knight of resignation. And note also – though we can hardly miss this, since Johannes keeps repeating the point – that the third aspect under which the two knights can be compared is that whereas infinite resignation can be understood, faith remains an enigma – to Johannes and other outsiders, at least.

But there is another dimension worth exploring. In contrast to resignation, several recent commentators have stressed that one of the knight of faith's main features is his joy (FT 65);[28] and again, a joy taken *in the finite*. A particularly good example here is Johannes' earlier image of the 'mundane' knight of faith: the man who fantasises about a delicious meal that his wife might have prepared for him, yet who is just as joyous when he returns home to much plainer fare than he had imagined. To clarify further the idea of joy in the finite, it is useful to consider another Kierkegaardian pseudonym, Johannes Climacus, author of the *Postscript*, and his famous discussion of whether a religious person could legitimately enjoy a trip to the Deer Park, a Copenhagen amusement park. What is significant about this for us is that, like Johannes de silentio, Climacus also talks of the 'movement of infinity' and insists that a religious person must find a way of combining his 'God-relationship' with the finite ends and trivial activities of human existence, such as visits to the Deer Park. (It is significant here that the Deer Park was, according to George Pattison, considered 'the epitome of noisy, stupid vulgarity'.[29]) Climacus is suspicious of 'the monastic movement', the religious attitude that encouraged withdrawal from the world in order to pursue closeness to God. Such withdrawal is neither necessary nor even desirable: if made, Climacus insists, it should be done with 'a certain sense of shame' (CUP 414). (Climacus compares the person who can only pursue a God-relationship by withdrawal from the world with a woman who, unable to use the thought of her beloved to give her strength to go about her work, instead needs to go to *his* place of work and be with him continually.) Thus, Climacus goes further than Johannes, in describing as an 'illness' the inability to bring one's God-relationship into a further relationship with the finite (CUP 486). Yet Johannes' lad as knight of infinite resignation is incapable of this. We can thus assume that Climacus would pass the same verdict on such knights as he would on those heading for the cloister.

A second key feature of the knight of faith's joy is the *absence of blame and accountability* that feature in his view of the world.

Abraham never asks who is to blame for the call to sacrifice Isaac; the hungry 'mundane' knight of faith never blames his wife for the absence of a banquet. Indeed, note that in all of the first three 'sub-Abrahams' of the 'Attunement', blame is present as a central factor. Recall: the first sub-Abraham pretends to be a heartless monster, thinking it better that Isaac blame his father rather than God. The second – even after the appearance of the ram has made the human sacrifice unnecessary – 'saw joy no more' (FT 46) and effectively blames God for the whole ordeal. The third 'begged God to forgive his sin at having been willing to sacrifice Isaac, at the father's having forgotten his duty to his son' (FT 47). In other words, he considers the ethical to be the highest duty, and in so far as his willingness to sacrifice Isaac amounts to a momentary willingness to violate this highest duty, he thinks in terms of his *own* sin, guilt and blameworthiness. Yet in the Abraham who truly deserves the title 'knight of faith', blame has dropped out of the picture, to be replaced by joy.

We are now in a position to see why Johannes thinks that faith requires a 'paradoxical and humble courage' (FT 77). The humility inheres in the fact that while the movement of resignation can be performed by my own strength of will, the 'getting back' which faith provides is something I cannot bring about myself. To view someone or something (Isaac, or life itself) under the aspect of 'gift' is radically to transform my view of it – and myself.[30] The courage of faith is of a very different sort from that of the more standard kind of hero.

Thus we end up where we have been before: Johannes admires faith while professing a failure to understand it. His admiration, once again, is a counterbalance to the desire of 'the age' to sell faith short, and fail to recognise it as an awesome mystery, 'the greatest and most difficult of all' (FT 80). Abraham's significance *qua* knight of faith should not be downgraded. There is no halfway house: 'let us either forget all about Abraham or learn how to be horrified at the monstrous paradox which is the significance of his life, so that we can understand that our time like any other can be glad if it has faith' (FT 81). The theme here is the first-person appropriation that is central to Kierkegaard's work. In line with this, Johannes emphasises that a major part of the point of considering the Abraham narrative is 'so that a person may judge for himself whether he has the inclination and courage to be tried in such a thing' (FT 81). Here is one of the clearest statements that relating to Abraham as an exemplar demands and requires *self-examination*. Johannes presents his reader with the following question: Are *you* capable of what Abraham was capable of? This is what Johannes has been asking himself, and what he expects his reader to do also. It might still be crucial to ask, however, *in what sense* we are to take Abraham as exemplary. We shall return to this question in Chapter 6.

WHAT IS THE CONNECTION BETWEEN FAITH AND INFINITE RESIGNATION?

What the above account leaves unclear is what Johannes means when he claims that faith is a 'double movement'. Does the knight of faith make two distinct movements – first a movement of infinite resignation, identical to that made by the knight of infinite resignation, and then a second movement, that of 'faith'? Certainly, this is how Johannes' claim has often been read, and there are passages in the text that support such a reading. Johannes insists that 'anyone who has not made this movement [infinite resignation] does not have faith' (FT 75), and that the knight of faith makes 'one more movement' (FT 75) than infinite resignation. But the challenge for an account of this is to explain how the following problem can be avoided. If the very nature of resignation is the renunciation of the finite and the particular, and the very nature of faith is an embrace of the finite and the particular, how is the 'double movement' of faith, thus construed, possible? How can Abraham genuinely give up Isaac, while then making 'one more movement', the defining characteristic of which is that he believes that he will 'get Isaac back'? Does not the latter belief amount, ultimately, to the view that he will not, really, have to give up Isaac? Thus the movement of faith seems to amount to a renunciation of the movement of resignation. Can we make sense of this? As we have seen, it is in the light of such apparent contradiction that Johannes expresses incomprehension: he is 'aghast'; 'amazed' (FT 66); 'virtually annihilated' (FT 62). But must we rest content with being dumbfounded here? Must we rest content with talking, along with Johannes, of faith in terms of 'the absurd'?

There are several possibilities here. First, it could be that faith, by its very nature, is totally incomprehensible, and that Johannes' response is the right one for this reason. Second, it could be that Kierkegaard's view of faith is inherently confused. Third, it could be that *Johannes'* view of faith is limited. The most likely reason for this third possibility is that – as he readily admits – Johannes stands 'outside' faith. This leaves open the possibility that faith might look significantly different to someone on the 'inside'. Fourth, it could be that we need to read the Abraham story on an allegorical level, beyond what Johannes explicitly says. In what follows, I shall argue for a combination of the third and fourth possibilities – though I now think we can travel further with Johannes than I originally thought when writing the first edition of this book.[31]

The first possibility should surely be rejected if at all possible. If Abraham is utterly beyond comprehension, and if it follows from this that faith is utterly beyond comprehension, then what could there be to say about it? On this view, what would distinguish faith from any other incomprehensible form of behaviour? And if it cannot be so distinguished, why should anyone admire it or its exemplars? Yet admiration Johannes clearly has – which in turn would make Johannes (at least *qua* admirer of Abraham) pretty baffling. This would seriously hamper our ability to make sense of his text – or of understanding Kierkegaard's reasons for writing it. So if a case can be made for one of the other possibilities, we should surely, other things being equal, prefer it to this first possibility.

The problem with the second possibility is that, given the pseudonymity issue, we would not be able to draw any such conclusion from *Fear and Trembling* alone. An overall account of Kierkegaard's view of faith is beyond the scope of this book (though in fact I do not think the conclusion is warranted). But this does not greatly matter, since it is in a combination of the third and fourth possibilities that the best answer lies.

In what follows, then, I shall argue that there is a problem with taking at face value the idea that the movement of faith is incomprehensible. To be fair to Johannes, his explicit claim is that *he* does not understand Abraham – but it is very easy to slide from this into the view that (Abraham's) faith just *is* incomprehensible. It is certainly easy to reach this conclusion if we take Johannes to be saying that Abraham both believes and does not believe that he will have to kill Isaac. But perhaps this is not his view at all. (It is important to note, by the way, that the claim that there are limitations on what we can expect Johannes to be able to tell us about faith certainly does not render *all* that he says worthless: far from it. It does not follow from the fact that I have a *limited* understanding of a subject that everything I have to say about the subject is incorrect or confused. This will be important to bear in mind when considering what we can learn from Johannes – including the view of faith as 'eschatological trust' and 'radical hope' that I shall trail in this chapter and discuss in more detail in Chapter 6.)

In order to tackle this important issue, let us turn to some of the secondary literature. (Readers should be warned that this discussion of the secondary literature will take up the remainder of this chapter.) To begin with, I want to consider Mooney's understanding of faith, and some criticisms that have been made of it by Ronald L. Hall, before turning to a critique of the latter view (and my own earlier endorsement of it) made by John J. Davenport.

EDWARD MOONEY AND 'SELFLESS CARE'

Mooney's way of dealing with the apparent contradiction outlined above is to go for an allegorical reading that is, I shall argue, too weak. Mooney claims that faith needs to be understood in terms of 'selfless care' and the renunciation of proprietary claims. To illustrate this, Mooney asks us to consider an antique watch that we have cared for, and that is suddenly stolen. The likely response is both sorrow and anger. Not only would we be sad at its loss, we would also be angry that it had been *stolen*, as opposed to merely lost. This anger is inextricably linked to the fact that someone has violated our rights of ownership. As Mooney puts it, 'Care is linked to proprietary rights. It gets entwined with possessiveness and a capacity for hurt, should possession-related rights be violated.'[32]

This dimension of the capacity to be hurt, Mooney argues, could be cancelled by renouncing one's proprietary claims. If we did make such a renunciation of a possession, we could still be saddened by its loss, but we would 'be spared the added pain of knowing that our rights have been violated'.[33] Thus, 'Much of the stoic hardening of the self to disappointment and change can be interpreted as narrowing the area of proprietary claim.'[34] If I have already given something up, I cannot be hurt by its being taken away. Mooney links this way of thinking with the knight of resignation's being said to 'renounce his claim' on the princess: he 'infinitely renounces the claim to the love which is the content of his life' (FT 75).

This seems slightly misleading. The 'stoic' counsel of non-attachment that says 'Don't get too attached to anything: that way you will not be disappointed when it is taken from you' is not that of the knight of infinite resignation. As we have seen, such a knight's attachment is vitally important: an identity conferring commitment. The lad's love for the princess *is* 'the content of his life': this clearly distinguishes him from such stoical non-attachment. Thus it is misleading for Mooney to present infinite resignation as such a form of stoicism. Nevertheless, despite the centrality to his life of his love for the princess, the lad *qua* knight of resignation is prepared to 'resign' or 'renounce' that which is most important to him. Moreover, he does so in such a way that according to Mooney, as we have already seen, he pays a price for diminished hurt: diminished care.

Mooney now aims to contrast such a case of love or care with one that is not tied up with proprietary claims at all:

> I may enjoy and warmly anticipate the appearance of a sparrow at my feeder. Yet I would claim no rights over this object of my enjoyment. The matter of its life and death is something over which I have no claim. Of course, I would feel indignant were someone maliciously to injure it. But in the course of things, the sparrow will go its way. Meanwhile, I will adjust myself to its goings and comings.[35]

Mooney calls such a concern – 'that forgoes proprietary claim'[36] and has nothing to do with the assertion of rights – a 'selfless concern'.[37] Its alleged application to the difference between faith and infinite resignation is as follows:

> We can now see how the knight of faith can both renounce and enjoy the finite. He sees or knows in his bones that renouncing all *claims* on the finite is not renouncing all *care* for it. The knight ... cares for the worldly with a selfless care, for she has given up all proprietary claim, all vested or egoistic expectation. The knight of resignation, on the other hand, cannot distinguish, blurs together, these sorts of concern. The lad's care for the princess is sadly diminished as he renounces his claim. To *him*, it seems impossible that one might renounce all claim and yet in a *worldly* sense still love. For the lad as for Johannes himself, only on 'the strength of the absurd', through a capacity for 'the impossible', could one both resign and preserve one's love.[38]

On this view, then, what distinguishes the knight of faith from the knight of resignation is that the former *renounces all claims while retaining his care*. I shall turn to what I find unsatisfactory about Mooney's gloss shortly, but before doing so, I want to note an important feature about Mooney's claim with which I am in sympathy. This is the possibility, mentioned above, that Johannes or a knight of resignation is wrong to construe the defining feature of the existence of the knight of faith in terms of 'the absurd' or 'the impossible'. Mooney suggests that this is simply how things appear to someone *outside the sphere of faith*, which leaves open the possibility that the knight of faith could *reject* descriptions in terms of 'the absurd'. Instead, Mooney suggests that what *appears* as 'a wild hope or an unintelligible contradiction in beliefs'[39] – and therefore 'absurd' – can in fact be understood differently, as we shall shortly see.

Other commentators (for instance C. Stephen Evans), share Mooney's view that characterising faith in terms of 'the absurd' is a view from *outside* faith. Evans draws attention to a famous quote from Kierkegaard's reply to Magnús Eiríksson's critique of Kierkegaard's ostensible position on the relation between faith and reason based on a reading of *Fear and Trembling*. Included in Kierkegaard's response is the claim that 'neither faith nor the content of faith is absurd' for the believer (though its appearing so remains a continual threat, which Kierkegaard speculates may have been 'the divine will' [JP 6: 6598 (p. 301)]). Similarly, in a journal entry from the same year (1850), Kierkegaard adds:

> The absurd is a category, the negative criterion, of the divine or of the relationship to the divine. When the believer has faith, the absurd is not the absurd – faith transforms it, but in every weak moment it is again more or less absurd to him. The passion of faith is the only thing which masters the absurd ... The absurd terminates negatively before the sphere of faith, which is a sphere by itself. To a third person the believer relates himself by virtue of the absurd; so must a third person judge, for a third person does not have the passion of faith.
>
> (JP 1: 10)

It is pretty clear in Kierkegaard's reply that Johannes de silentio is intended to be such an observing third party (which Kierkegaard accuses Eiríksson of overlooking).

All this makes sense, according to Evans, once we realise that for Kierkegaard, what counts as 'reason' is socially and historically conditioned:

> In so far as God transcends the social order, and in so far as the social order tries to deify itself and usurp divine authority, there is a necessary opposition between faith and 'reason', just as there is a tension between faith and what in *Fear and Trembling* is called 'the ethical'.[40]

I shall not pursue this discussion any further here: suffice it to note that one can accept Mooney's scepticism about the accuracy of talk of faith in terms of 'the absurd' without committing oneself to his overall position, to which we shall now return.

What is wrong with Mooney's reading, wherein what distinguishes the knight of faith from the knight of resignation, is that the former renounces all claims while retaining his care? First, we need to ask what this amounts to in the Abraham case. The willingness to sacrifice Isaac is presumably the manifestation of Abraham's willingness to renounce all proprietary claim: the willingness to give to God the best that he has, that about which he cares most. But what does it mean to say that Abraham continues to care? Are we simply restating Abraham's anguish: that he will have to kill he about whom he cares most? In which case, has Mooney's gloss told us anything we didn't already know? In order to answer this let us investigate Mooney's reading in more detail.

Mooney suggests that what appears as 'a wild hope or an unintelligible contradiction in beliefs' should instead be understood as 'a complex test of care'.[41] He achieves this by the following allegorical reading. The belief that the princess is lost – that love is impossible – 'measures a capacity to acknowledge real loss, without which one's care would be shallow and weak'.[42] Whereas the belief that the princess will be returned – that love is possible – 'measures a capacity for joyful welcome of what may be given: a capacity to acknowledge the blessings of existence, appearing wondrously, without warning or rationale'.[43] Thus, the knight of faith's apparently contradictory beliefs that the princess is lost and yet that the princess will be returned – that love is both possible and impossible – actually boils down to a capacity for 'grief and dread' on the one hand and 'joy, welcome, and delight'[44] on the other. What appears 'absurd' (to Johannes or a knight of resignation) is in fact but an example of the human capacity to have contradictory emotions. This capacity, Mooney suggests, is undeniable: think, for instance, of the possibility of 'love–hate' relationships. Thus, Johannes' talk of the absurd is a 'polemical exaggeration'.[45] Mooney glosses what he takes faith to amount to:

It is not that God can both return and not return the princess. The capacity of faith is neither the capacity to believe God capable of two mutually exclusive actions, nor the capacity to believe two incompatible propositions. It concerns a capacity for care. Not only in religious faith, but also in the poetic faith implicit in expansion of our aesthetic sensibilities, care must be plumbed, and plumbed in opposed directions. So too, the faith that accompanies any radical growth or change of self. Care will be tested both as dread of what is about to be lost and as welcome of the new and uncertain, about to be received. These temperament- or character-defining beliefs or emotions will be ambiguously mixed and must be acknowledged as mixed.[46]

Again, we need to ask how this is supposed to apply in the Abraham case. Although Mooney devotes a section to this,[47] his answer is less than crystal clear. The general idea seems to be that Abraham's willingness to sacrifice Isaac shows, in a particularly dramatic way, what renouncing a proprietary claim could amount to.

Abraham gives up his own 'immortality project' of '"possessing" the son, and the son's sons, to eternity'.[48] Yet in doing so, he does not renounce his care: 'In severing the tie, a selfless care is renewed and released'.[49] But this is problematic in a number of ways.

First, does it mean that, as Abraham wields the knife, he continues to care? Exactly what would it mean to say that? Could it amount, as mentioned before, to anything other than a restatement of Abraham's 'anguish'? And might not Johannes' incomprehension at Abraham's actions be preferable to the endorsement of Abraham's effectively saying to Isaac 'Don't think the fact that I am about to kill you means that I don't care about you'? (This seems to turn Abraham into an even more extreme version of the self-deceived sadist headmaster of yore who, about to take a strap to a child, says 'This is going to hurt me more than it hurts you'.) Part of the problem here is that Isaac's point of view has been omitted. Quite what Isaac would make of the idea that Abraham represents 'selfless care' at the very point of standing willing to plunge the knife into his breast is a moot point.

Second, consider the claim that Abraham's willingness to go through with the sacrifice shows the renunciation of a proprietary claim. Can this really be so? The evidence is at least ambiguous. My willingness to take my son's life seems even more outrageous against the background of the claim that this shows me to have renounced my claim over him. The willingness to take Isaac's life seems to show precisely that Abraham has *not* renounced his claim, in so far as it shows that he still thinks of Isaac as, in some sense, 'his', to do with as he wants. Mooney might respond to this by saying that Abraham's action shows that he is giving Isaac up to God. But this merely defers the problem: is it not problematic that Abraham's only way of doing so is by treating Isaac as a 'possession', as '*his* best'?

Perhaps Mooney would respond to these criticisms by claiming that the real significance of the Abraham story is a symbolic or allegorical one, and that these objections are too concerned with the specific details of the story of Abraham's sacrifice of Isaac. But such a response would simply underline the fact that Mooney's gloss, and the perceived need to read the stories of Abraham and the lad and the princess as 'ordeals of love' or 'complex tests of care', comes at a high price. These stories may indeed fit such descriptions, but the question remains as to why we need *these stories specifically* to draw attention to such points, or to make a point about the possibility of possessing contradictory emotions.[50] In relation to a text that places so much stress on the importance of the particular and attention to detail, is not Mooney's account excessively general?

It is worth noting that Mooney's reading stems from trying to reconcile faith and resignation as a double movement: trying to understand what it could mean to claim that the knight of faith *first* makes the movement of resignation, and *then* makes the further movement of faith. In view of the problems with Mooney's reading outlined above, it is worth considering whether an alternative understanding of the 'movement' of faith is possible.

RONALD L. HALL: RESIGNATION AS AN 'ANNULLED' POSSIBILITY?

Ronald L. Hall offers such a reading. First, consider Hall's criticism of Mooney. Hall argues that Mooney's 'selfless care' – caring for the world while making no proprietary claims upon it, a mode of existence exemplified by Mooney's relation to the sparrow at his feeder – cannot be the mode of existence of the knight of faith. This is because it does not amount to what Hall calls a fully 'human embrace' of the world and of finitude. To see what he means by this, consider his comparison between Mooney's relation to the sparrow and 'a marriage as a covenant of existential faith'.[51]

Hall takes marriage as paradigmatic of a human relationship in which one shows one's acceptance of the world and of finitude by embracing one particular significant human other. His point against Mooney is that when applied to marriage, the model of 'selfless care' is found wanting:

> What kind of marriage would it be for one spouse to say to the other that he or she does not make any claims on the other, but will simply adjust to the other's comings and goings? And what would we think if both mutually acknowledged that in the course of things the other will go his or her own way? What does the disavowing of all proprietary

claims have to do with the covenant of marriage? Isn't it just the point of the wedding vows publicly to enter into the mutual proprietary claims of each on the other?[52]

Hall anticipates Mooney's possible response: that each spouse's autonomy and independence is compromised by their partner's making such proprietary claims on them. But he does not make the most obvious counter-response, which is surely to ask 'So what?' In other words, is it not part of the very nature of a serious commitment to marriage that the making of such a lifelong commitment comes at the cost of some autonomy and independence? The point to which Hall's discussion turns is the suggestion that a degree of jealousy (as opposed to mere envy) is entirely appropriate within a marriage, since jealousy 'implies a proprietary claim, a desire to protect what is one's own'.[53] A marriage with no hint of possible jealousy is only possible when neither spouse cares about the 'goings and comings' of the other – and that is no genuine marriage at all. This seems to me true, but it is surely ancillary to the more obvious point sketched above. Of course (to anticipate a possible response that Hall considers) marriage, *qua* lifelong commitment, reduces one's 'autonomy and independence' – but then what genuine commitment does not?[54] A certain reduction in independence is a corollary that follows from the very idea of commitment. But many consider this a price well worth paying for the benefits of marriage, which shows that they do not consider untrammelled autonomy and independence the *summum bonum* of what they value.[55]

Put at its strongest, I think, Hall's point is this. Marriage embodies 'existential faith' in so far as it is a freely entered into commitment in which I embrace and commit myself to one particular significant other. This commitment is reciprocal, and so, *pace* Mooney, it is false to claim that it involves the renunciation of proprietary claims. I make claims on my spouse, and recognise that she makes claims on me. Mooney's idea of 'selfless care' does not do justice to certain fundamental human relationships – precisely because such relationships involve *commitment*. Thus the very different relationship Mooney can have to the sparrow at his feeder will not capture 'a marriage as a covenant of existential faith'.

But consider the following objection. All that Hall has done is to give us an alternative picture to Mooney. He has *not* shown that marriage can be exemplary of existential faith. Suppose that Mooney's picture of faith (care without claims) is right. In that case, the mutual commitment and reciprocal claims that are integral to marriage properly understood make marriage incompatible with faith. True, this view runs up against a serious problem in making sense of Kierkegaard's infamous quote, about his own broken engagement, that 'Had I faith I would have stayed with Regine' (KJN 2; JJ 115). But it is sufficiently intelligible an objection to justify the demand for a fuller account of Hall's alternative to Mooney and how it might be supported. And this brings us back to our central concern about this debate, namely making sense of whether or not faith includes resignation in the sense outlined earlier.

So what alternative way of understanding the movement of faith does Hall propose? Before answering this question directly, we shall need to outline further aspects of Hall's understanding of the significance of the Abraham story. According to Hall, the main point of Abraham's sacrifice of Isaac is to show us the depth of Abraham's attachment 'to finitude, to his son, to historical particularity, to this world'.[56] This is the point of the claim that Abraham 'had faith for *this* life' (FT 53). Indeed, it is worth pointing out that later in the paragraph in which this phrase appears, Johannes makes a claim about Abraham's faith that seems sharply at odds with Mooney's 'selfless care' interpretation. He says: 'it was for this life that Abraham believed, he believed he would become old in his land, honoured amongst his people, blessed in his kin, eternally remembered in Isaac' (FT 54). This hardly sounds entirely 'selfless'. Hall claims that the Abraham story teaches us the following lessons about 'existential faith'.

First, faith requires the deepening, not the withdrawal, of our commitment to finitude. For the reasons given above, this includes the *claims* that stem from such commitments. This seems to be the thought behind Hall's insistence that Abraham must deepen 'his claim on his son (and finitude in general)'.[57] Hall reads Johannes' claim that faith is the paradox 'that the single individual is higher than the universal' (FT 84) as a claim about the importance of 'particularizing and personalizing'[58] such claims. What he means by this, I think, is that it is important to see that the claims that stem from our various commitments apply to each of us in the first person. (Hall thinks that this is hinted at by the fact that God addresses Abraham personally ['Abraham, where are you?'], and Abraham replies likewise ['Here I am'].) As we have already noted, this stress on what Hall calls 'the particularity of first-person presence'[59] is an important theme elsewhere in Kierkegaard, most memorably perhaps in the *Postscript* but also in Kierkegaard's direct addresses to his reader ('How is it with you, my listener?') in the upbuilding discourses.

In other words, Hall seems to be saying, each of us is called upon to deepen the particular commitments of our lives. Faith is not 'a technique for transcending the contingencies and vulnerabilities of personal historical particularity'.[60] To live in faith 'is not to live above the threat of loss, of suffering, of death'. It does, however, involve becoming aware of such 'negative possibilities: to become conscious of the fact that such a transcendence, such refusal of our own personal presence in the world is possible'.[61]

Hall's second and third points are closely related and can thus be treated together. Such first-person commitment is ongoing and continual. In the face of continual temptation to avoid the hurts, pains and difficulties of such a fully human life, the knight of faith must *continually* refuse such temptation. Thus, 'faith is an intrinsically temporal modality of existence'.[62] But why talk of 'temptation' here? The reason is that 'the faithful reception of the world from the hands of the Eternal *presupposes an ongoing possibility of doing otherwise* – an ever-present temptation not to receive it'.[63] For Hall, this means that 'resignation' is a constant temptation. But human existence is 'intrinsically subject to possibility, and hence to anxiety, to vulnerability, to loss'.[64] In a passage influenced by Martha Nussbaum, Hall adds:

> The faithful self does not put these elements to rest, she plunges forward through them. The faithful self is continually called to embrace the world in all of its fragility, for she recognizes that it is, at any moment, in her power to refuse. The knight [of faith] knows that such a refusal would bring with it a form of existence that would be other than the human; to this possibility she must continually say 'no!'[65]

This temptation to 'refuse' the life of faith that Hall sees as fully human plays a crucial role in his understanding of the movement of faith, as we shall now see.

Recall our original question: 'What alternative way of understanding the movement of faith does Hall propose?' We are now in a position to consider an intriguing suggestion of Hall's, which would explain Johannes' claim that faith is a 'double movement' the first stage of which is infinite resignation. Reprising our earlier discussion, Hall asks,

> if faith is not simply a matter of adding a second step to the first step of world-denial, if the knight of infinite resignation fails not because he does not go far enough but because he goes in the wrong direction completely, then how can we make sense of the claim that resignation and refusal are necessary elements *within faith*?[66]

Hall's suggestion is that the sense in which faith *includes* resignation is as an 'annulled possibility'. This is an idea he takes from *The Sickness unto Death*, and what he calls Kierkegaard's 'logic of paradox'. The basic idea here is relatively simple, once one penetrates the notoriously confusing language of *Sickness*. A similar paradox to the one we are currently considering occurs in *Sickness*. (As a preliminary, we need to remember not to conflate terms like 'faith' across different Kierkegaardian texts, and also to know that faith in *Sickness* is understood as a mode of self-relation in which the self is 'relating itself to itself ... willing to be itself ... rest[ing] transparently in the power that established it' [SUD 14].) The paradox we are interested in occurs when Anti-Climacus (the pseudonymous author of *Sickness*) claims that such faith involves 'a state of the self *when despair is completely rooted out*' (SUD 14, Hall's italics). However, he later goes on to say that despair is in some sense *essential* to faith ('the *first element in faith*' [SUD 116n]). Hall defuses this apparent contradiction by noting the following further quote: 'Not to be in despair must signify the destroyed possibility of being able to be in despair; if a person is truly not to be in despair, *he must at every moment destroy the possibility*' (SUD 15, italics added).

In other words, despair is necessary for faith as an annulled possibility: something which, at all times, the person of faith 'at every moment, destroys, negates, annuls, as a possibility'.[67] If it helps, consider this. In the *Postscript*, Climacus famously describes faith as like being out on 70,000 fathoms of water (CUP 204). If we combine the two images, despair is the desire to give up and stop treading water: survival (that is, faith) is only possible by refusing that temptation – and doing so *continually*!

Thus, the answer to our problem – 'In what sense could faith be a "double movement" that includes resignation?' – is again, according to Hall: 'as an annulled possibility'. As he puts it, 'the full import of the faithful embrace of the world comes in the concrete, existential recognition of the fact that we have the power to do otherwise; it is this power to do otherwise that is a permanent possibility within faith, a possibility faith must continually annul.'[68]

This permanent possibility includes the temptation to refuse human existence with all its hurts and in all its fragility: which as we have seen is here being read as to refuse the human in the manner of the knight of infinite resignation, the lad who renounces his princess, transcendentalising and abstracting – and therefore dehumanising – his love in the process. Marriage is a good illustration of this in so far as, if a marriage is to be successful over a lifetime, one must constantly renew one's commitment to it, in the face of various temptations. Such temptations are legion: the possibility of an affair with another partner, of walking out during a 'rough patch', of a withdrawal into oneself of such extremity that it ceases to be accurate to say that one is committed to one's partner or the marriage at all.[69] This, then, is the sense in which faith includes resignation, on Hall's reading: as an ever-present temptation that must be continually annulled.

But consider the following objection. One might think that Hall's use of marriage as an illustration of existential faith does not map on to parenthood – and thus Abraham and Isaac. Suppose what makes Hall's argument work for marriage is the fact that a marriage is (at least usually, in the Western context) the free commitment of adults. I *choose* my spouse – and she chooses me – in a way that I do not choose my parents. I am only given stewardship, as it were, of my children, so I do not have a right to expect as much in the way of commitment from my children as I do from my spouse.

But this objection does not work in the Old Testament context.[70] In the world of the Old Testament, children have a very strong obligation to 'honour the father and the mother'. Children have responsibilities that extend even beyond the parents' death. (One of the laws in Deuteronomy even permits a parent to take a 'stubborn and rebellious' son before the elders of the city and have him stoned to death.[71]) The overall point is simple: in the Old Testament context, the commitment and loyalty demanded in the parent–child relationship is in no way less than that involved in a contemporary marriage. So freedom of choice does not make the relevant difference. (In addition, recall from Chapter 1 the uncertainty as to whether Isaac is a child or an adult at the time of the *akedah* events, and thus the possibility of his being a willing, autonomous participant.)

JOHN J. DAVENPORT'S OBJECTION: RESIGNATION OR DESPAIR?

The above debate is one of the matters on which I have changed my views since the first edition of this Guidebook was published. While I still think that there is much of interest in Hall's view of faith, I now find compelling an objection brought against both Hall and myself (in the first edition) by John J. Davenport.[72] Davenport objects that the reading outlined above does not adequately distinguish between resignation and *despair*, and the 'all-things-considered judgment that Isaac is forever lost'[73] (which is what faith must continually annul) constitutes despair rather than resignation. Davenport argues that we must distinguish between resignation *simpliciter* and the complex form of resignation that *Sickness* describes as a form of despair, that is, 'to be unwilling to hope that an earthly need, a temporal cross, can come to an end' (SUD 70). The latter is resignation plus the refusal to 'hope in the possibility of help, especially by virtue of the absurd, that for God everything is possible' (SUD 71). It is this attitude (and not resignation per se) that is incompatible with faith. Arguing that faith must build *cumulatively* on continuing resignation (which, as we have noted, Johannes does seem to suggest), Davenport seeks an alternative conception of resignation, compatible with Johannes' assertion that '[i]nfinite resignation is the last stage before faith, so that anyone who has not made this movement does not have faith' (FT 75).

Davenport's full answer rests on a reading of faith as what he calls 'eschatological trust'. In order to unpack this adequately, we will need first to continue with our reading of the rest of *Fear and Trembling*, before returning to Davenport in Chapter 6, where I will outline the 'eschatological trust' view of faith, and seek to build upon it further through a discussion of what Jonathan Lear has called 'radical hope'. As noted, what faith must continually annul is not resignation but despair – and this explains the importance of hope. But, for present purposes, it will help to outline Davenport's two suggested types of infinite resignation and how each is compatible with either despair or faith.

Davenport labels these two types of resignation 'Beouwulfian' and 'elegaic' (viewing both Abraham and the young lad as instances of the latter). What both types have in common is a longed-for end, valued as good, but which the agent cannot see how they can bring about under their own powers. *Pace* Mooney, Davenport also thinks that in both types of resignation, the agent *continues to value this end fully*.[74] Where the two types of resignation differ is that in the first ('Beowulfian' resignation), the agent continues to strive for the longed-for end, but without the hope that this striving will contribute to bringing it about. His examples include heroic battles in which defeat is considered 'no refutation' and Socrates' continuing to press his case with the jury while knowing all too well what the outcome will be.[75] In the second ('elegaic' resignation), the agent gives up actively striving for the longed-for end, while nevertheless not diminishing his love or care (again, contra Mooney above). But what remains humanly impossible – unachievable under the agent's own powers – remains 'eschatologically' possible – achievable through the God for whom all things are possible. For more of what this means we must wait, as I say, for Chapter 6. But what the above has sketched is a conception of resignation *compatible with either despair or faith* and which suggests that what really needs to be continually annulled in faith is not resignation but despair – thus underlining the importance of *hope* in faith.[76] In so far as resignation, thus conceived, does not require a devaluation of the finite, this suggests a way in which the movement of faith can indeed be built cumulatively on to the movement of resignation, thus preserving in a more straightforward way the idea of faith as a 'double movement'.

WHAT DOES ABRAHAM BELIEVE AT THE POINT OF DRAWING THE KNIFE?

There is a further problem we should now face head on: namely, the question of what Abraham believes at the point of drawing his knife. On the view I wish to defend, Abraham must *not actually come fully to accept that he is going to have to kill Isaac*: rather, such a despairing conclusion is what he must continually fight against. Yet later in the text, in Problema III, Johannes seems to insist that he must accept this:

> he must know at the decisive moment what he is about to do, and accordingly must know that Isaac is to be sacrificed. If he doesn't definitely know that, he hasn't made the infinite movement of resignation, in which case his words are not indeed untrue, but then at the same time he is very far from being Abraham, he is less significant than a tragic hero, he is in fact an irresolute man who can resolve to do neither one thing nor the other, and who will therefore always come to talk in riddles. But such a *Hæsistator* [waverer] is simply a parody of the knight of faith.
>
> (FT 143)

Andrew Cross draws heavily on this passage to argue for a reading of *Fear and Trembling* central to which is the idea that Abraham *does* believe that Isaac is lost.[77] Cross's reading, to which I shall now turn, is an interesting and important one, because it tackles head on issues that many overlook. Yet ultimately, I shall argue, Cross gets this matter the wrong way round. In what follows, I shall aim to show firstly what Cross achieves, but second why I think his interpretation is flawed, and why we should prefer an alternative that I shall outline.

So what does Abraham believe at the point of drawing the knife? Cross argues that Abraham's actual belief is 'that Isaac will die (at the appointed hour, etc.), and believes only that'.[78]

Whereas in my view, Abraham's belief is – ultimately – that he will *not* have to sacrifice Isaac (or that Isaac is not ultimately lost), despite the enormous evidence (to 'worldly understanding') to the contrary. I shall flesh out both interpretations below, but note the following important preliminary. Both readings have a significant advantage over a common traditional interpretation, which has Abraham believing two incompatible things: first, that he will have to sacrifice Isaac (and so Isaac will die), and second that somehow he will not have to sacrifice Isaac (and so Isaac will not die). The former belief shows Abraham's obedience to God, while the second belief shows his ability to continue to take joy in Isaac. This is how Johannes' remarks about Abraham's faith being 'on the strength of the absurd' are often interpreted: it is absurd because it involves simultaneously believing two mutually contradictory propositions.

The problem with such a reading should be obvious. Cross puts the problem very clearly. Such an interpretation

> should be adopted only as a last resort, since adopting it means attributing a radically and patently untenable position to de silentio (and, possibly, to Kierkegaard). The problem isn't just that a conception of faith as involving the simultaneous and explicit affirmation of contradictory propositions is wildly implausible as an ideal (although it is that). The problem is that such a conception is incoherent on its face. There is nothing that it is to hold contradictory beliefs in this manner; to hold the one just is to deny the other.[79]

Hence we can agree with Cross that we should try to find another reading of the text if at all possible. Both Cross's reading and mine avoid this 'contradictory beliefs' problem. But which of them is to be preferred? Cross's reading, in a nutshell, is as follows. Abraham acts on the basis of faith – that is, acts as if he *won't* lose Isaac – while all the time fully believing that he *will* lose Isaac. His orientation to Isaac's survival is 'practical, rather than cognitive'.[80] Despite his belief,

> he goes on being as wholeheartedly committed to Isaac as before. Rather than finding peace and security by abandoning his interest in the finite (his love for Isaac), a security that would consist in his

being sheltered from the kind of personal devastation that would occur if he lost that upon which the meaningfulness of his life is based, he goes on loving Isaac just as before, fully recognizing the devastation he thereby subjects himself to.[81]

His faith is manifested in

a sustaining wholehearted attachment to, and identification with his relationship to, Isaac at the same time that he believes that Isaac's loss is certain and recognizes that that loss would destroy him. Any irrationality here is practical, not epistemic. He is knowingly subjecting himself to an overwhelming harm, a harm whose occurrence he believes to be certain, and which could be avoided by his repudiating his involvement in the finite and retreating to the self-protective stance of the knight of resignation.[82]

My reading has things the other way round. As I see it, at the point of pulling the knife Abraham, while 'convinced of the impossibility, humanly speaking' (FT 75) of keeping Isaac, has such faith and trust in God that he believes – despite the overwhelming evidence to the contrary – that he will *not* lose Isaac. On this view, as with that of Cross, belief 'on the strength of the absurd' does not mean believing two contradictory propositions. Rather, Abraham's belief is 'absurd' from the perspective of 'human' reason (especially that of an outside observer such as Johannes): he continues to trust God despite the utter lack of evidence (to 'worldly understanding') that this makes any sense.

Why accept my reading over that of Cross? I shall try to make this case by considering Cross' objections to a similar reading. Let me start with two preliminaries by way of clarification, the second of which is particularly important. I do not mean to endorse either of two readings, considered and rejected by Cross, that might look superficially similar to mine. The first of these is the idea that Abraham simply does not *entertain* the thought that Isaac might have to die. As Cross rightly says, this would make Abraham 'either so blind or so deluded that he belongs in the category of mere unreflective immediacy'[83] – a primitive form of what Kierkegaard calls 'the aesthetic'[84] that is a million miles from 'faith'.

But that is not my view: far from never being entertained, the thought of losing Isaac is always ever-present in Abraham's mind: hence his 'anguish'.

But this brings us to the second picture, of an Abraham who 'recognizes but discounts the threat to Isaac's continued existence ... letting his wishes blind him to the plain and evident facts of his situation'.[85] I don't want to endorse such an Abraham either, but it is important to note that Cross blurs some important distinctions in this part of his discussion. He claims that: 'An Abraham who continues to think that, perhaps by some miraculous circumstance, Isaac will not be lost is, in de Silentio's view, not properly facing up to his situation'.[86] In fact, I don't see any textual evidence for the claim that Johannes thinks that Abraham's belief in the possibility of divine miraculous intervention would be a form of cowardly self-deception.[87] The textual evidence Cross provides here is inadequate. He rightly notes that Johannes distinguishes Abraham from 'the miserable [*usle*] hope that says "Who knows what may happen, it's possible certainly"' (FT 66). But this 'caricature of faith' (FT 66) – which *does* look like a form of self-deception, of hiding one's head in the sand – surely does not capture all possible manifestations of a belief in the possibility of divine grace. Neither would such a belief be what Johannes is aiming to exclude in contrasting faith with 'the improbable, the unexpected, the unforeseen' (FT 75). (As if a plausible reaction to the idea of God becoming man in the form of Christ could be: 'I didn't see *that* coming'.) The picture I am endorsing is of an Abraham who trusts in God, who believes in the possibility of divine grace even in this, the most terrible of situations. This cannot be dismissed as identical to an Abraham who, at the point of unsheathing the knife, says 'Of course, it's *improbable* that I won't have to kill Isaac'. *Pace* Cross, an Abraham who believes in divine grace – in the providence of a trustworthy God – cannot be ruled out (at least, not without further argument) simply on the grounds of being a self-deceived 'dissembler'.[88] It is sheer caricature to suppose that such an Abraham could be captured as someone 'going through certain motions, calling God's bluff as it were, all the time telling himself, "Of course this is just pretend, I'm not really going to have to give Isaac up".'[89]

The main point here is that belief in divine grace need neither be self-deceptive nor entail the kind of spiritual 'laziness' that Cross is rightly concerned about. In his journals, Kierkegaard makes clear his commitment to the view that belief in divine grace does not obviate the need for continued 'striving': 'It is detestable ... for a man to want to use grace, "since all is grace", to avoid all striving' (JP 2: 1909). It is true that the 'dissembling', self-deceived Abraham seems guilty of some version of this spiritual laziness: the laziness of not fully facing up to his situation. But Cross has not provided us with reason to think that the Abraham I have in mind – one who trusts in the possibility of divine grace even in the most terrible trial he can imagine – need be such a figure.[90]

My interpretation is in fact similar in most respects to one that Cross describes as 'common':[91]

> Abraham overcomes his belief that Isaac's death is certain, in the sense of ceasing to have that belief and coming to believe instead that Isaac will not die. His faith either consists in or makes possible his holding the latter belief in spite of his awareness that it is contradicted by all available evidence – in spite of his recognition that it is an absurd belief to hold in his circumstances. He believes that Isaac will remain with him, believes this 'on faith alone', where this may mean that he believes it in the absence of epistemic support, in the face of overwhelming counterevidence, in virtue of his confidence in God's good will, or some combination of the three.[92]

I do not want to claim that Abraham comes to replace one belief (Isaac will die) with another (Isaac will live). Rather, as I see it, the former is what unaided human reason dictates – what the evidence thus amassed supports – but Abraham's faith is such that he believes the latter. Nevertheless, that qualification aside, the above *is* basically my view. Cross' reasons for rejecting it are twofold: 'An Abraham who believes that Isaac's death will not come about is not performing a genuine sacrifice, and is irresolute in the bargain.'[93] But these are not good reasons. First, the issue is not best described in terms of whether Abraham is performing a genuine sacrifice. What matters is whether he *would be* willing to go through with it if push came to shove. I see no problem with imagining an Abraham who would be prepared to go through with the sacrifice if need be, but whose trust in God is such that he continues to believe that Isaac will be spared. Note, crucially, that in the Problema III passage quoted earlier, the future tense is used: Abraham 'must know at the decisive moment what he *is about to* do, and accordingly must know that Isaac *is to be* sacrificed' (FT 143, my emphasis). This clearly allows for the possibility that – despite how things look – all is not yet lost. But is such an Abraham 'irresolute', a 'waverer'? Again, I see no reason to judge him thus. As we have seen, it is not that he is trying to have his cake and eat it by believing two incompatible things. Rather, he believes one thing – Isaac will be spared – despite the overwhelming evidence to the contrary. As Johannes explicitly says, 'he believed that God would not demand Isaac of him, while still he was willing to offer him if that was indeed what was demanded' (FT 65). My reading captures this exactly, whereas this passage is quite clearly a problem for Cross. (Though Cross does attempt to explain this, as we shall shortly see.) However, there is one apparent problem for my reading. In what follows, I shall try to show that this problem is only apparent.

The ostensible problem for my interpretation stems from the Problema III passage. Immediately after saying that Abraham must know that Isaac is to be sacrificed, Johannes adds, 'If he doesn't definitely know that, he hasn't made the infinite movement of resignation' (FT 143). Now, on my interpretation, if what this means is that he makes the movement of resignation, and then a second, temporally discrete movement of faith, then Johannes ought not to say this. But we do not have to read the passage this way. For there *is* a sense in which Abraham has made the movement of resignation. He has 'resigned' in the sense that he has steeled himself for the eventuality that *if* his faith is misplaced, then he will sacrifice Isaac. Further, from Davenport, we can add that he can no longer see any way that he can bring about his desired end (Isaac's continuing to live, in order to flourish and produce the promised offspring) under his own powers. Nonetheless, he still continues to value Isaac's life as before. Moreover, in so far as his resignation is 'elegaic', he gives up actively striving to bring about Isaac's survival (hence the trip to Moriah as commanded).

His entire trust is now in God. But — in so far as he has faith — he does *not* believe that this trust is misplaced.

The problem for Cross is more serious. Whereas the above passage comes at the end of a long digression about aesthetic concealment in Problema III (more of which in Chapter 5), the passage that poses such a problem for Cross is located absolutely centrally in the main part of the text that deals with faith and resignation. This, recall, is the passage stating that Abraham 'believed that God would not demand Isaac of him, while still he was willing to offer him if that was indeed what was demanded' (FT 65). How can Cross explain this?

Cross admits that he has a potential problem: 'How ... are we to make sense of de silentio's repeated claim that Abraham "believed" that Isaac would not be demanded?'[94] But since he holds that Abraham must believe that Isaac will die, he aims to interpret this 'belief' as 'a noncognitive state of commitment ... an expression of an attitude of confidence, commitment, or trust, directed toward some nonpropositional entity such as a person'.[95] (He does this partly on the basis of the observation that the Danish term translated as 'believe' in the passages in question — *tro* — is the same as that translated as 'had faith' in others.)

First, note that this does not answer Cross' own question, which was explicitly posed about 'believing *that*'. But there is a further problem. Who Abraham 'believes in', of course, is God. He 'believes in God' not simply in the sense that he believes that such a God exists — that is taken for granted of all the sub-Abrahams of the Attunement, as well as 'the' Abraham. Rather, Abraham 'believes in God' in such a way that 'that phrase indicates an attitude of confident trust in this entity'.[96] But trust in God to do what, or in what sense? Cross' commitment to the idea that Abraham believes that Isaac will die means that 'it cannot be a trust in God to prevent Isaac's permanent demise from coming about'.[97] Thus he has to seek another dimension to this trust. In doing so, as well as failing to answer his own original question, he ends up with an implausible picture of trust, on which he bases an inadequate picture of the knight of faith. How so?

Cross draws on Annette Baier to give an account of 'the structure of trust'. Adult (as opposed to naive, childish) trust involves 'voluntarily and knowingly leaving oneself open to harm that the trusted person, in virtue of being trusted, is in a position to inflict upon one'.[98] So far, so good. But much less plausible is the further claim that 'relying upon a person who one thinks is almost certain to come through involves less trustfulness than relying on a person who one thinks is very likely to betray or disappoint one'.[99] This seems to treat trustfulness as a conscious state, whereas surely it can be the background against which a relationship operates. (My dealings with you are perhaps at their most trusting if I do not consciously ask myself whether I can rely on you, but just take it for granted that I can, perhaps because you have always shown yourself to be trustworthy in the past.[100]) On this rather shaky ground, Cross builds the following claim:

> the degree of trustfulness manifested in some performance is a function of two things: the trusting person's assessment of the likelihood that the trusted party will disappoint, and the extent of the loss that the trusting person expects to suffer in the event that the trusted party does disappoint. The maximum of trustfulness would be manifested in a person who voluntarily leaves herself open to the greatest possible loss or harm, and is certain that the harm she is counting upon not to happen will happen. *And that is precisely Abraham's stance.*[101]

But this hardly sounds like trust at all: more like sheer stupidity. Moreover, what this comes to in the Abraham case seems starkly at odds with faith, trust or hope: 'The knight of faith ... leaves his fate up to God, even as he takes it to be certain that God will disappoint.'[102] Two comments are appropriate here. First, leaving my fate up to a God whom I am certain will disappoint sounds far more like a kind of despair than faith. Such a person has *surrendered all hope* (and, presumably, any concomitant possible *joy*). So, second, for this reason, Cross cannot legitimately claim that such is the stance of the knight of faith. Far better to embrace as the knight of faith an Abraham who believes and trusts in the possibility of divine grace.

But I suggest that my interpretation fares better than that of Cross on another count. My interpretation avoids one of the most curious features of Cross' reading of the knight of faith. This is the idea that faith, as Cross thinks Johannes construes it, does not require theistic belief at all: 'In fact, belief in the existence and good will of an omnipotent agent threatens to undermine the stance of faith as de silentio describes it.'[103] Cross says this because of his insistence, which we have challenged above, that any Abraham who does not believe in the 'genuine impossibility' of Isaac's being spared must be the person who says 'Who knows what may happen, it's possible certainly.' And the idea that a future with Isaac is 'genuine impossibility' is undercut by belief in an omnipotent God for whom 'all things are possible'. Cross claims, 'If ... one recalls the various times in Abraham's life when God has come through for him when all seemed lost – as de silentio is happy to do – it comes to seem quite reasonable for him to believe that somehow or other Isaac will not be taken from him'.[104]

I don't think this will do. It requires us to believe that, following his three day ride to Mount Moriah – during which God has not intervened – and after binding Isaac – during which God has still not intervened – that Abraham, as he draws the knife, can consider it 'quite reasonable' that now is the moment that God will save the day. On my reading, Abraham *does* believe and trust that this is what will happen. But such a belief surely cannot accurately be described as 'quite reasonable'. *Pace* Cross, there is no problem at all in understanding how Johannes, a person who lacks Abraham's faith, can contemplate such a possibility and be 'aghast'. He can be aghast quite simply because Abraham's expectation is *not* 'quite reasonable'.

Even more importantly, however, the idea that Abraham's faith does not require theistic belief flies in the face of the text. The Abraham story only makes sense *at all* against an understanding that Abraham is in dialogue with his God. So in reaching the conclusion that theistic belief actually undermines the *Fear and Trembling* conception of faith, Cross shows just what an enormous price he is prepared to pay to support his reading. By contrast, the alternative interpretation I have offered pays no such price.

All of the above provide reasons to think that, at the point of drawing the knife, Abraham believes, against overwhelming evidence, that somehow Isaac will be spared. But a vital part of his faith is the need continually to annul the temptation to give in to despair: to take heed of the evidence, lose hope and trust in God, and resign himself to the loss of Isaac. That Abraham does *not* do this is a vital part of what makes him, for Johannes, the paradigm exemplar of faith. As promised, we shall flesh out this sketch further in our discussion of faith as 'eschatological trust' and 'radical hope' in Chapter 6.

NOTES

1. As noted in Chapter 2, an alternative translation of this term would be 'anxiety'.
2. Abraham has traditionally been valorised in Christian thought as a great exemplar of righteousness, based largely on Paul's remarks in Romans 4. We shall return to this issue in Chapter 5.
3. We might think that Johannes has come dangerously close to this himself in the 'Speech in Praise of Abraham': recall his threefold account of Abraham's 'greatness' at the start of that section. We shall return to this issue in Chapter 7.
4. Of course, these might not be the only distinctions necessary. One live question, already alluded to, which *Fear and Trembling* typically sparks, is how Abraham differs from the contemporary killer or would-be killer who claims a religious motivation. We shall return to this in Chapter 6, in our discussion of 'divine command' interpretations of *Fear and Trembling*, with particular reference to the difference between Abraham's situation and the contemporary one.
5. Recall the warnings as to the likely target of the term 'Hegelian' in Chapter 2.
6. Carlisle plausibly suggests that the idea here is that philosophy should recognise its own limitations (2010: 79), drawing a parallel with the humility of Socratic ignorance.
7. Hegel claims that speculative philosophy offers the same 'substance' as the Christian religion, but that the former speaks in a different language to that of the priests – a language more 'appropriate to the advanced consciousness of the modern world' (Dickey 1993: 309).
8. Hegel would claim that 'by raising the truth of Christianity to the level of philosophical consciousness, and by putting Christian values in a more-teachable form, he had made that truth and those values more, rather than less, accessible to Christians in the modern world' (Dickey 1993: 315–16). Kierkegaard's response would be that in doing so, the Hegelians had distorted the Christian message beyond recognition. On the 'comic' dimension of this, see Lippitt 2000: Chapter 2.
9. Compare, for example, Martha Nussbaum's claim that certain novels have an indispensable role to play in ethics: '[C]ertain truths about human life can only be fittingly and accurately stated in the language and forms characteristic of the narrative artist. With respect to certain elements of human life, the terms of the novelist's art are alert winged creatures, perceiving where the blunt terms of

ordinary speech, or of abstract theoretical discourse, are blind, acute where they are obtuse, winged where they are dull and heavy' (Nussbaum 1990: 5).
10 Here I prefer Walsh's and the Hongs' translation 'in the capacity of' to Hannay's 'in the guise of', 'guise' perhaps misleadingly implying semblance or pretence.
11 One could also say, as Walsh does, 'regained his original condition'.
12 The precise relation between the tragic hero and the knight of infinite resignation has puzzled commentators, but the language of 'heroism' in describing the latter, together with the fact that Johannes, as we have seen, describes himself as operating 'in the capacity of a tragic hero' [*i Qualitet af Tragisk Helt*] and yet also as having 'immense resignation' [*uhyre Resignation*], suggests that there must an overlap between the two figures, even though they are not identical.
13 See Davenport 2012: 148–9.
14 On the importance of life as a divine gift, see also the discourse 'Every Good and Every Perfect Gift Is from Above' in EUD. This is, along with 'The Expectancy of Faith' (more of which in Chapter 6), one of the two 'upbuilding discourses' published in May 1843, five months before *Fear and Trembling*.
15 '[W]ork out your own salvation with fear and trembling' (Philippians 2:12).
16 Tietjen 2013: 106.
17 Some commentators take the fact that both movements are said to be made 'continually' to mean that they must both be simultaneous. But the text is not clear on this: at one point, for instance, Johannes says: 'I make the movements of infinity, whereas [*medens*] faith does the opposite, [after] having performed the movements of infinity it makes those of finitude' (FT 67, translation adjusted). The 'after', only implicit in Hannay's translation, is explicit in Walsh's – and justifiably so, as the Danish *efter* is explicitly in the original.
18 However, we should be careful here. In some readings of *Fear and Trembling*, the story of the lad and the princess seems to get almost as much attention as does the story of Abraham in illustrating faith. Kierkegaard explicitly cautions against this in an unpublished draft of a text critical of the reading offered by Theophilus Nicolaus (a pseudonym of the Icelandic theologian Magnús Eiríksson). Here Kierkegaard describes the lad and the princess narrative as 'a minor illustration, an approximation' used 'merely to illuminate Abraham, not to explain Abraham directly' (JP 6: 6598 [p. 302]).
19 I notice that such 'realists' are still around. I once read a guide to relationships featured in a British newspaper that advised readers to take a frank look at themselves and to rate their attractiveness on a scale of 1 to 10. Readers were informed that long-term success in a relationship is most likely when the partners' level of attractiveness is 'within two points' of each other. If you are only a 'six', say, you are probably wasting your time in dating a 'nine'. So now you know.
20 Mooney 1991: 49.
21 Mooney 1991: 52, 156n37.
22 Mooney 1991: 53. Readers familiar with the first edition of this Guidebook will note that this is one of the points on which I have subsequently changed my view: more on this later.

23. Mooney 1991: 53.
24. Hence Carlisle's suggestion that the difference between resignation and faith is ultimately a question of autonomy (2010: 92).
25. Cf. Evans 2004: 71.
26. Kierkegaard makes very clear in his response to Eiríksson that the difference is between what is 'humanly possible' and what is possible for God (JP 6: 6598 [pp. 303–4]).
27. For an illuminating account of this in relation to Kierkegaard's discourse on the book of Job, see Mooney 1996: Chapter 3.
28. See, for instance, Kellenberger 1997; Evans 2004: 71; Miles 2011: 255–6. Joy [*Glæde*] is a major theme in Kierkegaard's later religious writings: see especially the discourses on the lily of the field and the bird of the air in WA.
29. See Pattison 1999: 99.
30. For more on this, see Lippitt 2015a, 2015b, and in press.
31. For the full picture, see also Chapters 6 and 7.
32. Mooney 1991: 53.
33. Mooney 1991: 53.
34. Mooney 1991: 53.
35. Mooney 1991: 53.
36. Mooney 1991: 53.
37. Mooney 1991: 53.
38. Mooney 1991: 54.
39. Mooney 1991: 56.
40. Evans 1993: 25.
41. Mooney 1991: 56.
42. Mooney 1991: 56.
43. Mooney 1991: 56.
44. Mooney 1991: 56.
45. Mooney 1991: 57.
46. Mooney 1991: 58.
47. Mooney 1991: 58–61.
48. Mooney 1991: 59.
49. Mooney 1991: 59.
50. For the record, let me add that, in general, I have much sympathy with Mooney's line (as quoted above) about the importance of recognising, and learning to live with, ambivalent emotions. (For more on this in a different context, see Lippitt 2015c.) But in the case of unpacking *Fear and Trembling* specifically, I think we need to dig deeper.
51. Hall 2000: 31.
52. Hall 2000: 31.
53. Hall 2000: 31.
54. Hall 2000: 31.
55. However, both Hegel and Kierkegaard's Judge William (the author of *Either/Or* Part II) argue that in marriage one attains a sort of 'higher' freedom. For Hegel, marriage involves 'the free consent of the two to become one person.

They give up their natural and private personality to enter a unity, which may be regarded as a limitation, but, since in it they attain to a substantive self-consciousness, is really their liberation' (Hegel 1996: §162). More on Hegel and freedom in Chapter 4. (Unless otherwise stated, all endnotes to Hegel texts are to paragraph, not page, number.)

56 Hall 2000: 33.
57 Hall 2000: 33.
58 Hall 2000: 33.
59 Hall 2000: 33.
60 Hall 2000: 34.
61 Hall 2000: 34.
62 Hall 2000: 34.
63 Hall 2000: 34, my emphasis.
64 Hall 2000: 35.
65 Hall 2000: 35.
66 Hall 2000: 35.
67 Hall 2000: 36.
68 Hall 2000: 37.
69 Stanley Cavell has discussed such themes – marriage as 'remarriage' – in relation to various films. See Cavell 1981 and Hall 2000: Chapter 4.
70 I am grateful to Hugh S. Pyper for discussion of this point.
71 See Deuteronomy 21:18–21.
72 Sharon Krishek has offered a similar objection to Hall and a reading of the relation between resignation and faith which in many ways parallels and is indebted to that of Davenport (Krishek 2009: 81–107, especially pp. 99–101, 104–7).
73 Davenport 2008a: 226.
74 Davenport 2008a: 228–9.
75 Davenport 2008a: 228–9.
76 Luther too (1964: 93–5) stresses the choice between hope and despair (by which 'nearly all people are tempted' [1964: 94]). See also Carlisle 2015: 51ff.
77 Cross 1999.
78 Cross 1999: 236.
79 Cross 1999: 238.
80 Cross 1999: 239.
81 Cross 1999: 239.
82 Cross 1999: 240.
83 Cross 1999: 234.
84 'The aesthetic' is a rich and complex category in Kierkegaard. The best-known embodiment of the aesthetic as a mode of existence – one of the Kierkegaardian 'stages on life's way' or 'existence-spheres' – is the young man known only as 'A', who is the author of at least most of the disparate collection of papers that make up Part 1 of *Either/Or*. *Either/Or* contrasts the aesthetic and ethical existence-spheres via the attitudes and worldviews of 'A' and Judge William respectively. Any brief account of the aesthetic mode of existence is likely to be

an oversimplification. However, with that warning in mind, it suffices for our purposes here to note that the aesthete is quite prepared to employ various forms of concealment in pursuit of what he perceives as 'the interesting' and to avoid boredom (described by 'A' as a 'root of all evil' [EO 227]). Kierkegaard often associates 'the interesting' in this 'aesthetic' sense with disengaged spectatorship, as opposed to the 'passion' of ethical or religious engagement. For probably the clearest brief picture of the aesthetic attitude, see A's essay 'Crop Rotation'; for the extremes of concealment to which an aesthete may be prepared to go, see 'The Seducer's Diary'. Both are contained in Part 1 of *Either/Or*, though it is unclear whether or not we are supposed to suspect A of having written the latter. For more on the aesthetic worldview, see 'In Vino Veritas' in *Stages on Life's Way*.

But what of the reference to 'unreflective immediacy'? In *Either/Or*, such a form of 'immediate' aestheticism – exemplified by the pure sensuousness of Don Juan or Don Giovanni – is contrasted with its polar opposite, the super-reflective aestheticism of Johannes the Seducer. To understand the contrast, read 'The Immediate Erotic Stages or the Musical Erotic' alongside 'The Seducer's Diary'.

85 Cross 1999: 234.
86 Cross 1999: 234.
87 Such a belief has a lengthy pedigree in the Christian tradition: recall especially the passage from Hebrews 11:17–19 cited in Chapter 1.
88 Cross 1999: 234.
89 Cross 1999: 234.
90 At the risk of getting ahead of ourselves, an additional point against Cross's reading can be gleaned from a passage in Johannes' discussion of the contrast between Abraham and the 'tragic hero' in Problema I. Of the tragic heroes he discusses (more of which in Chapter 4), Johannes says if at the decisive moment of having to sacrifice their son or daughter 'these three men had added to the heroism with which they bore their pain the little words "It won't happen", who then would understand them? If in explanation they added: "We believe it on the strength of the absurd", who then would understand them better?' (FT 87). It is clearly implied that 'It won't happen' is precisely what Abraham holds: this is what distinguishes him from the tragic heroes. More fully, *pace* Cross, I think this passage clearly suggests that Abraham believes it won't happen and believes this 'on the strength of the absurd' (in the ways explained above).
91 Puzzlingly, however, Cross cites no examples of commentators who have held it, apart from one quote from Mooney which does not make entirely clear whether or not he is ascribing this whole view to Mooney.
92 Cross 1999: 237.
93 Cross 1999: 237.
94 Cross 1999: 241.
95 Cross 1999: 241.
96 Cross 1999: 242.

97 Cross 1999: 242.
98 Cross 1999: 242. The reference is to Baier 1994.
99 Cross 1999: 243.
100 Kierkegaard's twentieth-century compatriot Knud Ejler Løgstrup is interesting on trust as a default human attitude (Løgstrup 1997).
101 Cross 1999: 243.
102 Cross 1999: 243.
103 Cross 1999: 250.
104 Cross 1999: 251.

4

SUSPENDING THE ETHICAL
PROBLEMATA I AND II

PROBLEMA I: IS THERE A TELEOLOGICAL SUSPENSION OF THE ETHICAL?

Johannes ends his Preamble with a promise that what follows will show 'how monstrous a paradox faith is, a paradox capable of making a murder into a holy act well pleasing to God ... which no thought can grasp because faith begins precisely where thinking leaves off' (FT 82). We might think that by now we had been made well aware of 'how monstrous a paradox faith is'. But what Johannes is promising is a look at the same problem from a different angle. He will, he claims, 'extract from the story ... its dialectical element' (FT 82), though in fact even in what follows, its 'anguished' dimension is never far from his concerns. Nevertheless, there is a change of emphasis at the beginning of Problema I. Each of the three problemata begins with the assertion, with only very minor differences in wording in each case, that 'the ethical ... is the universal [*det Almene*]' (FT 83: cf. 96, 109). It is easy to be misled by this. It might appear as if Johannes is offering us a *definition* of 'the ethical', whereas in fact the problemata – indeed, the whole book – may well be written in order to question the very assumption that the ethical is the universal. So if this is the very claim that *Fear and Trembling* places under scrutiny, what does it mean?

At the start of the first problema Johannes glosses the idea that the ethical is the universal in two ways, which he presents as versions of the same point. As the universal, the ethical 'applies to everyone, which can be put from another point of view by saying that it applies at every moment' (FT 83). Some of the secondary literature has concerned itself with whether the conception of the ethical under scrutiny is predominantly Kantian or Hegelian. This will not be the predominant purpose of the following. For the record (and as will become clearer), I think it is predominantly Hegelian, though I also think that *some* of what Johannes has to say is also relevant to a Kantian conception, so I shall also briefly discuss that.[1]

Exactly what is it about Abraham that makes him offensive to the view of the ethical Johannes has in mind? There are arguably four features, though all of them are interrelated. First, Abraham is an *exception*. In being prepared to obey God's command, he seems to be excluding himself both from the ethical requirement not to kill an innocent human being, and more specifically, from his particular responsibility to his son. ('Abraham's relation to Isaac, ethically speaking, is quite simply this, that the father should love the son more than himself' [FT 86; cf. 98].) Abraham's status as an exception segues into the second, and probably most significant, of the ways in which he appears scandalous. His putting himself above what ethics dictates amounts to 'the paradox' that 'the single individual' is 'higher than the universal' (FT 95). He fails in what is, according to the view of the ethical under scrutiny, 'the individual's ethical task': 'to abrogate his particularity so as to become the universal' (FT 83). What makes him 'higher' is, third, his direct relation to God. (Recall the way Genesis presents direct conversations between Abraham and God, such as over the fate of Sodom and Gomorrah.) And, fourth, this extraordinary God-relation means that Abraham is unable to *explain* himself to others in the public arena of language. Taken together, these four reasons are why Johannes considers Abraham to be a scandal to those who hold that 'the ethical is the universal'. But we need to say more about each of these points.

ABRAHAM AS EXCEPTION

One of the major resonances of the term 'universal' in moral philosophy derives from Kant. In his *Grounding for the Metaphysics of Morals*, one of the ways in which Kant formulates his famous 'categorical imperative' is as follows: 'I should never act except in such a way *that I can also will that my maxim should become a universal law*.'[2] This has become known as the 'formula of universal law'.

Kant's famous example of lying shows how he intends this to work. I can conclude that I should not lie because I could not coherently will lying as a universal law: that is, applying to everyone, at all times. Why not? Because, if *everyone* were to lie,

> there would really be no promises at all, since in vain would my willing future actions be professed to other people who would not believe what I professed, or if they over-hastily did believe, then they would pay me back in like coin. Therefore, my maxim [a universal law of lying] would necessarily destroy itself just as soon as it was made a universal law.[3]

So in speaking of 'universal law' does Kant mean 'universal' in the sense of applying to everyone, at all times? Contemporary exponents of Kant's ethics are keen to dispel the stereotypical picture of him as an inflexible worshipper of exceptionless rules. Typically, they argue that Kant's ethics allows for far more flexibility and attention to the particular than is commonly supposed. (See, for example, the 'casuistical questions' he raises at various points of *The Metaphysics of Morals*, on issues such as what *counts* as an instance of morally culpable suicide[4] or of 'defiling oneself by lust'.[5]) Nevertheless, when it comes to killing an innocent human being, things are fairly clear-cut. On Kant's view, I would not be allowed to kill an innocent human being, even if commanded to do so by God.[6] Hence Kant's explicit condemnation of Abraham in *The Conflict of the Faculties*. The comment on Abraham already noted in Chapter 2 is prefaced by the following claim:

If God should really speak to a human being, the latter could still never *know* that it was God speaking. It is quite impossible for a human being to apprehend the infinite by his senses, distinguish it from sensible beings, and *be acquainted with* it as such. But in some cases the human being can be sure that the voice he hears is *not* God's; for if the voice commands him to do something contrary to the moral law, then no matter how majestic the apparition may be, and no matter how it may seem to surpass the whole of nature, he must consider it an illusion.[7]

It is then in a footnote on Abraham that he adds:

Abraham should have replied to this supposedly divine voice: 'That I ought not to kill my good son is quite certain. But that you, this apparition, are God – of that I am not certain, and never can be, not even if this voice rings down to me from (visible) heaven'.[8]

Moreover, such killing is prohibited in virtue of the fact that the innocent in question is another rational being. (In Kantian language, my killing such a person would violate their status as an *end*: I cannot legitimately treat them only as a *means* to an end.) But it would be wrong to infer from this that Kant is committed to the absurd position of holding that Abraham's 'anguish' consisted solely of the destruction of another 'rational agent': that the fact that the intended sacrificial victim was his son was unimportant. Kant is quite prepared to allow for a variation in the degree of benevolence felt towards certain individuals on the basis of particular attachments of love. He distinguishes between 'benevolence in *wishes*', which really only involves 'taking delight in the well-being of every other and does not require me to contribute to it'[9] and 'practical benevolence (beneficence)', which amounts to 'making the well-being and happiness of others my *end*.[10] In the latter case, 'I can, without violating the universality of the maxim [to "love thy neighbour as thyself"], vary the degree greatly in accordance with the different objects of my love (one of whom concerns me more closely than another)'.[11] Nevertheless, the main point that matters for our purposes is that for Kant, as the quote from *Conflict* shows, Abraham puts himself beyond the ethical pale by being prepared to sacrifice Isaac. Not even an ostensible divine command makes Abraham a justified exception. So it seems that – in respect of killing an innocent – there are to be *no exceptions*. Onora O'Neill puts it like this:

> In restricting our maxims to those that meet the test of the Categorical Imperative we refuse to base our lives on maxims that necessarily make of our own case an exception. The reason why a universalizability criterion is morally significant is that it makes of our own case no significant exception.[12]

The relevance of this to Abraham – treated in *Fear and Trembling* as the exception *par excellence* – should be obvious. For Kant, *nobody* may take the life of another innocent human being. Since Abraham is therefore not a justified exception, his willingness to sacrifice Isaac must be morally condemned. Abraham does indeed 'suspend the ethical' – and so must be condemned, rather than praised as the 'father of faith'.

But there is no good reason to think that Johannes' primary target is Kant. Given the importance of the Danish Hegelians as Kierkegaard's primary philosophical opponents, we can be sure that whomever else he may also have had in mind, in at least some major respects it is a 'Hegelian' position that is under scrutiny. We next need to ask, then, in what sense the ethical is 'the universal' for Hegel.

THE SINGLE INDIVIDUAL AS HIGHER THAN THE UNIVERSAL

As the second of our points from earlier shows, the primary opposition here is between 'universal' and 'particular' or 'individual'. But to understand the specifically Hegelian resonances of this, we need to consider Hegel's distinction between *Moralität* ['morality' or 'individual morality'] and *Sittlichkeit* ['ethical life'].

Hegel voices a famous objection to Kant's categorical imperative, which he takes over from his precursor J. G. Fichte. It is, he charges, merely formal and abstract: 'duty which must be willed only as such, and not for the sake of a content, is [only] a formal identity excluding all content and specific character'.[13] The weakness of Kant's position is that it

> lacks all organic filling. The proposition, 'Consider if thy maxim can be set up as a universal rule' would be all right, if we already had definite rules concerning what should be done. ... But in the Kantian theory the rule is not to hand, and the criterion that there should be no contradiction produces nothing.[14]

In other words, the categorical imperative – indeed, any principle universally binding on all rational beings, if there were such – would be too empty and abstract to constitute a substantive ethical code by which any actual human being could live her life. This is the charge of 'formalism'. Fichte held a more particularistic view than Kant's. For Fichte, moral duty must be recognised in each individual case by conscientious reflection on the particular circumstances of each individual case.

Kant and Hegel both agree that to be moral is to be rational, and that rationality is central to our nature as humans.[15] Where they differ is on what this rationality amounts to. Hegel objects to what he takes to be Kant's view that the rationality that grounds morality is an *individual's own* rational thought. But important to Hegel's story of the development of ethics is the distinction between *Moralität* and *Sittlichkeit*. (One commentator describes this as 'perhaps the most prominent theme in Hegel's ethical thought'.[16]) *Moralität* is to do with an individual agent's inner will and intention. The task of the individual self is to get his own particular will to conform to the universal will. Here, it is through its *own* will and action that the subject aims to actualise itself. But, crucially, *Moralität* – which Hegel tends to associate with Kant's moral theory and views as relatively abstract – must ultimately be subordinated to *Sittlichkeit*, the 'ethical life' of one's society (and hence sometimes translated as 'social' or 'customary morality'). That is, the content of our moral duties is specified by actual concrete relationships to other individuals and to institutions. Stewart glosses *Sittlichkeit* as 'the concrete realm of customs, duties, institutions, and mores that are generally accepted in any given society'.[17] As Hegel puts it in the *Phenomenology of Spirit* (signalling his agreement with 'the wisest men of antiquity'), 'wisdom and virtue consist in living in accordance with the customs [*Sitten*] of one's nation'.[18] It is important to note that what Hegel is recommending is not the *unreflective* acceptance of the *status quo*, the customs and institutions of one's own society. Rather, the educated member of a modern state accepts these customs and institutions because he has reflected upon how they may be rationally justified.[19] Hegel's own philosophy, indeed, aims to provide such a justification.

Note how this affects the sense in which 'the ethical is the universal' for Hegel. The ethical life [*Sittlichkeit*] is 'universal' in so far as it comprises the laws, customs and institutions of a particular society. On this understanding of 'the universal', Abraham's being a single individual who is 'higher' than the universal amounts to the idea that he considers his own private, individual relation to God to have priority over his duties as a social creature and a good citizen.[20] To our contemporary social morality, the idea of a father being prepared to sacrifice his son on the basis of a supposed divine command appears morally outrageous.[21] And our social morality is no different from either Hegel's or Kierkegaard's in this respect. Hence we can understand why Johannes insists that Hegel should really have condemned Abraham unequivocally. (Hegel, he says, should have protested 'loudly and clearly against the honour and glory enjoyed by Abraham as the father of faith when he should really be remitted to some lower court for trial and exposed as a murderer' [FT 84] – that is, as soon as his actions were to conflict with the law.[22]) But there are additional reasons why this is so. To see what, we need briefly to consider aspects of Hegel's view of language. This will show the connection between the third and fourth features that make Abraham appear scandalous.

PRIVACY AND LANGUAGE

Language, for Hegel, is an essentially public sphere, employing sharable concepts. Abraham's inability to make himself understood in language is thereby deeply problematic. Hegel is deeply suspicious of the possibility of an individual having a direct, inexpressible relation to 'the absolute' or the divine: such an idea, to Hegel, smells suspiciously of *Meinung*.

Hegel associates talk of *Meinung* [opinion, view] with idiosyncrasy. A *Meinung* is

> a subjective representation, a random thought, a fancy, which I can form in any way I like, while someone else can do it differently. A *Meinung* is mine; it is not an intrinsically universal thought that is in and for itself. But philosophy is objective science of truth, science of its necessity, conceptual cognition, not opining and spinning out opinions.[23]

This is in line with Hegel's opposition to what he saw as the tendency of his German contemporaries 'to organize philosophy around feeling and fantasy':[24] around excessive subjectivity, in one popular sense of that term, a particular target here being Romantic individualism's positing 'the arbitrary will of the individual as the absolute criterion of moral judgement'.[25] To this Hegel opposes speculative philosophy, to fight against 'what in *The Encyclopedia* he called the "knight-errantry" of philosophical "willfulness", a willfulness that Hegel contended had led to "the mania" of "everyone [wanting] to have his own system" of philosophy'.[26] In the *Phenomenology of Spirit*, Hegel expressly contrasts what I *mean* – my particular idiosyncratic meaning – with what can be *said*, in the publicly available, 'universal' resources of language. Subjective idiosyncrasy cannot be expressed in the universal resources of language. As Michael Inwood succinctly puts it, 'Hegel invariably champions the rationality of language and depreciates *Meinung*.'[27]

We can see more clearly the significance of this by considering Hegel's worries, in his discussion of *Moralität*, of the dangers of conscience. 'Act according to your conscience' was the central tenet of Fichte's ethics. But in the *Philosophy of Right*, Hegel argues that the self-centredness of conscience is dangerous. The danger is that 'man holds his own will as for himself valid and authoritative'.[28] Hegel is worried about 'pure inwardness of will', which 'may possibly convert the absolute universal into mere caprice. It may make a principle out of what is peculiar to particularity, placing it over the universal and realising it in action. This is evil.'[29] The significance of this message for our purposes will be clear if we recall Johannes' talk of Abraham as 'the single individual' standing in 'an absolute relation to the absolute'. For Hegel, any appeal to conscience needs to avoid this danger, and here is where the universal, public resource of language can help: 'Language is self-consciousness existing *for others* ... and as *this* self-consciousness is universal ... It perceives itself just as it is perceived by others'.[30]

This is precisely what is impossible for Abraham. Johannes insists that he cannot 'speak', cannot explain himself in the public arena of language. It should be clear, then, why Abraham is such an important case in dividing Johannes from Hegel. God's command inheres in an entirely personal relation between God and Abraham, a relationship anathema to Hegel. The radical privacy of Abraham's trial looks like a clear-cut case of *Meinung*. Relatedly, it is also worth noting that in his mature thought (albeit not in the so-called *Early Theological Writings*) Hegel associates faith [*Glaube*] with 'immediate certainty' [*Gewissheit*]: 'a subjective certainty that does not entail truth'.[31] Also relevant here is Hegel's criticism of an ethics of conviction, in which 'my good intention and my conviction that the act is good make it good',[32] a view that Hegel considers absurd.

For these reasons then, Hegel, like Kant, would not be prepared to tolerate Abraham as a justified 'exception' to the demands of the ethical, his circumstances so unique as to be incommunicable.[33] Thus, though the term 'universal' has different resonances in Kant and Hegel, both insist that ethical demands are, in some sense, universal, and that reason requires us to submit to these demands.[34] Abraham's failure to do so means that he must stand condemned.

THE PRIMACY OF THE ETHICAL

However, Johannes is making a further important point here. The ethical, understood in this way, *is its own justification*. This is what Johannes means by the claim that the ethical 'rests immanently in itself' (FT 83). Its end or purpose [*telos*] is not external to it; rather it 'is itself the *telos* for everything outside' (FT 83). Everything is to be understood in relation to, and is subordinate in importance to, the ethical. It is vital that we understand this. Consider, by contrast, a form of 'divine command ethics' which identifies what is morally good with what God wills or commands. On certain versions of such a view, what is morally good is morally good simply *in virtue of the fact that God wills it thus*. In such a case, the ethical (that is, in this example, 'what is morally good') *does* have a *telos* external to itself: namely, the will of God. The reason that I should refrain from killing innocents is that God wills it thus. By the same token, if God wills that I should kill an innocent, then that is what, morally, I should do. Yet if this is so, Johannes wants us to see, the ethical cannot be its own *telos*: there is a higher court of appeal (the will of God). So one way of putting the question exercising Johannes throughout is to ask *whether there is any higher court of appeal than the ethical*. That is, could there be anything 'higher' in virtue of which 'the ethical' – an individual's responsibilities to a 'universal' requirement – could be suspended?

It is not hard to see why some have thought that the above form of divine command ethics is precisely what Johannes is supporting in *Fear and Trembling*. On this reading, the answer to the question of the first problema – 'Is there a teleological suspension of the ethical?' (in the Abraham case) is 'no', since Abraham does what is ethically right: he obeys the command of God (a personal God who makes promises and issues commands). The answer to this question is 'no' because the answer to the question of the second problema – 'Is there an absolute duty to God?' – is 'yes'. We shall consider interpretations of *Fear and Trembling* according to which it supports a form of divine command ethics in Chapter 6.

Lest there be any unclarity, then, what is under Johannes' scrutiny is the view that answers our question – 'Is there any higher court of appeal than the ethical?' – in the negative. It is because of this that 'the individual's ethical task is ... to abrogate his particularity so as to become the universal' (FT 83). Moreover, if there is nothing 'higher' than the ethical, there is nothing to prevent us from conflating religious with ethical terminology, effectively taking the view that the religious boils down to the ethical. This is what Johannes has in mind when he says:

> As soon as the single individual wants to assert himself in his particularity, in direct opposition to the universal, he sins, and only by

recognizing this can he again reconcile himself with the universal. Whenever, having entered the universal, the single individual feels an urge to assert his particularity, he is in a state of temptation, from which he can extricate himself only by surrendering his particularity to the universal in repentance.

(FT 83)

The significance of this passage is precisely that it appropriates religious terminology to describe an offence against the ethical. Johannes' question now is whether such a view is 'the highest'. That is, does the above adequately capture a Christian-religious view? If it does, then 'the ethical and a person's eternal blessedness, which is his *telos* in all eternity and at every moment, are identical' (FT 83). In other words, attaining salvation involves leading an ethically blameless life. (On the most common readings of his philosophy of religion, this is also Kant's view.[35]) If this were so, Johannes says, two things would follow. First, Hegel would be right to say that viewing man 'as the single individual' is a 'moral form of evil' which must be 'annulled in the teleology of the ethical life' (FT 83). In other words, on the Hegelian view, by thinking of himself not in his particularity but subsuming himself as part of the social whole, the individual attains redemption from the 'sin' of thinking of himself predominantly as an individual. This, for Hegel, is what the moral life consists in: one attains one's highest dignity as a rational being by submission to the demands of the ethical universal. Second, though, if Hegel were indeed right, then despite Hegel's claim that this philosophy is Christian, Judaism and Christianity would in fact be redundant. Although Hegel and – as we have seen in the above quote – Johannes, in paraphrasing a broadly Hegelian way of thinking on these matters, have talked in terms of sin, temptation and redemption, such biblical terminology is actually surplus to requirements. If the ethical life is indeed 'the highest', 'then one needs no other categories than those of the Greek philosophers' (FT 84). That is, the ethical life as a person's highest *telos* can be understood entirely from the point of view of Greek paganism. (This is a point Johannes will go on to underline by drawing on Greek tragedy in his forthcoming discussion of the tragic hero.) This is one of the ways in which Kierkegaard would want to attack Hegel's claim that the latter's was a Christian philosophy.

This, then, is how Johannes reaches the conclusion we alluded to earlier: that, if Hegel were consistent, he should have protested 'loudly and clearly against the honour and glory enjoyed by Abraham as the father of faith when he should really be remitted to some lower court for trial and exposed as a murderer' (FT 84). Either the Hegelian or Abraham must be wrong.

IS ABRAHAM AN IMMORALIST?

So does Abraham, as Johannes portrays him, completely ignore 'universal' ethical demands? No. To see this, we should note an important qualification that Johannes makes here. He describes Abraham as 'having been in the universal' (FT 84). One manifestation of an individual setting himself 'apart as the particular above the universal' is obvious: the downright immoralist, who consciously rejects the requirements and demands of morality. It is important for Johannes' purposes that he distinguish such a figure from Abraham — and this is what he is aiming to do in this qualification. We are to take it that Abraham takes the demands of the ethical seriously, and for the most part considers himself bound by them: this is why the discussion is about the 'teleological suspension', not the total abandonment, of the ethical.[36] Nevertheless, the claim seems to be that there are certain exceptional circumstances in which the ethical can indeed be suspended. According to Johannes, to believe and act on this is a vital feature of faith.

Johannes' way of expressing this is to say that:

> Faith is just this paradox, that the single individual as the particular [*den Enkelte som den Enkelte*] is higher than the universal, is justified before the latter, not as subordinate but superior, though in such a way, be it noted, that it is the single individual who, having been subordinate to the universal as the particular, now by means of the universal becomes that individual who, as the particular, stands in an absolute relation to the absolute. This position cannot be mediated, for all mediation occurs precisely by virtue of the universal; it is and

> remains in all eternity a paradox, inaccessible to thought. And yet faith *is* this paradox.
>
> (FT 84–5)

This important passage will take some unpacking. First of all, the meaning of the claim that 'the single individual as the particular is higher than the universal' and 'stands in an absolute relation to the absolute' should by now be pretty clear. What this claim amounts to, at its most basic, is that an individual can have a relation to 'the absolute' – understood by Johannes as (Abraham's) God – in a more direct way than by being 'mediated' through the universal. Whereas for Hegel, a person cannot approach the divine without some kind of intermediary. In the case of 'revealed religion', as Hegel calls Christianity in the *Phenomenology*, this intermediary is the incarnate form of Christ (who is 'Spirit as an individual Self'[37]). In fact, in the *Phenomenology* Hegel explicitly describes Christ as 'the Mediator' [*der Vermittler*][38] – unsurprisingly, given that Christ effectively describes himself this way ('I am the way, the truth and the life: no man cometh unto the Father but by me'[39]). The Abraham story offends such a consciousness in that Abraham's relation to God seems far more 'direct'. Rather than God's will being revealed through such intermediaries as a priest, a holy book or the incarnate son of God, in the Genesis narrative Abraham has *direct* access to God.

However, we should note that Johannes seems to be using the term 'absolute' in a way quite different to Hegel. As mentioned above, for Johannes 'the absolute' seems to mean 'God': Abraham's God. For Hegel, as for many in the post-Kantian German philosophical tradition 'the absolute' is ultimate, unconditioned reality: in a sense, 'the absolute' is identical to the universe, considered as a whole. But since this includes you and I, Johannes and Abraham, 'the absolute' is not something to which we can stand in a range of possible relations. For Hegel, then, to say that Abraham stands in 'an absolute relation to the absolute' quite literally makes no sense.

But we need to say more than this in order to understand what 'mediated' means. Moreover, in what sense does mediation occur 'by virtue of the universal'?

Mediation [*Vermittlung*] — a key term in Hegel — is, in Alastair Hannay's words, the process of 'resolving conceptual oppositions into higher conceptual unities' (FT 154n58). This is an important part of Hegel's philosophical method. For example, one might naturally think that duty (obligation) and desire (inclination) are in opposition: one's desires (say, for a night on the tiles) often appear to be opposed to one's duty (say, to stay in and look after one's young child). One manifestation of the apparent opposition between desire and duty is an example discussed by both Hegel and Kierkegaard's Judge William in *Either/Or* and also mentioned by Hannay. This is the often expressed idea that personal freedom is opposed to public service. You cannot enter into any binding relationship or commitment, you inform me, because this will 'tie you down', restrict your freedom. (Kierkegaard's most famous presentation of this view is the aesthete A's essay 'Crop Rotation' in *Either/Or*.) Hegel — and Judge William — aim to show that this is a superficial view of freedom, and that a genuine understanding of freedom shows that it is *dependent upon* public service. How so?

The basic idea is as follows. A person is free, for Hegel, if and only if he is 'independent and self-determining, not determined by or dependent on something other than [him]self'.[40] But one cannot assume that acting on one's desires is a manifestation of freedom, because one's desires are often imposed from outside. There are various versions of this idea. Consider, for instance, the thought that one's most basic bodily desires — what Plato's Socrates, in the *Republic*, calls 'the agitations of sex and other desires, the element of irrational appetite'[41] — are not what one's true, or highest, self consists in. On this view, my desires are not really 'me': my true self is to be identified not with my 'irrational appetites', but with my rationality. However, Hegel thinks that the ascetic option of restraining one's desires is often excessive, since in civilised adults, desires are rarely merely bodily or brutish, but are infused with the influences of culture and *Sittlichkeit*. The underlying problem in all this is the issue of where we should draw the boundary between the self and what is external to the self. Hegel's general line is to argue that the attempt to attain freedom by ignoring or abolishing that which is felt to constrain one's true self — such as in Plato's anti-bodily asceticism – won't work. Rather, freedom lies in recognising what is felt as 'other' than oneself as *identical* to oneself. When this 'other' is public service, therefore, the solution is to recognise the contribution that public roles and commitments play in creating the self. The cares and commitments that I develop as a result of taking seriously my roles as husband, father and local doctor, for example, are an important part of my identity, my sense of myself. After all, could I even *have* an identity without some such roles? And *all* of us have *some* such roles – son, daughter, brother, sister, citizen, neighbour. But by 'owning' such roles, public service and personal freedom can be reconciled into a 'higher unity'. This is an example of 'resolving conceptual oppositions into higher conceptual unities'.

The second key feature of mediation – and here we need to recall the points made earlier about *Meinung* and language – is that it is a *conceptual* operation, taking place in the public arena of language and concepts. I think this is what Johannes means when he says that 'all mediation occurs precisely *by virtue of the universal*'. The highlighted phrase here refers to the idea that concepts are publicly accessible – 'universal' in that sense. As we have seen, Johannes insists that Abraham cannot 'speak': cannot explain his actions in the public arena of language and concepts. If one takes 'thought' to consist in concepts that must be publicly available for comprehension, it would thus be trivially true that Johannes' Abraham is 'a paradox inaccessible to thought'.

In summary, then, Johannes' claim seems to be that mediation cannot 'solve' the Abraham case. What is, to the Hegelian, the incoherent idea of a 'single individual' standing in an 'absolute relation to the absolute', a direct relation to God, cannot be resolved – somehow made coherent – via mediation. In this context, Johannes' final insistence in our quote – 'And yet faith is this paradox' – should be read as meaning that, despite all this, such a mode of existence as Abraham's is *possible*. Exemplars of faith can and do exist. Thus, if we are to be able to take the Abraham story seriously (by which Johannes means literally – and more of the significance of this later), we need to take seriously the possibility of a direct, unmediated relation between God and an individual human being such as Abraham.

In fact, Johannes could be accused of misrepresenting – perhaps misunderstanding – Hegel's view of mediation. 'Mediated', for Hegel, has resonances such as 'complex' or 'developed', and stands in opposition to 'immediate', which has resonances such as 'simple' or 'given'. But absolute, unmediated immediacy is a chimera: in this sense, *everything* is mediated, conceptual. On the other hand, Hegel claims that the very opposition between mediation and immediacy *itself* requires mediation, so that ultimately nothing is either purely mediated or purely immediate. So there are greater and lesser degrees of mediation and according to Inwood, 'Hegel's arguments are often obscured by the different levels of mediation and immediacy that come into play: e.g., absolute, wholly unmediated, immediacy (which never occurs), relatively bare immediacy, and mediated immediacy'.[42] We do not need to get into the full intricacies of this for our purposes. But we do need to say this much. According to Hegel, my knowledge of my own existence is (relatively) immediate, whereas my knowledge of God is (relatively) mediated. But to say this is not necessarily to claim that the only way to God is through Christ, a holy book or a priest. There is another important dimension of mediation that applies to the Abraham case, and that Johannes seems to be overlooking. Since *nothing* is purely immediate, this means that without any mediation at all, Abraham's God would be just a strange, disembodied voice. It is only through mediation that this voice becomes recognisable to Abraham *as God*: He who has created the world, expelled Adam and Eve from the Garden of Eden, sent the great flood, made a covenant with Abraham, destroyed Sodom and Gomorrah and so on. So in this sense of 'mediation', it is misleading of Johannes to say that Abraham's standing in an absolute relation to God is a position that 'cannot be mediated'. A degree of mediation must already be present for Abraham to be able to identify his interlocutor as God at all.[43]

So we should distinguish three different dimensions of mediation relevant to our concerns. First, in the broadest sense in which Abraham's interaction with God is mediated (that which I have just described), Johannes is simply wrong to say that Abraham's relation to God 'cannot be mediated'. It already is. But there are two further senses in which he might have a case. The first of these is the idea that a human being cannot approach God without an intermediary such as Christ, the Bible or a priest. This idea is certainly part of Johannes' target. The second is Hegel's idea that because everything is mediated (in the sense of conceptual), nothing is ineffable. Thus Hegel would have to dispute Johannes' apparent claim that Abraham cannot 'speak' – communicate – at all. However, we shall later see reason to question whether Johannes is able consistently to stick to this view himself.

There is one important respect in which Johannes wants to up the ante from my description in the last paragraph but two above. Rather than Abraham being *an* important exemplar of faith, he seems to present Abraham as *unique* – or nearly unique. Intensely sceptical of those who would find analogies to the Abraham story, Johannes says that 'I doubt very much whether one will find in the whole world a single analogy, except a later one that proves nothing' (FT 85). We shall return to one aspect of this puzzling, cryptic remark in Chapter 6 – but for the time being, we need to turn our attention to another type of character to whom Abraham might appear similar but, Johannes insists, is not. To our earlier discussion of the knight of infinite resignation, we now need to add a fuller discussion of the 'tragic hero'.

AGAMEMNON AND OTHERS: THE TRAGIC HERO

As we have seen, Johannes stresses that Abraham 'cannot be mediated': he is 'either a murderer or a man of faith' (FT 85). Johannes now tries to make this case by aiming to show that, unlike the predominantly 'ethical' figure of the tragic hero, Abraham's actions cannot be explained and justified in 'universal' ethical terms. In other words, Abraham is not just another 'tragic hero'.[44]

But who is the 'tragic hero'? As we saw, Johannes briefly mentioned such a figure in the Preamble, but now he considers three examples. First is Agamemnon, especially as portrayed in Euripides' play *Iphigenia in Aulis*. Agamemnon, leader of the Greek forces in the Trojan War, is attempting to sail to sack Troy. But the lack of winds being sent by the goddess Artemis makes this impossible. In exchange for winds favourable to the fleet, Agamemnon is commanded to summon his daughter Iphigenia to Aulis under the pretext of her marrying the hero Achilles. But in reality, she is to be sacrificed to Artemis. The tragic dilemma Agamemnon faces is between his civic duty *qua* king ('the universal', in something like Hegel's sense) and his love for Iphigenia (the particular). The question is whether Agamemnon can bring himself to command the death of his daughter in the service of a 'higher', because 'universal', good. In Euripides' version of this story, Agamemnon does give the necessary command, but at the very point of sacrifice, Iphigenia is carried off to dwell with the gods.[45] But the point is that, like Abraham, Agamemnon is prepared to go through with the sacrifice: 'it is with heroism that the father has to make that sacrifice' (FT 86). He is willing to sacrifice his daughter 'for the well-being of the whole' (FT 86).

Johannes' second example is the story of Jephthah, from the Old Testament's book of Judges.[46] Jephthah, a leader of Israel against the Ammonites, vows to God as follows:

> If thou shalt without fail deliver the children of Ammon into mine hands, Then it shall be, that whatsoever cometh forth of the doors of my house to meet me when I return in peace from the children of Ammon, shall surely be the Lord's, and I will offer it up for a burnt offering.[47]

God answers Jephthah's prayer, and the Ammonites are slaughtered. But the tragic twist is that on his return, it is his only child – his daughter – who greets him.

There has been disagreement amongst biblical scholars as to how this should be interpreted. The text does not explicitly say whether Jephthah actually puts his daughter to death, though several early Jewish and Christian interpreters claim that he did so. Another reading emphasises 'the principle of dedication symbolized by the burnt offering'.[48] That is, Jephthah's vow to God is read as an offer to dedicate his daughter to God – and what the biblical text explicitly says is that she was pledged to eternal virginity, Jephthah thus depriving himself of an heir. This latter reading, perhaps, makes Jephthah's situation rather less tragic than the former, and Johannes' treating this story on a par with Agamemnon and Brutus – of whom more imminently – suggests that it is the former interpretation that he has in mind.

'Brutus', the third of Johannes' tragic heroes, is Lucius Junius Brutus, a first consul of Rome. He is probably most famous for his strict sense of justice and condemned two of his sons to death for suspected treason. This is what Johannes has in mind when he says: 'When a son forgets his duty, when the State entrusts the father with the sword of judgement ... then it is with heroism that the father must forget that the guilty one is his son' (FT 87).

Each of these stories, then, has a father who is at least prepared to sacrifice the life of his son or daughter for something 'higher'. It is easy to see, therefore, why one might think the Abraham story analogous to this. So why, according to Johannes, would this be a mistake?

Johannes seems to take Agamemnon, Jephthah and Brutus as being ethically in the right: we are told in each case that everyone would admire these tragic heroes. This is far from obvious, and some of his claims seem contentious to the point of being ridiculous. For instance, if Iphigenia had *really* been on the verge of getting married, we are told, 'the betrothed would not be angered but proud to have been party to the father's deed' (FT 86).[49] But whatever our response to claims such as this, to make too much of them would obscure Johannes' main point. This is simply that, in each of the 'tragic hero' cases, a justification for the action *within* the ethical is possible. If we recall what we have said about the ethical earlier, we can see that part of such a claim is that the actions of the tragic hero are publicly understandable. It is quite clear to us what Agamemnon's dilemma is: can he really afford to put his love for his daughter above his duties as a king and military leader? Agamemnon could justify his willingness to sacrifice Iphigenia in terms of the demands of the state trumping those of the family. Similarly, Jephthah has made a publicly understandable vow to God, and so can explain his decision in terms of the importance of honouring a promise. (Keeping his promise also has a pragmatic dimension: if he broke it, 'would the victory not be taken once more from the people' (FT 87)?) Brutus can explain his decision in terms of the importance of upholding the law. But in Abraham's case, Johannes insists, no such ethical – publicly comprehensible – reason can be given. The private nature of Abraham's God-relationship makes it utterly incomprehensible to anyone else why he is prepared to kill Isaac. The difference Johannes sees between the tragic hero on the one hand, and Abraham on the other, is that if the former had replied, as did Abraham, 'It is a trial in which we are being tested' (FT 87), we could not have understood him. In other words, the claim is, we only understand the actions of these 'tragic heroes' because we can see that there could be an ethical justification for their actions (such as 'the well-being of the whole' or 'to honour a promise'). And this point stands even if we disagree that this justification is overriding. For instance, perhaps we belong to a culture for which family loyalties matter more than 'the well-being of the whole', so that we disagree – perhaps violently – that Agamemnon's was the right decision. None of this really affects Johannes' main point that such a disagreement is a disagreement *within the ethical*. Johannes' position seems to be that however violently we disagree with the justification offered, we could come to understand why its defender holds it. An argument about the relative merits of each ethical alternative could take place. Johannes' point is that nothing of the sort can happen in the Abraham case, if all that Abraham can offer by way of justification are *non*-justifications such as 'It is a trial in which I am being tested' or 'I believe on the strength of the absurd'. In conclusion, if the ethical is 'universal', public, then Abraham stands outside the ethical altogether: 'In his action he overstepped the ethical altogether, and had a higher *telos* outside it, in relation to which he suspended it' (FT 88).

This is why Johannes claims that 'Abraham's whole action stands in no relation to the universal, it is a purely private undertaking. While, then, the tragic hero is great by his ethical virtue [*sin Sædelige Dyd*], Abraham is great by a purely personal virtue [*en reen personlig Dyd*]' (FT 88, translation adjusted).[50] That is, as we have said, he stands in 'an absolute relation to the absolute'. To describe this as a 'trial' or 'temptation', Johannes implies, is potentially misleading. A 'temptation' usually involves *not* carrying out an ethical duty (FT 88) – but in the Abraham case, the ethical is *itself* the temptation, in that it is tempting to want to make oneself understood. Thus the ethical, understood as the universal, the public, cannot accommodate Abraham. Hence Johannes claims that we need 'a new category for understanding Abraham' (FT

88): a category – 'faith'? – in which an individual's relationship to God can be private and (in at least one sense of the term) unmediated.

Like the knight of infinite resignation, then, the tragic hero can be understood. The knight of faith, by contrast, 'cannot speak' (FT 89). Our earlier references to Hegel on language show what this means. 'To speak' means 'to express the universal': 'The moment I speak I express the universal, and when I do not no one can understand me' (FT 89). (In the same vein, Johannes later says that 'if when I speak I cannot make myself understood, I do not speak even if I keep talking without stop day and night' [FT 137].) That Johannes has some sympathy for this Hegelian view is suggested by his saying that 'while Abraham arouses my admiration, he also appals me' (FT 89).

Finally, Johannes stresses the lack of comfort that Abraham can take in virtue of his inability to make himself understood. (This is another reason why the ethical – speaking so as to justify oneself – is 'the temptation'.) Moreover, he wonders how such a person can assure *himself* that he is justified (FT 90). The contemporary Hegelian refrain that he is to be 'judged by the outcome' is no consolation. This is partly because 'the outcome' comes last, and one obviously cannot learn from what has yet to happen. (There might, though, be an important difference between Abraham's perspective and ours, to which we shall return in Chapter 6.) Johannes seems to associate this concern with 'the outcome' with the disengaged, spectator perspective of a category of people he calls 'the lecturers' [*Docenterne*] (FT 91). His references to 'the outcome' also flag the worry that Abraham is somehow supposed to be justified by the fact that he 'passed' God's test. Does this mean that if Abraham had gone through with the sacrifice – if God had not provided the ram – Abraham would have been 'less justified' (FT 92)? (Commentators will disagree on this, as we shall also see in Chapter 6.) Johannes' primary concern here is that the Abraham story should not simply become a matter of 'what happened': 'it is the outcome that arouses our curiosity, as with the conclusion of a book; one wants nothing of the fear, the distress, the paradox. One flirts with the outcome aesthetically' (FT 92). In other words, his concern here is another manifestation of his insistence that any consideration of the Abraham story should not 'leave out the anguish', 'the fear and distress in which the great are tried' (FT 93).

There follows a three-paragraph aside in which Johannes turns from the 'greatness' of Abraham to the 'greatness' of the Virgin Mary. A comparison between the Genesis narrative and that of Luke 1:26–38 (in which the birth of Christ is foretold to Mary) sheds light on these passages. Mary's amazement at the news of her impending motherhood, followed by willing acceptance of the will of God, echoes the response of Abraham and Sarah in Genesis.[51] Johannes also stresses Mary's isolation ('The angel came only to Mary, and no one could understand her' [FT 93]), again paralleling what he has been arguing about Abraham. Evans suggests that this should be read as a message to Kierkegaard's complacent contemporaries in 'Christendom', to the effect that in a sense, all Christians find themselves in a position analogous to Abraham's. While one might wistfully imagine that it would have been desirable 'to see Christ walking about in the promised land', that amounts to – once again – forgetting 'the anguish, the distress, the paradox' (FT 94) of such a circumstance ('Was it not a fearful thought that this man who walked among others was God?' [FT 94]). Rather, Evans suggests, 'To be a Christian is to believe God communicates through a particular historical individual, a message that always transcends *Sittlichkeit* and can come into conflict with it, forcing the person of faith to be "the single individual" who breaks with established ways of thinking.'[52]

In this sense, the message is that faith is in some respects no easier today than it was for Abraham.[53]

In summary, then, if the ethical is the universal, then 'Abraham's story contains a teleological suspension of the ethical' (FT 95). That is, the ethical, understood as the universal, is suspended for a higher *telos* (Abraham's commitment to his God). But as well as the fact that the Hegelian cannot accept such an exception, we also have the problem of what follows from this view. What follows, as we have seen, is that Abraham must have a private, unmediated relation to God. This is what Johannes means by saying that he has 'as the single individual, become higher than the universal'. And this is 'the paradox that cannot be mediated'. '[I]f this is not how it is with Abraham, then he is not even a tragic hero but a murderer' (FT 95). In other words, unlike the tragic hero, he cannot give even an ethical justification for his action, let alone a justification or *telos* 'higher' than the ethical.

PROBLEMA II: IS THERE AN ABSOLUTE DUTY TO GOD?

We have just seen that central to Problema I is the relation between the universal and the particular, and that for Johannes, valorising Abraham commits us to commending the idea that 'the single individual' could be 'higher than the universal'. Problema II addresses a related question – the status of specific, particular duties to God. As we shall see, it also reaches the same conclusion as Problema I about the relation between the 'single individual' and the universal.

As already mentioned, each problema opens with a dimension of what one is allegedly committed to in holding that the ethical is 'the universal'. Problema II's claim is at first glance perhaps the strangest. Its opening claim is that: 'The ethical is the universal and as such, in turn, the divine' (FT 97).

The basic issue turns out to be the nature of our duty to God, and Johannes deals with this as follows. It could be claimed that all duties are ultimately duties to God.[54] But what, Johannes wonders, would be the cash value of such a claim? If *all* duties are duties to God, what room does this leave for specific, particular duties to God – a God, moreover, with whom one can enter into an intimate personal relationship – of the kind faced by Abraham? Is 'duty to God' in fact merely shorthand for ethical duty, duty to 'the universal'? If so, Johannes suggests, 'God becomes an invisible, vanishing point ... his power is to be found only in the ethical, which fills all existence' (FT 96). In which case, wouldn't the view under investigation ultimately amount to boiling 'God' down to 'the ethical'? (Compare our earlier discussion of this in relation to Problema I ['The primacy of the ethical'].) Kant comes pretty close to saying this in *Religion within the Boundaries of Mere Reason*: 'The proposition "We ought to obey God rather than men", means only that when human beings command something that is evil in itself (directly opposed to the ethical law), we may not, and ought not, obey them'.[55] He also claims that 'there are no particular duties toward God in a universal religion; for God cannot receive anything from us; we cannot act on him or for him.'[56] Views such as this, Johannes seems to be saying, even if paying lip service to God, are well on the way to those familiar in our 'secular age'.

Johannes aims to explain why faith is a paradox. His discussion mostly focuses on dimensions of 'the universal' already discussed in relation to Problema I, and his explanation is in terms of the *public* nature of 'the universal'. In Hegelian philosophy, Johannes tells us, the outer is higher than the inner: as we have seen, an external, public manifestation is higher than *Meinung* or 'mere' subjectivity. From such a standpoint, faith – here defined as the condition in which 'interiority is higher than exteriority' (FT 97) – is indeed a paradox. In 'the ethical view of life' – understood, remember, in terms of the 'universal' – 'it is the individual's task to divest himself of the determinant of interiority and give it an expression in the exterior' (FT 97). But Abraham's trial, in its radical privacy, is 'an interiority that is incommensurable with the exterior' (FT 97). Thus, unless one is to dismiss faith as being sub-ethical – perhaps a return to a childish or 'aesthetic' form of immediacy – the paradox of faith can also be expressed in either of the following two ways. Either 'the single individual is higher than the universal' (FT 97), or 'the single individual ... determines his relation to the universal through his relation to the absolute, not his relation to the absolute through his relation to the universal' (FT 98). As we suggested in relation to Problema I, this latter way of putting it means that the individual's ethical relation ('his relation to the universal') stems from his relation to the God of promises and commands ('the absolute'), rather than the other way round. Johannes immediately follows this up by offering another variant, the only one that adds anything substantially new: 'The paradox can also be put by saying that there is an absolute duty to God' (FT 98). In other words, he answers Problema II's question in the affirmative. Because, in faith, the individual's God-relationship involves an absolute relation to the absolute, it follows that 'the ethical is reduced to the relative' (FT 98). If what matters absolutely is my commitment to God, then my commitment to the ethical (in so far as it is not identical to God) is of only relative importance. Thus in saying that there is an absolute duty to God, Johannes means, first, that such a duty exists over and above one's duty to the ethical and, second, that in relation to the duty to God, the duty to the ethical is relativised. Only such a standpoint will enable us to justify Abraham.

(For completeness, we should add that Johannes puts his point about faith's paradoxical nature in yet another way when he says that 'the single individual is quite unable to make himself intelligible to anyone' (FT 99) – again, as we have already seen, because of the radical privacy of Abraham's trial. Our earlier discussion of *Meinung* already suggests why, and we shall defer further discussion of this aspect for the time being, since it is a central theme of Problema III.)

Johannes next considers another biblical passage, this time from the New Testament, which also concerns the implications of an absolute duty to God. In Luke 14:26, Jesus says: 'If any man come to me, and hate not his father, and mother, and wife, and children, and brethren, and sisters, yea, and his own life also, he cannot be my disciple.' It is important to note that Johannes' treatment of this passage parallels his treatment of the Abraham story, in so far as he insists that it not be watered down, that it be *taken literally*. He holds in contempt the biblical exegete who, armed with a knowledge of Greek, comes to the conclusion that 'hate' really means something like 'love less' or 'give less priority to' (FT 100). Such evasion, he insists, 'ends up in drivel rather than terror' (FT 101). The comparison with the Abraham story, then, is twofold. First, Johannes insists that both the Luke passage and the Abraham story be taken literally: 'if the [Luke] passage is to have any sense, it must be understood literally' (FT 101). This same assumption lies behind Johannes' whole treatment of the Abraham story: recall his contempt in the 'Preamble' for the preacher for whom the message of this story is something so vague as that we should give to God 'the best'. Second, what unites these two pieces of scripture, if taken literally, is their capacity to induce terror: their capacity to shake the foundations of their hearer's world-view. (It is precisely this that makes such hearers want to interpret them other than literally.) Once again, we are back with the 'distress and fear' (FT 103) of the paradox of faith.

At the point of Abraham's willingness to sacrifice Isaac,

> the ethical expression for what he does is this: he hates Isaac. But if he actually hates Isaac he can be certain that God does not require this of him; for Cain and Abraham are not the same. Isaac he must love with all his soul. When God asks for Isaac, Abraham must if possible love him even more, and only then can he sacrifice him; for it is indeed this love of Isaac that in its paradoxical opposition to his love of God makes his act a *sacrifice*. But the distress and anguish in the paradox is that, humanly speaking, he is quite incapable of making himself understood.
>
> (FT 101)

Consider the last line of this passage. Abraham's 'distress and anguish' lies in the fact that 'humanly speaking, he is quite incapable of making himself understood'. One might be forgiven for thinking that, on the contrary, making oneself understood was some way down the distress and anguish scale in comparison to the prospect of having to kill one's own son. This underlines how public expression and communicability – 'making oneself understood' – are central to Johannes' way of seeing.

Next, Johannes again contrasts Abraham with the tragic hero. Once again, the theme of making oneself understood is combined with the central theme of universal and particular. 'The tragic hero renounces himself in order to express the universal; the knight of faith renounces the universal in order to be the particular' (FT 103). But the latter is neither easy to do, nor the same thing as rejoicing in one's idiosyncrasies. What distinguishes a knight of faith from mere 'stragglers and vagrant geniuses' (FT 103) is that the former 'knows ... that it is glorious to belong to the universal' (FT 103). That is, as we saw in relation to Problema I, he understands and feels the attractions of the universal, including the capacity it brings for openness, being 'readable for all' (FT 103). This, recall, is why the ethical is, for the knight of faith, 'the temptation'. Making himself understood by returning to the universal is a *continual* temptation in the knight's 'constant trial' (FT 105). Johannes' discussion here highlights, at some length, the *isolation* of the knight of faith: 'alone about everything' (FT

106), he 'is always absolute isolation' (FT 106), 'the individual, absolutely nothing but the individual' (FT 107) who 'walks alone with his dreadful responsibility' (FT 107). (Recall here the parallels between Abraham and Mary – both in their own ways isolated figures – discussed in Problema I above.)

Problema II ends, like Problema I, with an either/or. At first glance, the text reads as if Johannes is presenting us with *four* options, but in fact the last three are variations on the same theme. The first of these latter three possibilities is that 'faith has never existed because it has existed always' (FT 108). In other words, faith is nothing as extraordinary as that exemplified in Abraham. This option presents us with an instance of the 'watering down' of faith. So this first option is similar to the third: that the Luke 14 passage must be watered down, explained away, as by the 'tasteful exegete', in the manner that ends up in 'drivel'. Since faith would become something radically different – far more readily amenable to 'worldly understanding' – from what Abraham manifests, these two options really amount to the second of our trio: that 'Abraham is done for' (FT 108). Thus the real either/or is as follows. *Either* there is an absolute duty to a promise-making God with whom an individual can enter into a personal, intimate relationship, in which case the paradox that 'the single individual as the particular is higher than the universal and as the particular stands in an absolute relation to the absolute' (FT 108) *or* Abraham is indeed 'done for'. In other words, this 'paradox' is the only alternative to watering down faith or dismissing Abraham as a callous murderer.

SUMMARY

Let us recap. If the above summarises the message of Problema II, the message of Problema I can be summarised as follows. If 'the ethical is the universal' – the hypothesis Johannes is putting under scrutiny throughout the problemata – then Abraham's story contains a 'teleological suspension' of the ethical. Abraham offends this conception of the ethical in four related ways: he is an exception; he embodies the paradox that a 'single individual' can be 'higher' than the universal; he has a direct relation to a personal God; and he is unable to explain himself in the public arena of language. In these respects, he allegedly differs from a tragic hero such as Agamemnon, whose dilemma is within 'the ethical', and who can explain himself in the public arena of language. 'And yet faith is this paradox': the figure of Abraham means that we need to take seriously the possibility of a direct, 'unmediated' (in one sense, at least) relation to God through which an individual can be higher than the universal.

That, at least, seems to be what Johannes is saying. However, we shall see in Chapter 6 that there is a huge variety of ways in which the ostensible message of *Fear and Trembling* has been unpacked. Before considering this, though, we should first turn to the third and final problema, and Johannes' further reflections upon Abraham's silence and concealment.

NOTES

1 I have aimed here to clarify my position further than did the first edition, as some have misunderstood my earlier claims. Merold Westphal, for instance, claims that I suggested 'the contrast is between faith and Kantian or Hegelian ethics more or less equally' (2014: 43n8), though in fact that claim was never made.
2 Kant 1993: 14.
3 Kant 1993: 15. See also Kant 1996b: 182–4.
4 Kant 1996b: 177–8.
5 Kant 1996b: 179–80.
6 The qualification 'innocent' is important here, given that Kant famously supports capital punishment on retributivist grounds.
7 Kant 1996a: 283.
8 Kant 1996a: 283.
9 Kant 1996b: 201.
10 Kant 1996b: 201.
11 Kant 1996b: 201.
12 O'Neill 1989: 156.
13 Hegel 1996: §135.
14 Hegel 1996: §135.
15 For a brief but clear account of morality in Hegel, to which the present paragraph is indebted, see Inwood 1992: 191–3.
16 Wood 1993: 222.
17 Stewart 2003: 311.
18 Hegel 1977: §352.
19 See Hegel 1996: §258. Evans adds that 'Hegel believed that modern states had achieved or were achieving a social system in which the demands of reason

would no longer be in opposition to the demands of society, because those societies were themselves the realization of those demands of reason' (2004: 68).

20. That is, to the extent that these make sense given Abraham's context. Johannes says that 'Abraham's relation to Isaac, ethically speaking, is quite simply this, that the father should love the son more than himself' (FT 86). What is probably in the background here is the Hegelian idea that *Sittlichkeit* is expressed in the family, civil society and the state and that, for Abraham, there is nothing 'higher' than the family. Hence the slightly later remark that 'There is no higher expression of the ethical [*det Ethiske*] in Abraham's life than that the father shall love the son. The ethical [*det Ethiske*] in the sense of the ethical life [*det Sædelige*; cf. *Sittlichkeit*] is quite out of the question' (FT 88). It is 'out of the question' in the sense that these 'higher' expressions of *Sittlichkeit* have minimal application to Abraham (except in so far as future nations and states are 'latent' in Isaac's 'loins' [FT 88]). See also Problema III, where Johannes explicitly states that 'for Abraham the ethical had no higher expression than that of family life' (FT 136).

21. And perhaps we are right to judge it thus, as we shall see when, in Chapter 6, we consider the difference between Abraham's situation and our own.

22. Stewart 2003: 315.

23. This quote comes from the Introduction to Hegel's *Lectures on the History of Philosophy*: cited by Inwood 1992: 48.

24. Dickey 1993: 306.

25. Stewart 2003: 312.

26. Dickey 1993: 307.

27. Inwood 1992: 48.

28. Hegel 1996: §138.

29. Hegel 1996: §139. While the state can support some forms of moral conscience, it cannot go as far as to allow acts that contravene universally valid civil law (cf. Stewart 2003: 314–15).

30. Hegel 1977: §652.

31. Inwood 1992: 46.

32. Hegel 1996: §140.

33. Hegel's remarks about Abraham in his early essay 'The Spirit of Christianity and Its Fate' – an essay unavailable to Kierkegaard – are savage. He comes to some of the same conclusions as Johannes, but judges Abraham far more negatively as a result. He portrays Abraham as being in 'opposition' to 'the whole world', and 'it was through God alone that Abraham came into a mediate relation with the world, the only kind of link with the world possible for him' (Hegel 1971: 187). (Compare the idea of Abraham as the 'single individual' viewing himself as 'higher' than the universal.) 'Love alone was beyond his power; even the one love he had, his love for his son, even his hope of posterity – the one mode of extending his being, the one mode of immortality he knew and hoped for – could depress him, trouble his all-exclusive heart and disquiet it to such an extent that even this love he once wished to destroy; and his heart was quieted only through the certainty of the feeling that this love was not so strong as to render him unable to slay his beloved son with his own hand' (Hegel 1971: 187).

34 Evans suggests that a more contemporary way of putting the point that Abraham cannot justify his behaviour to others in his society (because 'a justification must appeal to the accepted values of a society that are embedded in its language') is to say that Abraham cannot appeal to 'public reason' in a Rawlsian sense (2015: 73). For Westphal, neither does Abraham have access to a Habermasian justification (2014: 56).
35 This view of Kant on religion is discussed, but in some cases questioned, by some of the essays in Phillips and Tessin 2000.
36 This point is further discussed in Problema III, where Johannes aims to show the difference between Abraham's concealing his purpose from those most directly affected by it and various forms of 'aesthetic' (that is, sub-ethical) concealment. See especially the distinction between 'first' and 'later' immediacy (FT 109).
37 Hegel 1977: §762.
38 Hegel 1977: §785.
39 John 14:6.
40 Inwood 1992: 110.
41 Plato 1974: 439d.
42 Inwood 1992: 186.
43 Compare here Kant's point in the first of the quotations from *The Conflict of the Faculties* above.
44 Recall the point about the overlap between the tragic hero and the knight of infinite resignation in Chapter 3 above (note 12).
45 Or so the messenger who delivers this news to Clytemnestra (Agamemnon's wife and Iphigenia's mother) interprets it. Euripides' play has an intriguingly ambiguous ending. According to the messenger's speech, all present at the sacrificial ceremony hear the slitting of Iphigenia's throat, but when they look up, what they see is not a dead girl, but a dead deer. This is interpreted as a sign that Iphigenia's heroism has been rewarded by being transported to live with the gods. However, Clytemnestra is left wondering whether this was just a story concocted for her benefit.
46 See Judges 10:6–12:7.
47 Judges 11:30–1.
48 See the notes to the King James Study Bible, pp. 427–8.
49 Perhaps, recalling the historically contextual nature of the Hegelian 'ethical life', there is such a context which makes this seem less preposterous. Thus, Evans again (as part of his argument for the claim that the conception of the ethical in *Fear and Trembling* is broadly Hegelian and not Kantian): 'These characters reside in ethical worlds in which their ethical duties are derived from the social institutions in which they participate, and it is taken as obvious that one's duties to the state trump those duties grounded in the family' (2015: 72).
50 Walsh's translation seems to me here more straightforwardly faithful to the Danish. Hannay translates *ven sin Sædelige Dyd* as 'his deed's being an expression of the ethical life', but this loses the fact that the term 'virtue' [*Dyd*] is explicitly mentioned as a descriptor of both the tragic hero and Abraham.

51 The predicted birth of John the Baptist to Zechariah and Elizabeth in their old age (Luke 1:5–23) also echoes the theme of Abraham and Sarah becoming parents in old age.
52 Evans 2006: xxv.
53 Evans 2006: xxv. Westphal argues that *Fear and Trembling* contains a kind of ideology-critique directed against a prevailing Christendom that is more Hegelian than Christian (2014: 80–1).
54 Compare Kant's definition: 'Religion is (subjectively considered) the recognition of all our duties as divine commands' (1998: 153).
55 Kant 1998: 110n.
56 Kant 1998: 153n.

5

THE SOUND OF SILENCE
PROBLEMA III

The third problema consists of perhaps the hardest part of *Fear and Trembling* to understand, and in courses in which the text is taught, I suspect probably the least commonly read. Though the opening leads us to suggest something similar in style to the first two problemata, what follows is a much longer and more rambling discussion. In line with Problema I and II, Johannes begins by picking out another feature of the ethical understood as the universal, namely that it is 'the disclosed' or revealed [*det Aabenbare*]. As we have seen, the ethical demands that its adherents speak about – explain – their actions. Yet Abraham remained 'silent'. Hence Johannes' question: 'Was it ethically defensible of Abraham to conceal his purpose from Sarah, from Eleazer, from Isaac?'[1]

Johannes opens the problem thus:

> The ethical as such is the universal; as the universal it is in turn the disclosed. Seen as an immediate, no more than sensate and psychic being, the individual is concealed. So his ethical task is to unwrap himself from this concealment and become disclosed in the

> universal. Thus whenever he wants to remain in concealment, he sins and is in a state of temptation, from which he can emerge only by disclosing himself.
>
> (FT 108)

We have already said enough in Chapter 4 to understand why Johannes associates the ethical with disclosure. He echoes Judge William's view (in a passage quoted by Climacus in the *Postscript*), that the aesthetic existence-sphere[2] can be demarcated from the ethical by the idea that pivotal to the latter is the insistence that 'it is every man's duty to become open' (CUP 254). The most fundamental reason why concealment is ethically culpable is that communication between moral agents is necessary if a moral community is to be possible. As Mark C. Taylor puts it, 'to remain silent and to refuse to express oneself in an honest and forthright way is to negate the very possibility of moral relationships ... moral community is impossible without communication'.[3] Silence is ethically culpable in so far as it involves clinging to the mysterious inwardness of one's particularity rather than aiming to justify oneself using the 'universal' resources of language. To say this, of course, is not to deny the obvious fact that you might not accept my explanation for why I did what I did, or recognise my reasons *as* reasons. But as with the case of the tragic hero, this does not affect Johannes' point, which is not to deny the possibility of moral disagreement, but rather that there is no hope of mutual understanding if utter silence is maintained.

So if disclosure is a mark of the ethical, and Abraham dwells in concealment, then there is an obvious problem. What prevents us from judging Abraham as a mere reversion to the aesthetic, the sphere of concealment or 'hiddenness'?[4] This is the central question that motivates Problema III, and this is why Johannes says:

> Unless there is a concealment which has its basis in the single individual's being higher than the universal, then Abraham's conduct cannot be defended ... If, however, there is such a concealment, then we face the paradox, which cannot be mediated, just because it is based on the single individual's being, in his particularity, higher than the universal.
>
> (FT 109)

Again, what is under scrutiny is the Hegelian's alleged desire to have his cake and eat it. Since 'the Hegelian philosophy assumes there is no justified concealment' (FT 109), Johannes alleges, it should not praise the concealing Abraham as the father of faith. These, then, are the questions and issues motivating the 'aesthetic inquiry' (FT 109) that takes up most of Problema III. As Johannes puts it, 'the point is to show how absolutely different the paradox [i.e. faith as exemplified in Abraham] and aesthetic concealment are from one another' (FT 112).

It is important to recognise that the use Johannes is here making of the term 'aesthetics' is closer to its standard usage than it is to the 'aesthetic life' as embodied in 'A', the 'aesthete' of *Either/Or*. This becomes clear in the examples Johannes gives after the above quotation. These are 'aesthetic' in the sense of being possibilities one might find in a light drama or romantic comedy: the young girl secretly in love who, perhaps out of duty, marries another, keeping silent about her true feelings; the young man who keeps silent because he knows his love will 'ruin an entire family', hoping that perhaps his beloved might find happiness with another. The concealment of such individuals 'is a free act' (FT 112). However, Johannes suggests, 'aesthetics' is unlikely to rest content with such sorrowful stories, for 'aesthetics is a respectful and sentimental discipline which knows more ways of fixing things than any assistant house-manager' (FT 112). Thus, in each example, the respective beloveds 'get wind of the other party's noble decision' (FT 112), and following the necessary explanations, the girl and boy get their beloveds, 'as a bonus the rank of real heroes as well' (FT 112) and all live happily ever after. Thus such silence and concealment plays a role in an entertaining yet undemanding evening at the theatre.

But such stories lack ethical depth and seriousness. Johannes insists that 'ethics knows nothing either of this coincidence or this sentimentality' (FT 112–13). Ethically, for the reasons discussed above, what is demanded of individuals in such stories is disclosure. Hence Johannes' conclusion that 'aesthetics called for concealment and rewarded it. Ethics called for disclosure and punished concealment' (FT 113).

However, there can be circumstances in which 'even aesthetics calls for disclosure' (FT 113). Unlike the above examples, in which 'the aesthetic illusion' leads the boy or girl to suppose that their silence can save another, there can be circumstances in which our old friend the 'tragic hero' is required to 'interfere' in another's life, in such a way as to require disclosure. Yet this will only turn out to show another difference between a story viewed aesthetically and the same story viewed ethically. Johannes brings us back to Agamemnon, about to order the sacrifice of Iphigenia. Aesthetics also wants to have its cake and eat it. On the one hand, it demands Agamemnon's silence, since 'it would be unworthy of the hero to seek another's consolation' (FT 113). That is, the dramatic stakes are raised by Agamemnon's having to face his fate in lonely solitude. Yet on the other hand, the dramatic stakes are also raised if he is tested by 'the terrible temptation incurred by the tears of Clytemnestra [his wife] and Iphigenia' (FT 113) – the temptation, that is, to override his (perceived) duty *qua* king and spare his daughter's life. How can aesthetics maximise the tension by having both these options? How are Clytemnestra and Iphigenia to find out if Agamemnon does not speak? Aesthetics once again resorts to coincidence: 'it has an old servant standing by who discloses everything to Clytemnestra. And now everything is as it should be' (FT 114). In other words, now the sobbing and dramatic tension can (and does) really reach its height. (Clytemnestra tearfully begs and pleads with Achilles to intervene on her daughter's behalf in such a way as to inspire a member of the chorus to remark that 'No animal fights fiercer than a mother for her child'.)

Yet ethics 'has no coincidence, and no old servant standing by' (FT 114). The difference between the ethical demand for disclosure and its only superficially similar aesthetic cousin is that the former would require *Agamemnon himself* to explain to Iphigenia her fate, despite temptations to remain silent. For the reasons in favour of the need for disclosure discussed above, Agamemnon *qua* tragic hero will only remain 'the beloved son of ethics' (FT 114) if he 'express[es] the universal' by explaining to Iphigenia – in the public space of language – that she must be sacrificed and why.[5] Moreover, part of Agamemnon's tragedy is that, in doing what the ethical (allegedly) demands, he must not be deflected from what he perceives as his duty by his daughter's pleas and tears. That is, he must not let *her* use of language deflect him. *The need to take personal responsibility in the public sphere of language and justification* is what distinguishes this 'ethical' Agamemnon from the 'aesthetic' version described above. This is what Johannes means when he summarises thus: 'Aesthetics required disclosure but availed itself of a coincidence; ethics required disclosure and found satisfaction in the tragic hero' (FT 114).

It is very easy to miss the significance to what follows of a passage that Johannes throws in at this point:

> The tragic hero, the darling of ethics, is a purely human being, and he is someone I can understand, someone all of whose undertakings are in the open. If I go further I always run up against the paradox, the divine and the demonic; for silence is both of these. It is the demon's lure, and the more silent one keeps the more terrible the demon becomes; but silence is also divinity's communion with the individual.
> (FT 114)

The sense that this is a throwaway passage is heightened by Johannes' apparently then going on to change the subject ('Before coming back to the story of Abraham, however, I would like to present some poetic personages'). But this passage is crucial not only to understanding the discussion of these 'poetic personages' (which will take up most of the rest of Problema III) but also to their significance in relation to Abraham. So before following Johannes any further, let us pause to take stock of what this paragraph is apparently telling us. First, our discussion so far has taken us far enough to understand the first sentence. The tragic hero is 'the darling of ethics' because he is not swayed from obeying the demand of the universal. If we again take Agamemnon as our example, we can see that not only does he put aside personal inclination (to *spare* his daughter) and particularity (to spare *his daughter*). He also obeys the ethical's demand for disclosure, in so far as, as we just saw, he accepts it as part of his duty that *he himself* must tell her of her terrible fate. All this is 'in the open', and thus Johannes can understand it. But anything 'hidden' runs up against 'the paradox' of silence. This silence, Johannes seems to be telling us, can be either 'demonic' or 'divine'. The difficulty is in distinguishing these radically different kinds of silence.

Johannes is struggling with trying to work out the differences between Abraham's silence – 'divine' silence – and 'demonic' silence. The latter, we shall shortly see, features importantly in two of Johannes' 'poetic' stories – Agnete and the merman, and Sarah and Tobias.[6]

FOUR POETIC PERSONAGES

Johannes' variations on and discussions of these four stories take up the majority of Problema III. Yet despite this, his attitude towards them appears to be somewhat 'take it or leave it'. They are introduced in a less than promising way, with the claim that 'in their anguish they might perhaps bring something or other to light' (FT 115). And, once the discussion of them is over, the claim made for them is no less modest: 'none of the stages described contained an analogue of Abraham, they were elaborated only so as to indicate, from the point of view of their own sphere, the boundary of the unknown land by the points of discrepancy' (FT 136).

The latter quote indicates the role these stories have. Johannes hopes that they might serve the purpose of getting him closer to understanding Abraham, but still only negatively. That is, these stories continue Johannes' overall negative project of aiming to get closer to understanding faith by comparing it with superficially similar instances that are nevertheless not faith. One sense in which the four stories are superficially similar to Abraham, the first quote suggests, is that they all deal with people suffering 'anguish'.

Johannes only seems to need the bare bones of each story to get going.

THE DELPHIC BRIDEGROOM

The first story, borrowed from Aristotle's *Politics*, is of a bridegroom at Delphi.[7] Johannes can summarise his raw material in a sentence: *'The bridegroom, for whom the augurs had predicted a misfortune as a result of his forthcoming marriage, at the crucial moment, when he is to fetch the bride, suddenly changes his plans –* he won't go through with the wedding' (FT 115). Johannes now employs the same kind of imaginative identification we have seen him using in relation to Abraham, as he tries to imagine himself into the shoes of the young bride (see FT 116). It is worth noting that Johannes' discussion here is guilty of the same crime of which he has accused 'aesthetics' earlier: a reliance on coincidence. As the troubled bridegroom steps out of the temple, the bride 'demurely ... turned her gaze down' (FT 116), with the result that she does not see the troubled look on his face. Yet in seeing her beauty, he concludes that this is the reason for the augurs' prediction: 'heaven must be jealous of her loveliness and his good fortune' (FT 116). Thus a mere averted gaze guarantees that, at the very moment he reaches this conclusion, the bride remains blissfully unaware of the rejection that is about to follow. Perhaps it is this reliance on coincidence that leads Johannes to break off from his imaginative leanings with the phrase 'I am not a poet, I only practise dialectics' (FT 116).

He then goes on to make three points and to consider four possible courses of action available to the bridegroom. It is hard to see the first of these points as anything other than self-justification of Kierkegaard's own actions in relation to Regine. Johannes claims that since the couple are not yet married (even if the ceremony is only minutes away), the bridegroom 'is pure and blameless, [he] hasn't bound himself irresponsibly to the loved one' (FT 116–17). The remaining points, though also having a potentially self-justificatory role, are more significant. The second aims to show that the bridegroom's action has a *religious* significance (thus taking the story closer to Abraham than would be a merely 'aesthetic' tale). Since the augurs speak with religious authority, it is on the basis of 'a divine utterance' that the bridegroom has to act. Thus his refusal to go ahead with the wedding is not merely 'conceit' (FT 116). And thirdly, his actions make him even unhappier than the bride, since he and his actions are the 'occasion' for their mutual unhappiness. (This idea seems to rely on something like the Socratic idea that it is worse to be the perpetrator of a wrong than to be its victim.)

Johannes then considers four options for the bridegroom. The first is to remain silent and get married. On this scenario, the bridegroom could hope that the misfortune would not follow immediately, thus preserving the possibility of a period of marital happiness, however brief, for his wife. He could also tell himself that he had been 'true to [his] love and not afraid to make [him]self unhappy' (FT 117). Central to this possibility is silence in the sense of concealing his reasons from his bride *despite marrying her*. Johannes gives this possibility short shrift, on the grounds that it 'insults the girl' (FT 117). He explains this as follows: 'By keeping silent he has in a way made her guilty, for had she known the truth she would never have given her consent to such a union' (FT 117). This explanation seems to be at its most plausible if we relate it to the idea, which Johannes mentions slightly earlier, that the augurs' prediction is of a misfortune *for the bridegroom*. If that is so, then his wife's 'guilt' can be seen to inhere in her going through with something that leads to her husband's (as opposed to her own) downfall. Hence Johannes' conclusion that, on this option, the bridegroom 'will have to bear not only the misfortune but also the responsibility for not having said anything, as well as her righteous anger at his not having said anything' (FT 117).

The second option is 'to remain silent and not get married' (FT 117). While this option, unlike the first, does not make his intended bride 'guilty', Johannes dismisses it as also involving 'an insult to the girl and the reality of her love' (FT 117). The reasons for this claim are not made explicit, perhaps because Johannes' main focus here is on the fact that 'aesthetics might approve' (FT 117) of this option. This is because it would require the bridegroom to 'enter into a deception in which he annihilates himself in relation to [his bride]' (FT 117). That is, the focus could be put on the suffering inwardness of the hero who, tragically, is unable to reveal the truth to his love, motivated as he is by what he perceives to be in her best interests. Dramatic tension could be heightened by such heroic suffering, culminating in 'last moment ... explanations' (FT 117) – that is, disclosure – which nevertheless do not prevent the 'aesthetic' necessity of the hero's tragic death. Johannes gives short shrift to this option too – perhaps simply because he views as 'an insult' anything less than honesty to the girl.

The third option is the one Johannes commends: the bridegroom should 'speak'. The bridegroom's disclosure will reveal the situation to his bride, and they will become like Axel and

Valborg, a couple forbidden by the church to marry because of their close kinship: 'a couple whom heaven itself has put asunder' (FT 117). In a footnote, Johannes considers but quickly dismisses a fourth option: to give up on the idea of marriage but nevertheless 'live in a romantic relationship with her' (FT 118n). This too is dismissed as an insult to the girl, because such a love 'doesn't express the universal' (FT 118n). To understand this remark, we need to recall that Judge William defends marriage as a paradigmatic expression of the universal.[8] Relatedly Climacus, in his review of Kierkegaard's writings, describes marriage as 'the most profound form of life's disclosure' (CUP 254).

Johannes concludes that the bridegroom should speak simply because such disclosure is what ethics demands (FT 118). Johannes' basic claim in relation to this first story, then, is that the bridegroom is *not* an exception to the demands of the ethical. As if anticipating what we might be thinking once we come to this rather frustrating conclusion, Johannes asks: 'why this sketch if I nevertheless come no further than the tragic hero?' (FT 118). The answer is that it 'might still shed light on the paradox' (FT 118) – that is, on Abraham. Again, it does so negatively, the crucial difference being that 'the augur's utterance is intelligible not just to the hero but to everyone and results in no private relation to the divine' (FT 119). In other words, what an augur prophesies can be understood by everyone: 'there is no secret writing that only the hero can read' (FT 119). This, then, is the difference between this story and that of Abraham. The bridegroom would be akin to Abraham if 'the will of heaven ... had been made known to him in some quite private way, if it had placed itself in a quite private relationship to him' (FT 119). Once again we are reminded that the point about Abraham is that, because of this 'private relationship' to God's command (a crucial dimension of his 'absolute relationship to the absolute' [FT 119]), he *cannot* speak 'however much he might want to' (FT 119).

AGNETE AND THE MERMAN

Johannes' second story is the popular Danish folk legend of Agnete and the merman. Again, he is interested in the story because of its potential for variation.[9] He quickly dismisses the standard version of the story, in which the merman is 'a seducer who rises up from concealment in the depths' (FT 120) whose 'wild desire' plucks the 'innocent flower' Agnete who is listening to the roar of the ocean. The first change Johannes proposes effectively tells the story of a seducer himself being seduced by 'the power of innocence' (FT 120). Instead of being forcibly plucked from the shore and dragged into the depths of the sea, Agnete willingly submits to the merman. Johannes describes the Agnete of the original legend as 'a woman who hankers for "the interesting"' (FT 121). Perhaps it is for this reason – Johannes' exposition is confusing on this point – that she is willing to submit: the merman is said to have 'coaxed from her her secret thoughts' and to be 'what she was seeking, what she gazed down to find in the depths of the sea' (FT 120). The important point is that Agnete looks at the merman 'in absolute faith, with absolute humility, like the humble flower she deemed herself to be; with absolute confidence she entrusts to him her entire fate' (FT 120). It is this trusting innocence that the merman cannot stand. Because he is 'unable to resist the power of innocence', he thus becomes a seducer unable to seduce. In a symbol of the merman's loss of power, the sea becomes calm. Consequently, he conceals from her his true purpose, returning her to the shore and claiming that he only wanted her to see the beauty of a calm sea. Agnete believes him. But the merman knows that he has lost Agnete, since 'only as his prize can she become his' (FT 121): that is, he can only possess her by seducing her. Thus this first variation gives us another instance of suffering or anguished concealment – to be contrasted with the variations that follow.

Perhaps to improve upon the one-dimensionality of a merman who can only exist as pure seduction, Johannes next proposes to 'give the merman a human consciousness' (FT 121). The other details of the above variation remain the same: 'He is saved by Agnete, the seducer is crushed, he has bowed to the power of innocence, he can never seduce again' (FT 122). But now, for this more human merman, two possibilities enter the frame: 'repentance [alone] and repentance with Agnete' (FT 122). (Presumably, what the merman repents of is his past as a seducer, and the fact that he was willing to seduce and destroy Agnete.) The significance of these two possibilities for Johannes' wider discussion immediately becomes clear: if it is 'repentance alone' that possesses the merman, then this is concealment; if it is 'repentance and Agnete', then this is disclosure. What difference does this make?

The significance of repenting, but concealing what he repents of from Agnete, is that this introduces a new category: the 'demonic'. Such concealed repentance makes both Agnete and the merman unhappy. Agnete is unhappy because her trusting love apparently only receives in return a trip out to a newly becalmed sea. The real focus of Johannes' interest, though, is the merman. (Note that this parallels his greater interest in Abraham than in Isaac.) The merman's unhappiness is more complex: he is unable to possess the girl whom 'he loved ... with a multiplicity of passions' (FT 122), and yet he also has the guilt of knowing that he *had been* prepared to seduce and destroy her. Enter the demonic: 'The demonic side of repentance will now no doubt explain to him that this is precisely his punishment, and the more it torments him the better' (FT 122).

What would embracing this 'demonic side of repentance' amount to? To see, let us first recap. The merman's repentance stems from his being awakened by Agnete's loving trustfulness to the possibility of a more genuine love, in comparison to which his previous desires – indeed, perhaps his previous self – seem appalling. Thus he sees the punishment of his unhappiness as deserved. 'Demonic silence' stems from what Mark C. Taylor calls 'this understanding of the inward suffering occasioned by deceitful deeds'.[10] Yet paradoxically, as Taylor points out, such demonic silence can exert a peculiar attraction. Such a merman's

> relation to his suffering is ambivalent. On the one hand he is repelled by it and wants nothing more than to be free of it, while on the other hand, he is attracted to it and refuses to part with it. The attachment to one's own corruption and suffering that leads a person to guard silence and to turn his back on the possibility of forgiveness is what Kierkegaard means by the demonic.[11]

One can therefore imagine this version of the merman wallowing in self-punishing self-pity. It is important to see that this is compatible with the dimension of giving in to this 'demonic possibility' that Johannes stresses. In another passage that suggests Kierkegaard's self-justification before Regine, he considers the possibility of the merman's aiming 'to save Agnete ... by resort to evil' (FT 122). He aims to save her by 'tear[ing] ... her love away from her'. Instead of offering a 'candid confession' (FT 122) – disclosure – he might 'try to arouse all dark passions in her, scorn her, mock her, hold her love up to ridicule, if possible stir up her pride' (FT 122). That is, by treating her appallingly, he might cause her to view herself as being better off without him – Kierkegaard's own tactic in relation to Regine. Although such a course of action hardly looks like literal silence, it is still compatible with concealment, in that he conceals from her the truth of the matter.

Next comes a puzzling claim, the point of which seems to be to justify the above discussion in relation to the 'divine silence' of Abraham. Johannes claims that demonic silence has an analogous, but misleading, relation to divine silence. In his actions as described above, the merman 'would ... aspire to be the single individual who as the particular is higher than the universal. The demonic has that same property as the divine, that the individual can enter into an absolute relationship to it' (FT 122–3). But why does the merman's acting unethically, deceptively, in relation to Agnete amount to aiming to be 'the single individual who as the particular is higher than the universal'? I think the answer is that the merman's actions are more than just unethical. They are not just a falling short of the demand to express the universal. Rather, recall Taylor's explanation of the demonic as an 'attachment to one's own corruption and suffering that leads a person to guard silence and to turn his back on the possibility of forgiveness'. Such an orientation does not just fail to express the universal, in the manner of shooting at a target and missing. Rather, the merman demonstrates a *self-absorbed embrace* of his (demonic) hiddenness. In this respect – and unlike the person who, morally striving for a universally comprehensible aim, nevertheless falls short of his moral target – the merman might appear to resemble Abraham, in whose isolation his God-relationship is also hidden from view. But this resemblance is only superficial, 'misleading':

precisely because the merman's hiddenness is 'demonic' rather than 'divine'. And whereas the former is entirely self-absorbed, the latter is premised on a relationship to another: God.

But suppose the merman does resist the demonic. Johannes goes on to consider two more possibilities. The first is still an instance of concealment (he 'remain[s] in hiding' [FT 123]), in which the merman 'finds repose in the counter-paradox that the divine will save Agnete' (FT 123). In other words, he simply trusts in God to save Agnete from her unhappiness. The second possibility is the more significant, since this – 'repentance with Agnete' – is the main contrast to 'repentance alone'. Here the merman is saved in so far as he is disclosed, and so – recalling the idea that marriage is 'the most profound form of life's disclosure' – he marries Agnete. This might at first glance look like a straightforward case of the ethical, of realising the universal: a merman of whom Judge William could approve. But Johannes claims that it is not so straightforward. He insists that there is still something paradoxical about this version of the merman. Why? Because 'when *through his own guilt* the individual has come out of the universal, he can only return to it on the strength of having come, as the particular, into an absolute relation to the absolute' (FT 124, my emphasis). This puzzling remark is followed by some gnomic comments about sin that certain commentators have claimed are pivotal to the whole book.

One such commentator, Ronald M. Green, suggests that what Johannes means to imply here is that 'Abraham and the merman are counterparts, positive and negative expressions of the same problem. Both have suspended the ethical, one by obedience and one by sin, and both are saved only by a direct, supraethical relationship to God.'[12] Seen in this light, and provided we are prepared to conflate guilt and sin, the previous quotation would then mean that the individual in sin ('through his own guilt') requires a direct relationship to God (coming 'as the particular, into an absolute relation to the absolute') in order to avoid being lost. We shall see in the next chapter that this is entirely in line with the Christian reading of the 'teleological suspension'. Central to Green's reading is the idea that Abraham functions 'as a figure for the problem of sin and atonement',[13] and that this mention of sin in the story of Agnete and the merman is 'not a chance aside but a window into *Fear and Trembling*'s deepest concerns'.[14] We shall return to this issue, and to Green's and related readings, in the next chapter.

The significance of this version of the merman seems to turn on the difference made by his own guilt. The difference this makes concerns how he can be saved from being 'lost'. This can happen only by his coming into an 'absolute relation to the absolute'. But another proponent of the Christian reading, Stephen Mulhall, points to something Green does not make explicit. If the merman marries Agnete, and thus allows her to save him, then despite the fact that this involves disclosure (in so far as it involves marriage), this is no merely ethical relation. Rather it is one in which 'what he values in the world [i.e. Agnete] will have been returned to him through what de silentio calls the paradox of the single individual attaining an absolute relation to the absolute'.[15] In other words, it looks strikingly like the *Fear and Trembling* conception of 'faith'. Abraham 'gets Isaac back', understood as a gift from God on a deeper level. Similarly the merman, by renouncing his previous relation to Agnete (as one to be seduced), also gets her back – again this time understood (in so far as he needs to enter into an absolute relation to the absolute to get to this point) as a gift from God.

It is easy to see why one might suggest, as does Sharon Krishek, that we should read 'repentance without Agnete' as infinite resignation and 'repentance with Agnete' as faith.[16] Krishek argues that the importance of the merman is that he is a figure 'closer to us' than is the exemplary Abraham. Like us, he might, 'demonically' choose actively the state of sin, choosing 'to lead an existence dominated by his demons':[17] the sinner who refuses to repent. Alternatively, he might make the movement of resignation, recognising his guilt and susceptibility, *qua* sinner, to fall back into his old, seductive ways, and so throw himself on the mercy of God. Thus he might find that certain peace of mind we have already seen to be characteristic of resignation. However, this means 'accept [ing] fully' that Agnete 'is lost for him'.[18] His third option, in which he allows himself to be 'saved through Agnete' (FT 124) corresponds to faith, on Krishek's reading. Agnete can save the merman through her love: by 'accept[ing] him (including his demons); by her power to become reconciled with her hurt pride and her fears about the future ... ; by being faith-full enough to have trust and hope, and to find joy in him and in their relationship of love'.[19] On the merman's part, 'repentance with Agnete' would mean re-establishing his relationship with finitude, 'expressed in his ability to find joy (including bodily, erotic joy) in [her]'.[20] ('Had I faith, I would have stayed with Regine.') Such a merman will live a love of 'joyful insecurity', in which he can 'find the strength to be hopeful and trustful' that despite the risks and vulnerabilities essential to human love, 'they will nevertheless, by the power of graceful infinitude, be capable of enjoying the gift of finitude bestowed upon them from above.'[21] Such a love is, Krishek suggests, a real possibility for all of us.

Yet Johannes insists that such a merman is still not Abraham. Why not? Simply because Abraham does not — unlike the merman — exist in a state of sin but is 'that righteous man who is God's chosen' (FT 124). Johannes seems to view the merman as comprehensible to us in a way that Abraham is not. The idea indeed seems to be that the merman, mired as he is in a state of sin (and consequent guilt), is closer to us, whereas the sinless Abraham is beyond our comprehension. At first, this seems strange. Presumably, Abraham is incomprehensible in part because for Johannes — and us — the idea of a state of sinlessness is incomprehensible. But why suppose Abraham represents sinlessness? Surely this goes against biblical chronology: in so far as Abraham post-dates the Garden of Eden, surely he too occupies a world of sin? There are two possible responses here. The first requires us to recall, as mentioned in Chapter 3, Abraham's status in Christian thought as a great exemplar of righteousness, based largely on Paul's remarks in Romans 4. As we noted in Chapter 1, Paul here presents Abraham as a supreme example of a person's being justified not by their works, but by their faith alone: 'Abraham believed God, and it was counted unto him for righteousness ... to him that worketh not, but believeth on him that justifieth the ungodly his faith is counted for righteousness'.[22] But righteousness is surely not the same thing as sinlessness. Rather, it means that a sinner can be 'justified', in Kierkegaard's Lutheran tradition, by faith — in God in Christ — alone. However, to say this leaves the precise relation between Abraham's faith (before Christ lived) and faith after the 'Christ event' unclear. So what of the second solution? This requires an *allegorical* Christian reading of *Fear and Trembling*, wherein Abraham symbolises God the Father. We shall return to this in Chapter 6. For the time being, note that for either version of the Christian reading, the discussion of Agnete and the merman is particularly significant, owing to Johannes' so far puzzling remarks on sin and repentance. We shall indeed need to return to this.

SARAH AND TOBIAS

Johannes' third story introduces yet another unhappy love match, that between Sarah and Tobias from the book of Tobit in the Apocrypha. In the original, Sarah has attempted to get married seven times, but all of her prospective bridegrooms have perished in the bridal chamber. Johannes seems right in his judgement that the tragic dimension of this story is clouded by the comical idea that such a thing could happen not once but seven times. So once again, he varies the story, making this Sarah's first betrothal. But 'she knows that the evil demon that loves her will kill the bridegroom on the wedding night' (FT 128). Characteristically, Johannes spends a page or so imagining and empathising with Sarah's situation in its full horror. Knowing of the threat, Tobias nevertheless goes through with the wedding, and he and Sarah pray together for God's mercy (FT 128–9). However, Johannes insists that however brave and noble Tobias would have been in so doing, it is Sarah who is the heroine. She shows 'love of God', 'ethical maturity', 'humility' and 'faith in God' (FT 129).

Johannes again contrasts the 'divine' and the 'demonic', by contrasting Sarah's heroic and faithful behaviour with the 'demonic' possibility that would be likely to arise if we 'let Sarah be a man' (FT 129). 'A proud and noble nature', we are told, 'cannot endure pity' (FT 129). In so far as a situation like Sarah's is bound to elicit pity, such a male Sarah 'would certainly be likely to choose the demonic, shut himself up in himself and say in his heart, as does the demonic nature, "Thanks, I am no friend of ceremony and fuss, I don't at all insist on the pleasures of love, I can just as well be a Bluebeard who gets his pleasure seeing girls die on their wedding night"' (FT 130). (It is hard to know which dimension of Johannes' gender stereotyping is worse here: the apparent belief that only men can have (proud and) noble natures – in stark contradiction to what he has just implied about the female Sarah's nobility of character – or the view of men contained in the above quote.) Such a demonic nature – most memorably portrayed in Gloucester (later Richard III), 'the most demonic figure Shakespeare ever portrayed' (FT 130)[23] – is 'aboriginally in the paradox' (FT 131). What does this mean? In a distinction that we are now in a position to see as echoing the discussion of Agnete and the merman, Johannes claims that such natures 'are either damned in the demonic paradox or delivered in the divine' (FT 132). This contrast suggests that we are here supposed to contrast Gloucester (the demonic) with Sarah (the divine). Gloucester is 'in the paradox' in the sense that it is impossible for him to realise the universal. As Johannes puts it, 'Natures like Gloucester's cannot be saved by mediating them into an idea of society' (FT 130). The aspect of Gloucester's nature that renders it impossible for him to realise the universal is his hunchback physique.[24] His inability to endure the pity that this inspires in others ensures that he can never feel fully 'at home' in society (FT 130). In this sense, Gloucester's nature makes it impossible for him to be 'saved' by the ethical, and so he must either embrace the demonic or the divine. Gloucester pursues the former. Sarah is also 'in the paradox' in the same sense: she too cannot attain the universal, in the sense that she cannot – for the reasons given – successfully marry. Thus, in this sense, Sarah is also compelled to live outside the security of the universal. (This needs to be understood specifically in the context of marriage. Johannes' point seems not to work if we ask ourselves what prevents Sarah from being part of the universal in some way other than through marriage.) There are two ways, according to Johannes, in which one can be 'put outside the universal from the start': by 'nature' or 'historical circumstance' (FT 131). Although it is possible to imagine circumstances in which what prevents Sarah from marrying is one form or other of the latter (such as illness or lack of opportunity), Johannes seems to imply that both Sarah and Gloucester come into the former category.[25] But the key contrast is between the two options of being 'damned in the demonic paradox or delivered in the divine [paradox]'. Whereas Gloucester's resentment at the pity he inspires, combined with his natural pride, leads to the former fate, Sarah represents the latter. And 'what love for God it takes to want to be healed when one has been crippled from the start for no fault of one's own' (FT 129). The point about such figures is that since ethics cannot save them, if they are to be redeemed at all (which Sarah is and Gloucester isn't), it must be by the divine.[26]

THE SYMPATHETIC FAUST

The final 'poetic personage' Johannes considers is a version of Faust. This Faust is 'a doubter' (FT 132) – and doubt, if unleashed, can be terrifying. Recall here that *Fear and Trembling* begins with a brief discussion of doubt, as a precursor to its discussion of doubt's ostensible opposite, faith. In a journal entry of 1835, Kierkegaard describes Faust as 'the personification of doubt' (KJN 1 AA: 12 [p. 14]). As we noted in Chapter 2, doubt is the central theme of the unpublished text, *Johannes Climacus*, in which a figure with the same name as the author of *Philosophical Fragments* and its *Postscript* is portrayed as a young student, 'ardently in love ... with thinking' (PF/JC 118).[27] Johannes Climacus continually hears the refrain *De omnibus dubitandum est* ['Everything must be doubted'], but notes that those who say this do not seem to take seriously what they say. The young student wonders what it would mean really to take doubt seriously, rather than saying 'Everything must be doubted' from a lectern[28] and then continuing to live, once the lecture is over, as if this were not true. In a paragraph added to the draft of *Johannes Climacus*, Kierkegaard explains that this text is intended to be an attack on speculative philosophy. Johannes Climacus' significance is said to be as follows:

> Johannes does what we are told to do – he actually doubts everything – he suffers through all the pain of doing that ... When he has gone as far in that direction as he can go and wants to come back, he cannot do so. He perceives that in order to hold on to this extreme position of doubting everything, he has engaged all his mental and spiritual powers. If he abandons this extreme position, he may very well arrive

at something, but in doing that he would have also abandoned his
doubt about everything. Now he despairs, his life is wasted, his youth
is spent in these deliberations. Life has not acquired any meaning for
him, and this is the fault of [speculative] philosophy.[29]

This, then, is the danger of taking doubt seriously. But – returning to *Fear and Trembling* – since Johannes de silentio's imagined Faust has 'a sympathetic nature', and because he is aware of the damaging effects that his doubt, if unleashed, could have on others, 'he remains silent, he hides his doubt in his soul' (FT 133). That is, by facing alone the sufferings that accompany genuine doubt, 'he makes himself a sacrifice to the universal' (FT 134). In other words, Faust protects others by sacrificing himself to the sufferings of doubt. Note that such a Faust *lives* his doubt, in the way praised in the Preface to *Fear and Trembling*, and in stark contrast to those 'speculative philosophers' (Martensen and his ilk?) whose doubt is presented as superficial; merely theoretical.

But ethics, because it requires disclosure, will condemn him for his silence (FT 135). Moreover, part of the doubter's torture will be that, if everything is to be doubted, this includes his own motives. He cannot be absolutely certain that 'it wasn't some hidden pride that prompted [his] decision' (FT 135).

There is, however, a way out – given in an initially baffling paragraph:

If on the other hand the doubter can be the single individual who as the particular stands in an absolute relation to the absolute, then he receives authorization for his silence. In that case he must make his doubt into guilt. In that case, he is within the paradox. But then his doubt is cured, even though he can acquire another.

(FT 135, translation adjusted)

What this means, I suggest, is as follows. The only possible 'justification' for Faust's silence is on the basis of an absolute relation to the absolute. Ethics, demanding as it does disclosure, *cannot* provide a justification – so any justification there is must be 'higher'. To achieve this relation would require Faust to 'make his doubt into guilt'. That is, he needs to recognise himself as guilty: for an absolute relation to the absolute (a relation to God unmediated by the ethical) to be possible, he must accept himself as a sinner. To do so puts him 'within the paradox'. What could this mean? Johannes could simply be restating the by now familiar idea that the single individual being in an absolute relation to the absolute is a paradox. But that seems unlikely, since if all he is doing is repeating this in the penultimate sentence, it is unclear what the intermediate sentence has added. We therefore need an alternative meaning of being 'within the paradox'. Such a meaning is provided by Faust's standing in relation to the 'absolute' paradox of Christ the 'god-man', through whom – according to Christianity – sin can be forgiven. In which case, Johannes would mean that if Faust was to understand himself as a sinner and relate himself to He who can forgive sin then 'his doubt is cured': that is, his sins are forgiven. Why conflate the curing of doubt with the forgiveness of sin? We cannot be sure about this reading, but some support for it is given by a journal entry of about this time in which Kierkegaard claims that 'Doubt is conquered not by the system but by faith' (JP 1: 891). It is clear from the reference to Christianity that immediately precedes this quote in the journal that Kierkegaard is here talking about specifically Christian faith. Excessive doubt is a manifestation of a state of sin as yet unredeemed by faith in Christ. If this reading is on the mark, note that this is one more piece of evidence for the idea that *Fear and Trembling* has an underlying Christian subtext – and thus heightens the need for us to consider Christian interpretations in Chapter 6.

RETURNING TO ABRAHAM

This long excursus has taken up a significant proportion of Johannes' book. In returning to discuss Abraham towards the end of the third problema, Johannes almost seems embarrassed about this: 'I have not forgotten, and the reader may now be pleased to recall, that this was the point to which the whole preceding discussion was intended to lead' (FT 136). So this seems a good point at which to recap. The question Problema III is trying to address is as follows. If the mark of the ethical is openness or disclosure, and Abraham (the exemplar of faith) is marked by concealment, is this just a reversion to the aesthetic? In order to show that the answer to this is 'No', Johannes continues his overall negative strategy of comparing Abraham with other cases in order to point out the differences: 'My procedure here must be to let concealment pass dialectically between aesthetics and ethics, for the point is to show how absolutely different the paradox and aesthetic concealment are from one another' (FT 112). The overall idea, then, has been to distinguish the allegedly necessary silence of Abraham's faith from superficially similar silences, some of which are blameworthy.

None of the narratives in Problema III (the Delphic bridegroom, Agnete and the merman, Sarah and Tobias or Faust) is really analogous to Abraham. Johannes thinks that describing them serves the purpose of getting closer to Abraham, but only negatively. Perhaps more useful than the specifics of each of the four main stories is the overall conclusion Johannes appears to think he can draw from his discussion of them. There emerges from all this a new figure, the 'aesthetic hero'. In the foregoing, Johannes claims, aesthetics 'demanded silence of the individual when by remaining silent he could save another' (FT 136). (Recall the Delphic bridegroom.) Johannes draws a disanalogy between such an 'aesthetic hero' – that is, someone who is a hero from an aesthetic point of view in keeping silent in order to save another – and Abraham. Abraham's silence is *not* in order to save another: it is precisely silence in the face of the command to sacrifice another. 'His silence is not at all to save Isaac, as in general the whole task of sacrificing Isaac for his own and God's sake is an outrage aesthetically. Aesthetics can well understand that I sacrifice myself, but not that I should sacrifice another for my own sake' (FT 136–7). In other words, the disanalogy between Abraham and the aesthetic hero shows that Abraham would offend 'aesthetics' as well as 'ethics'.

The difference between the 'aesthetic hero' and the – ethical – 'genuine tragic hero' is that the former's silence is 'on the strength of his accidental particularity' (FT 137): that is, the specifics of the situation of the bridegroom, for instance, cause him to stay silent. Whereas the 'tragic hero' such as Agamemnon 'sacrifices himself and everything he has for the universal' (FT 137) and, in this public manifestation of his commitments, is thus 'revealed'. In summary, then, the aesthetic hero can speak but will not (to save another).

The ethical 'tragic' hero can and should speak – the ethical's demand of disclosure – and does. Abraham is different from both of these: hence we need a 'new category' for him.

It is important to emphasise here that Johannes is not merely claiming that Abraham *does* not speak – but that he *'cannot ... therein lies the distress and anguish'* (FT 137). What he means by this is made clearer by the next sentence: 'For if when I speak I cannot make myself understood, I do not speak even if I keep talking without stop day and night. This is the case with Abraham' (FT 137). In other words, what Johannes is talking about is not Abraham's inability to utter words – he is not literally struck dumb – but his inability to *communicate* his situation: 'there is one thing he cannot say and since he cannot say it, i.e. say it in a way that another understands it, he does not speak' (FT 137).

Let us recap. As we have seen, Abraham's failure to *speak* is particularly damning from a Hegelian point of view: recall our earlier discussion of *Meinung*. To say something, I need to utilise the publicly available, 'universal' resources of language. This is precisely what Abraham cannot do. That this is what Johannes has in mind is made clear by his remark that: 'The relief of speech is that it translates me into the universal' (FT 137). Whereas the tragic hero can do 'justice' to 'all counter-arguments' (FT 137–8) – make and defend his case publicly – Abraham cannot. Once again, then, the focus is on his isolation: 'to contend with the whole world [as the tragic hero does] is a comfort, but to contend with oneself dreadful' (FT 138).[30]

As well as our four poetic personages, Problema III gives us one more negative parallel to Abraham: the 'intellectual tragic hero', exemplified by Socrates (FT 140–1). Johannes' treatment of this figure is likely to strike the reader as puzzling, given that it seems to take back some of what Johannes has been insisting upon about the significance of Abraham's ability to 'speak'. The difference between a tragic hero such as Agamemnon and his intellectual counterpart is that whereas Agamemnon could go through with the sacrifice in heroic silence, Socrates, when on trial for his life (as portrayed in Plato's *Apology*), 'is required to have sufficient spiritual strength at the final moment to fulfil himself' (FT 141). He needs to *speak*. Johannes suggests the following as his 'decisive remark':

'the death-sentence is announced to him, that instant he dies and fulfils himself in the famous rejoinder that he was surprised to have been condemned with a majority of three votes' (FT 141n).[31]

Puzzlingly given what Johannes has been saying all along, the link between this and Abraham is now said to be that unlike Agamemnon, but like Socrates, Abraham too needs to 'hav[e] something to say' (FT 141). Though Johannes says that he could imagine himself into Socrates' position and provide a 'decisive remark' if Plato's report of the trial had not provided one, he has been insisting all along that Abraham is too stern a test for his imaginative capacities. So his claim that he could not have imagined what Abraham could say should therefore come as no surprise. Yet here too, the relevant text provides us with a 'last word' from Abraham. Now things get very strange indeed. Having insisted that Abraham 'cannot speak' – cannot make himself understood – Johannes points out that Abraham *does* say something: 'My son, God will provide himself a lamb for a burnt offering' (FT 139, 142). This ambiguous response, Johannes tells us, 'has the form of irony, for it is always irony to say something and yet not say it' (FT 142). By 'irony', Johannes here seems to have in mind something like what Gregory Vlastos calls 'complex irony', in which 'what is said both is and isn't what is meant: its surface content is meant to be true in one sense, false in another'.[32] On the most common reading of this, Abraham's utterance is false in the sense that he does not really expect God to provide, literally, a lamb; but true in the sense that Isaac is himself the 'sacrificial lamb'. However, a further layer of irony is added, of course, by the fact that in the event God *does* provide a sacrificial animal, albeit a ram rather than a lamb. But can we really say that this utterance is accurately described by the phrase 'saying something and yet not saying it'? Previously, Johannes has stressed Abraham's utter isolation, his complete inability to make himself understood. But an ironic utterance with only two or three possible meanings hardly amounts to utter isolation, hardly amounts to putting Abraham way beyond the reach of language. Certainly, Abraham's utterance is more gnomic than the straightforward utterance – 'It is you who are to be sacrificed' – that Johannes tells us he could not have made at the crucial moment. (This is so both because if Abraham could say this at all, he could have done so earlier, and also because such a 'straight', easily comprehended utterance takes him 'out of the paradox' and into the universal (see FT 142).) But does the double- (or triple-) edged nature of his actual remark really amount to total incomprehensibility?

Something strange is going on here. Johannes seems to be making some kind of error.[33] But what is the significance of this? Is it simply a flaw in the text – or does that flaw have some greater significance? The latter possibility is considered in detail in Stephen Mulhall's reading of *Fear and Trembling* as a self-subverting text – a reading which we shall consider in Chapter 7. So we shall return to Johannes' curious remarks about Abraham's 'last word' then.

Problema III ends, then, with a restatement of the by now familiar paradox: 'that the single individual as the particular stands in an absolute relation to the absolute, or Abraham is done for' (FT 144).

EPILOGUE

After the problemata, *Fear and Trembling* closes with a brief 'Epilogue' that returns to the economic imagery with which the book began. Johannes mentions a tactic used by Dutch spice merchants during a slump in the market: dumping cargo at sea in order to 'force up the price' (FT 145) of what was left. Johannes claims: 'That was a pardonable, perhaps necessary, stratagem. Is it something similar we need in the world of spirit?' (FT 145). Note how this echoes the book's opening: that the age is putting on 'a veritable clearance sale' (FT 41), selling faith at a knock-down price. In the Epilogue, Johannes insists – twice – that faith is 'the highest passion in a human being' (FT 145, 146). While acknowledging that Johannes does not tell us precisely what he means by passion, Westphal offers an account of passion as 'what matters to us ... what we care about deeply enough to be part of our identity'.[34] Despite what the 'Hegelian' mantra of the age would have us believe, Johannes insists that one cannot 'go further' than faith (FT 147).[35] As we know by now, Johannes is opposed to the Hegelian view of history as the process of the self-actualisation of Spirit, and faith as something all can possess in virtue of our participation in *Sittlichkeit*. This leaves out something crucial: 'However much one generation learns from another, it can never learn from its predecessor the genuinely human factor. In this respect every generation begins primitively [*primitivt*], has no task other than that of any previous generation, and comes no further' (FT 145, translation adjusted).

This 'genuinely human factor' is 'passion'; a human being's 'highest passion' is faith; and here 'every generation begins from the beginning' (FT 145). In this important sense, the human task is always the same, in the sense we noted towards the end of our discussion of Problema I. Faith requires openness to the possibility that a call from God might clash with, require us to 'suspend', what our prevailing social morality dictates – and in this sense, the situation of the individual in any age is not so different from Abraham's. But in another sense, the nature of that trial might be – indeed, almost certainly will be – very different. As we shall suggest in Chapter 6, the way in which Abraham can act as a 'guiding star to save the anguished' might not be in his willingness to plunge the knife, but in the form taken by his trust and hope in God.

Fear and Trembling, then, is a text that aims to 'force up the price' of faith. This reference, though, is potentially confusing. What the spice merchants' action does, surely, is *artificially* inflate the price of the remaining spices. Is that what Johannes has been doing in relation to faith – artificially raising its price? Such an interpretation would support those readings that cast doubt on Johannes' reliability (of which more in Chapter 7). Or are we to read Johannes as giving us what he sees as the *true* value of faith, as a reaction to the tendency of his contemporaries to devalue it? In which case, his action is a 'necessary stratagem' in what are – for faith – desperate times. We cannot really answer this question until we have considered the issue of Johannes' reliability – which in turn depends upon considering various different interpretations of his text. It is to that task, then, that we must now turn.

NOTES

1 Daniel Conway notes that each of these acts of concealment occurs with respect to the three figures later described as 'ethical authorities [*Instantser*]'

(FT 136), and at the beginning (Sarah), middle (Eleazer) and towards the end (Isaac) of Abraham's journey, Sarah and Eleazer being left behind at earlier stages (2015b: 212). Note also that the issue of concealment does not arise for the version of the story in the Qur'an, in which Abraham reveals the content of his dream directly to his son.

2. See Chapter 3, note 84.
3. Taylor 1981: 180.
4. See especially CUP 253–4 on the aesthetic as the sphere of hiddenness.
5. However, Johannes here seems to overlook the fact that Iphigenia already knows her fate at this point of Euripides' play, presumably having been given the news by her distraught mother.
6. It is worth noting that silence is by no means always presented as a problem by Kierkegaard. Though here 'silence' is a major source of Abraham's anguish and distress, in *For Self-examination*, he presents it as necessary to hear God's Word (FSE 46–51). Similarly, in his late discourses on the lilies and the birds, silence is presented as one of the key things we need to learn from these 'divinely appointed teachers' (see WA 7–20): it is precisely because of the human ability to speak that 'the ability to be silent is an art' (WA 10). The problem this part of *Fear and Trembling* is discussing, then, is not silence per se but the alleged impossibility of making oneself 'understood'.
7. Note that of the four stories three involve male–female relationships and two explicitly involve marriage. This is perhaps the part of the text over which Kierkegaard's broken engagement to Regine hovers most obviously – in ways that will shortly become apparent.
8. See especially 'The Aesthetic Validity of Marriage' in *Either/Or* Part 2.
9. Deleuze and Guattari see this as acting 'like a precursor of the cinema', offering different versions of the story of Agnete and the merman 'according to variable speeds and slownesses' (1987: 281). Recall here the Attunement's different versions of the Abraham story, some of which, we already noted, are more 'filmic' than others.
10. Taylor 1981: 174.
11. Taylor 1981: 174–5.
12. Green 1993: 202.
13. Green 1993: 202.
14. Green 1993: 202.
15. Mulhall 2001: 385.
16. Krishek 2009: 184.
17. Krishek 2009: 185. Krishek has set up this part of her discussion with an interesting analysis of the Stanley Kubrick film *Eyes Wide Shut* and the novella on which it was based (2009: 179–83).
18. Krishek 2009: 185.
19. Krishek 2009: 186. Carlisle suggests that this 'saving' action of Agnete includes forgiveness, noting the fact that the name of Agnete (Agnes, in the Hongs' and Walsh's translations) is a form of the Latin term *Agnus*: as in 'the Lamb of God [*Agnus Dei*] that takes away the sin of the world' (John 1:29; Carlisle 2010: 151–2).

THE SOUND OF SILENCE 145

20 Krishek 2009: 187.
21 Krishek 2009: 187. Note that Krishek here touches on the importance of trust and hope, notions which I shall aim to develop further in Chapter 6.
22 Romans 4:3, 5.
23 The reference, of course, is to Shakespeare's *King Richard the Third*.
24 Note the emphasis Johannes gives to his pitiful speech about this (FT 130).
25 This is what Kierkegaard also felt about himself: see Keeley 1993: 147–8.
26 I am grateful to Anthony Rudd for help in clarifying this point.
27 Significantly, the Hongs claim that *Johannes Climacus* was most likely written between November 1842 and April 1843, that is, just before Kierkegaard began writing *Fear and Trembling*. (See the 'Historical Introduction' to PF/JC, p. x.)
28 Recall here Stewart's claim that the likely target of this jibe was Martensen and his followers. Johannes passes this judgement on 'scientific doubters' at FT 134; similar criticisms are made of speculative philosophers and 'assistant professors' or 'lecturers' elsewhere in Kierkegaard's oeuvre.
29 Cited in the 'Historical Introduction' to PF/JC: xiii.
30 Battles with oneself are a significant theme in some of Kierkegaard's upbuilding discourses from this period. For instance, in 'The Expectancy of Faith' (more of which in Chapter 6), he claims that the battle with the future is really a battle with oneself, since the only power the future has over us is the power we give it (EUD 18).
31 Johannes' account of this is a bit misleading in that Socrates makes this remark after he has just been found guilty and Meletus, one of his accusers, has proposed that the penalty should be death. But at this point the jury has not yet voted in favour of this penalty. (In Athenian courts at the time, the jury voted on alternative penalties proposed in turn by the accuser and the accused. Famously, Socrates' suggested alternative penalty was free maintenance at the state's expense.)
32 Vlastos 1991: 31.
33 On this point, see Conway 2008: 183, who notes that Johannes 'slides effortlessly' – and problematically – 'from *what Abraham intended* to *what Abraham knew would transpire*'.
34 See Westphal 2014: 102–20, especially the conclusion at p. 120. The passage cited is at p. 106.
35 Note the way the book ends, with a discussion of a would-be disciple of Heraclitus, who, attempting to 'go further' than his master, ends up regressing to a doctrine Heraclitus had abandoned (FT 147).

6

WHAT IS *FEAR AND TREMBLING* REALLY ABOUT?

Having worked our way through the text, it is now time to take stock. Is there a central claim of *Fear and Trembling*, and if so, what is it? Is it really that a command from God should override an ethical obligation, even if the divine command is to kill one's child? Or does such an interpretation miss the point, putting the emphasis in the wrong place? By now the vast majority of interpreters take the latter view (as do I). Of this group, some have also suggested that *Fear and Trembling* has a 'secret' or 'hidden' message. So our aims in this chapter will be threefold. First, I shall briefly sketch something of the 'reception history' of *Fear and Trembling*, chiefly to illustrate something of the sheer diversity of that reception. Second, I shall dig a little deeper into a selection of such readings, paying particular attention to what have been labelled 'higher ethics' readings of the text.[1] In response to such readings, I shall go on to explore the importance of *trust* (particularly what Davenport has called 'eschatological' trust) and – a relatively underexplored theme – *hope* in faith. Finally, I shall address an important dimension of the question of whether the 'surface' message commonly attributed to *Fear and Trembling* is its true message, through a consideration of specifically Christian readings of its 'indirect' message.

INTRODUCING ITS RECEPTION HISTORY

As well as philosophers and theologians, the range of figures influenced by Kierkegaard – very much including by *Fear and Trembling* – include artists such as Edvard Munch ('To read Kierkegaard is to experience oneself[2]), writers such as Franz Kafka and W. H. Auden, and political figures as diverse as György Lukács and Martin Luther King, Jr.

The political context gives something of the flavour of the sheer range of interpretation. Take Lukács. Andras Nagy locates a period in Kierkegaard reception in Hungary in the early twentieth century, in which a radical understanding of Kierkegaardian paradox is given Marxist answers. Lukács praises Kierkegaard as the figure who helped him 'to lose God'.[3] According to Nagy, the First World War gave new meaning to the dilemmas of *Fear and Trembling*, understood by Lukács to mean that 'on the basis of a mystical morality one must become a cruel politician and thus violate the absolute commandment: "Thou shalt not kill!"'.[4] But as Nagy notes, there is one crucial difference: 'the object of the sacrifice was lost forever; in the secularized – historically shaped – universe there was no longer anyone to save "Isaac".'[5] By contrast, in Russia during the years of *perestroika*, Abraham was co-opted for a diametrically opposed purpose, in which the individual 'dominating the universal' is taken by Kierkegaard translator Sergey Aleksandrovich Isayev to be a statement 'very brave and timely in the country that was only recently freed from political oppression'.[6] But both 'readings' might remind us of Gabriel Marcel's warning that 'there will always be the danger that what, for exceptional individualities, presents itself as a tragic philosophy, with its own undeniable grandeur, may become at the mass level a mere pragmatism for the use of middlemen and adventurers'.[7] Such a worry lies behind the perennial question – to which I shall return later in this chapter – of whether there are any grounds for distinguishing the actions of Abraham from contemporary terrorists and other killers who claim a religious inspiration for their deeds. Let us take it as a given that we need readings more nuanced than these.

Turning to the literary context, as well as countless figures from within Scandinavia,[8] writers beyond that region who discuss *Fear and Trembling* include W. H. Auden, Jorge Luis Borges, Franz Kafka and Walker Percy.[9] The relation between Kierkegaard and Kafka has gained particular attention. From his thirties onwards, Kafka read Kierkegaard with great interest. In light of his own tortured engagement to Felice Bauer (broken more than once), Kafka seems to have been fascinated in Kierkegaard's tactics in breaking his engagement. But according to Nicolae Irina, 'what apparently prompted Kafka's full-fledged interest in Kierkegaard's writings are the ethical and religious questions raised by Kierkegaard's portrayal of Abraham in *Fear and Trembling*'.[10] In a correspondence with his friend Max Brod, Kafka reports an ambiguous view of Kierkegaard, in which 'admiration' mingles with 'a certain cooling of my sympathy'. Urging Brod to read *Fear and Trembling*, Kafka nevertheless warns that Kierkegaard's

> affirmativeness turns truly monstrous and is checked only when it comes up against a perfectly ordinary helmsman. What I mean is, affirmativeness becomes objectionable when it reaches too high. He doesn't see the ordinary man (with whom, on the whole, he knows how to talk remarkably well) and paints this monstrous Abraham in the clouds.[11]

Kafka's ambivalence between admiration and deep scepticism about Kierkegaard's portrayal of Abraham seems to have continued for some time.[12]

There is an interesting link between Kafka's interest in Kierkegaard and the philosophical take-up of the latter's work. The range of philosophers, theologians and religious thinkers who have engaged with Kierkegaard is hugely diverse, including such figures as Karl Barth, Simone de Beauvoir, Maurice Blanchot, Dietrich Bonhoeffer, Martin Buber, Stanley Cavell, Jacques Derrida, Emmanuel Lévinas, Alasdair MacIntyre, Iris Murdoch, Gillian Rose, Jean-Paul Sartre, Paul Tillich, Miguel de Unamuno and Ludwig Wittgenstein.[13] *Fear and Trembling* is often one of the main texts forming their perceptions of Kierkegaard. Infamously, Kierkegaard has often been presented as a proto-existentialist, and it has been claimed that it was his influence on Kafka that sparked the French existentialists' interest in him.[14] Simone de Beauvoir explicitly credits *Fear and Trembling* as having influenced her 1945 novel *The Blood of Others*, which addresses the anguished moral choices faced by a group of French resistance fighters.[15] Along the same lines, in his famous 1946 lecture *Existentialism and Humanism*, Sartre refers explicitly to Kierkegaard's treatment of Abraham as a model for his own account of radical freedom.[16] Aiming to gloss the key existentialist terms anguish, abandonment and despair, Sartre gives the following account of anguish:

> When a man commits himself to anything, fully realising that he is not only choosing what he will be, but is thereby at the same time a legislator deciding for the whole of mankind – in such a moment a man cannot escape from the sense of complete and profound responsibility.[17]

He further expands on this with an explicit reference to Kierkegaard's treatment of the *akedah*:

> This is the anguish that Kierkegaard called 'the anguish of Abraham'. You know the story: An angel commanded Abraham to sacrifice his son: and obedience was obligatory, if it really was an angel who had appeared and said, 'Thou, Abraham, shalt sacrifice thy son.' But anyone in such a case would wonder, first, whether it was indeed an angel and secondly, whether I am really Abraham. Where are the proofs? ... If an angel appears to me, what is the proof that it is an angel; or, if I hear voices, who can prove that they proceed from heaven and not from hell, or from my own subconsciousness [sic] or some pathological condition? Who can prove that they are really addressed to me?
>
> Who, then, can prove that I am the proper person to impose, by my own choice, my conception of man upon mankind? I shall never find any proof whatever[.][18]

Within a page or two, we have reached the famous claim that we are 'condemned to be free'[19] – and to take responsibility for our choices — and the much-cited example of the young man in the Second World War needing to choose between joining the Free French to fight the Nazis or staying at home to help his ailing mother.[20] In a sense, where Abraham leads, we all must follow.[21] We are all in Abraham's situation, having to decide on our own without the possibility of justifying our decisions: hence 'Abraham's silence'. (As we shall see, Sartre's compatriot Derrida will later develop a related thought.) But in following Sartre down this path we leave the specifically religious context of Abraham's trial a long way behind (as with Lukács above). Thus it is not unreasonable for Manuela Hackel to ask 'whether Sartre's picture of Kierkegaard still resembles Kierkegaard — or whether it has already become too much of Sartre himself'.[22]

LÉVINAS: AGAINST KIERKEGAARD'S 'VIOLENCE'

Perhaps other thinkers also have brought too much of their own preoccupations to their critique of Kierkegaard. One influential philosopher who reads Johannes 'straight' — and reports thus finding Kierkegaard's thought 'violent' — is Emmanuel Lévinas. It is worth pausing to consider Lévinas's brief comments on *Fear and Trembling*, as there is considerable contemporary interest in the similarities and differences between his thought and Kierkegaard's. Jeffrey Hanson notes that notwithstanding his influence on the way Kierkegaard has been received in French philosophy, Lévinas's discussions on the Dane were 'comparatively few' and 'rarely in-depth'.[23] Indeed, Lévinas's account of central Kierkegaardian themes such as the existence-spheres is surprisingly simplistic. His first reference to Kierkegaard's 'violence' is as follows:

> Kierkegaardian violence begins when existence, having moved beyond the aesthetic stage, is forced to abandon the ethical stage (or rather, what it took to be the ethical stage) in order to embark on the religious stage, the domain of belief. But belief no longer sought external justification. Even internally, it combined communication and isolation, and hence violence and passion. That is the origin of the relegation of ethical phenomena to secondary status and the contempt for the

ethical foundation of being which has led, through Nietzsche, to the amoralism of recent philosophies.[24]

This passage blames Kierkegaard for quite a lot — and illicitly so. First, Lévinas accords the 'teleological suspension of the ethical' a status in Kierkegaard's wider authorship that he nowhere argues for. Second, he assumes, again without argument, that Johannes de silentio (and the other pseudonyms) speak unequivocally for Kierkegaard. Moreover, Lévinas seems to suppose that Kierkegaard is simply valorising Abraham for his willingness to kill Isaac. By now, we hardly need to point out that things are more complicated and ambiguous than this. There is no mention here of how Johannes, despite his 'admiration' for Abraham, is simultaneously 'appalled' by him. Nor does Lévinas consider either the possibility that Johannes is trying to wrestle with and clarify just what is at stake in commending Abraham as exemplary, or the possibility that he is putting a particular conception of the ethical under the microscope to see if it is adequate.

Lévinas repeats these charges against Kierkegaard in even more strident tones. Repeating the refrain that 'what shocks me about Kierkegaard is his violence', Lévinas again allies him to Nietzsche, and accuses him of an 'impulsive and violent style, reckless of scandal and destruction', which 'aspired to permanent provocation, and the total rejection of everything'.[25] He even goes on to associate this style with National Socialism, and this rot all allegedly sets in with Kierkegaard's 'transcendence [cf. "teleological suspension"] of the ethical'.[26]

Notwithstanding these excessive allegations, Lévinas does make an interesting suggestion about *Fear and Trembling*. In suggesting that its conception of the ethical is inadequate, he offers as an alternative his own now famous view of the ethical as being essentially 'the consciousness of a responsibility towards others'.[27] But he relates this to the idea that the real point of the *akedah* story may be quite different to what he takes Kierkegaard to suppose. Lévinas suggests an alternative emphasis to the command to sacrifice Isaac: 'the highest point of the whole drama may be the moment when Abraham paused and listened to the voice that would lead him back to the ethical order by commanding him not to commit a human sacrifice'.[28]

In other words, God's second voice is what matters: when the command to human sacrifice is replaced by God's provision of the ram that enables Isaac's life to be spared.[29] Other commentators, whose reading of the text is rather more careful than that of Lévinas, have also noted the significance of this factor – and given it a rather different significance. We shall return to this in considering, later in this chapter, a number of such readings of the text. According (amongst other readings) to the 'eschatological trust' reading that I shall discuss later in the chapter and support in broad outline, it is ironic that Lévinas fails to note that the second voice, and the provision of the ram, is crucial to *Fear and Trembling*, such that Johannes agrees with his judgement above.[30]

Overall, Lévinas's reading is rather unsubtle. But the point to note is that the reason he finds Kierkegaard 'violent' and therefore shocking is that he takes it for granted that the message of *Fear and Trembling* really is that a divine command should unquestionably override what the ethical demands. And many commentators have questioned this, and in a wide variety of ways.

TARQUIN'S POPPIES

It is not mere discomfort with such an ostensible conclusion that has led to a plethora of readings of *Fear and Trembling* as having a 'secret message'. Rather, such a suggestion is hinted at in the epigraph with which the book begins. There, Johannes (or is it Kierkegaard?) offers a typically gnomic remark from Hamann, a German thinker whom Kierkegaard greatly admired and who serves, in some of his writings, as an exemplary 'humorist'.[31] The remark is as follows: 'What Tarquin the Proud said in his garden with the poppy blooms was understood by the son but not by the messenger' (FT 39). This refers to the story of an early king of Rome whose son, having become a military leader in Gabii, sent a messenger back to his father asking advice on what to do next. Unsure whether he could trust the messenger, Tarquin gave no direct reply, but walked with him in a poppy field, striking the heads off the tallest poppies. On returning to Gabii, the messenger relayed this strange behaviour to Tarquin's son. The son – but not the messenger – understood its significance. The 'secret' message – communicated indirectly, note – was that the son should put to death or exile the leading citizens of Gabii. This he did, leading to the city's surrender to Rome. The point, then, is that a messenger may not understand the message he conveys. So why does this strange epigraph appear at the start of *Fear and Trembling*? How, exactly, does it apply to that text? Is Johannes the messenger – and what is it about the message that he fails to understand? Is it that his literal focus on the story of Abraham and Isaac obscures from him the real 'hidden' message of this story? Johannes repeatedly tells us that he lacks faith. So how much can we expect him to be able to tell us about it? It does not necessarily follow that the answer is 'nothing'. Perhaps an outsider's perspective, while limited, is still useful – in showing us what faith is not, or in showing us something of its formal structure, while nevertheless lacking the 'insider's' view of faith's 'double movement'.[32]

With this in mind, the rest of this chapter will offer a survey that aims to unpack various different interpretations of *Fear and Trembling*. Ronald M. Green describes the text as having been read on different 'levels'.[33] The following owes something to Green's investigations, but also offers some alternative foci.

A MESSAGE TO REGINE?

There is one 'hidden message' that we should get out of the way first. We briefly described in Chapter 1 the circumstances surrounding Kierkegaard's breaking off his engagement to Regine Olsen. We have also already mentioned, in Chapter 5, that *Fear and Trembling* – written, recall, shortly after the broken engagement – seems to have several self-justificatory passages. But recall in particular the tactics Kierkegaard claimed to have felt it necessary to use once it became obvious to him that he could not have made Regine happy had they gone through with the marriage. The least of all possible evils, he thought, was that she should come to consider him a scoundrel, utterly indifferent to her. That way she would be able, in contemporary pop psychological parlance, to 'move on' with her life. In this light, the first sub-Abraham of the 'Attunement' takes on a particular significance. This is the figure who, at the point of being willing to plunge the knife into Isaac's breast, tells Isaac that he is 'an idolator', and that killing him is his own desire, not God's command. He does this because 'it is after all better that he believe I am a monster than that he lose faith in [God]' (FT 45–6).

The significance of this passage to a 'biographical' reading is pretty obvious.[34] As Hannay puts it, 'If he can make Regine believe he is the sort of scoundrel you would expect to break off an engagement, Kierkegaard can save her from losing faith in the world'[35] – and, we might add, God. Not unreasonably, Hannay suggests that this is 'poor psychology ... indeed so poor for someone so feted for his psychological insight as to tempt one to doubt the honesty of the intention – or, failing that, the honesty of Kierkegaard's claim actually to have had it'.[36] Whatever we think of this, however, those who read *Fear and Trembling* as containing a 'secret message' to Regine tend to see this passage as being Kierkegaard's way of 'levelling' with her about his engagement-breaking tactics. If one reads the book this way, as a secret message to Regine, its central message is as follows. Just as Abraham is called by God to sacrifice that which is most precious to him (Isaac), so Kierkegaard is called to do the same (Regine). In Green's words, on this view Kierkegaard felt compelled to 'set aside his worldly hopes of happiness in order to undertake his solitary vocation as a religious author'.[37]

Another version of such a reading, offered for instance by Gregor Malantschuk, has Kierkegaard as the Isaac 'sacrificed' by his father. On this view, the hidden message to Regine – who needs to be told not *that* she was being sacrificed (obvious from the broken engagement itself), but *why* – was that Kierkegaard 'himself was being sacrificed, and therefore he had to sacrifice her',[38] at least in part because marrying her would involve initiating her into the terrible details of his relation to his father and the melancholy that he often associates with it.

Doubtless there are indeed 'autobiographical' features to *Fear and Trembling*. But its relevance to a sad, short-lived romance in the 1840s (or to Kierkegaard's relation to his father) can hardly explain the level of interest that the text has generated from commentators for more than one hundred and seventy years.[39] Let us start to explore, then, the different 'levels' on which the text has been read.

A CALL TO COMMITMENT: THEOLOGICAL SHOCK TREATMENT

The first of Green's 'levels' is simply a 'call to Christian commitment'.[40] On this level, Johannes is using the story of Abraham and Isaac as a kind of 'theological shock treatment'.[41] Kierkegaard saw his age as complacently conflating being a Christian with being born in 'Christendom' – being born in a 'Christian country' like Denmark, to Christian parents, and being baptised into the Danish State Church. Such a 'bourgeois' view of what religious commitment amounts to contrasts starkly with the courage of Abraham's raw, 'primitive' faith which involves acting and living in a certain way, even – indeed, especially – in the most exacting of circumstances. A more sophisticated version of the confusion of the age, Kierkegaard thought, came with the threat of Hegelianism. As we have seen, *Fear and Trembling* contains several jibes at the idea of 'going further' than faith: a reference to the Hegelian idea that faith was a relatively elementary stage of intellectual development that the Hegelian philosophy could surpass. Such a view subordinates the first person dimension of faith – stressed by Kierkegaard as so vital – to an understanding of the unfolding of *Geist* [Mind or Spirit] through world history.

Thus one of the most important points about *Fear and Trembling* read on this level is its use of the Abraham story starkly to point out that religious faith and a bourgeois life are not necessarily without conflict. Abraham's trial reveals the potential for a clash between 'ethical' and 'religious' commitments and duties. The story of the preacher who fails to take on board the implications of the Abraham narrative draws attention to contemporary Christendom's failure to see this. On this view, the central message of *Fear and Trembling* is that the 'present age' has devalued faith. (Recall here the text's use of economic imagery – especially at the beginning and the end.) Johannes' aim, on this view, is to draw attention to the true value – and potential cost – of faith.

THE PSYCHOLOGY OF FAITH

But this leaves unanswered our central question: does Johannes' talk of a 'teleological suspension of the ethical' amount to the claim that ethical requirements should be suspended in the light of the higher *telos* of the will of God? Though nothing we have said so far gives an unequivocal answer to this, Green's first level seems to be leaning in the direction of an affirmative answer. His second level, which is concerned with the 'psychology of faith', appears to answer this question in the negative. According to Green, such an inquiry 'starts with the first level's assumption that faith is a lived commitment but seeks to understand its precise mental content for the believer'.[42] Crucial to this is the distinction between the movement of infinite resignation and the movement of faith. At the end of his brief discussion of this, Green appears to endorse Mooney's view: that faith involves a 'selfless care' in which all 'proprietary claims' have been renounced. He concludes:

> If Mooney is right, this level of meaning of *Fear and Trembling* begins to suggest to us that the text as a whole is not quite the terrifying defense of religiously commanded homicide it seems to be. Rather, it begins to appear as a more traditional defense of selfless love as a central feature of the religious life.[43]

But this is clearly open to the objections we raised against Mooney earlier. On the first level, where the point was to shock the 'bourgeois' Copenhagen churchgoer out of his complacency, one can at least see that the Abraham–Isaac story was well-chosen, as a particularly striking way of showing the potential clash between 'ethical' and 'religious' commitments. But on this second level, where the message is simply that religious existence involves selfless love, this particular story seems badly chosen, for it is not clear why the story of Abraham and Isaac, specifically, is needed to make such a general and traditional point as this.

NORMS IN THE CHRISTIAN LIFE

Green's third level, on 'the normative shape of Christian existence', appears to address our central question more directly than the first two. It is at this level that *Fear and Trembling* becomes primarily a study in ethics, exploring 'the norms that should guide the conduct of a committed Christian',[44] and clearly at this level the Problemata (especially the first two) are central.

This level puts the focus squarely upon the issues we have been grappling with: the fact that, for Johannes, Abraham appears to stand outside the ethical understood as the universal, and that his behaviour cannot be explained or rationally justified.

Green puts the problem starkly:

> Reading *Fear and Trembling* as a work intending to offer at least a preliminary vision of the Christian moral life produces a jarring inconsistency. *Fear and Trembling* seems to hold up as exemplary and somehow worthy of imitation a kind of conduct that we cannot possibly encourage, defend, or understand in terms of general moral values.[45]

Green discusses various attempts to avoid this problem, of which I shall mention three. The first two consider the text to be attacking Kant and Hegel respectively, and the third sees Johannes (and perhaps Kierkegaard) as endorsing a divine command view of ethics.

KANTIAN 'ABSOLUTISM'

In the first version, discussed by Elmer Duncan, Johannes' target is taken to be Kantian absolutism: the idea, mentioned earlier, that there can be no exceptions to ethical demands. According to Duncan, Kierkegaard found this extreme position to be 'preposterous',[46] and reasoned that if a conception of the ethical fails to allow for exceptions, then space must be made for them outside the ethical – such as in the religious. But, Duncan argues, this move is unnecessary since there are available less radical approaches to the problem of exceptions that will find a space for them *within* the ethical.

Green raises two objections to this view: one good, one less so. First, he plausibly points out that ethical 'absolutism' *per se* does not appear to be Johannes' target. Recall that one of Johannes' main contrasts to Abraham is a tragic hero such as Agamemnon, and the tragic hero is said to act 'ethically' *despite* the fact that he does not obey Kant's ethical absolutes: he is prepared to take the life of an innocent human being, his daughter Iphigenia. Agamemnon, in other words, is quite prepared to kill in the interests of his duties *qua* king: an action of which a strict Kantian would not be able to approve.

Secondly, Green claims, Duncan's interpretation 'ignores Johannes' repeated affirmations that in suspending the ethical, Abraham moved entirely outside its sphere'.[47] From this, he infers that it is 'difficult to construe Abraham as seeking to break away from rigid ethical confines to express a more nuanced understanding of moral obligation'.[48]

But this conclusion is too hasty. Green seems to take it as obvious that we should view Johannes' ostensible understanding of the nature of the ethical at face value. But there is good reason to question this. As we have already suggested, the sentences that begin each of the problemata can be read as conditionals: that is, precisely the issue that the problemata bring into question is *whether or not* 'the ethical ... is the universal'. On this reading, Johannes is trying to draw out what the implications of commitment to such a view would be. One reason that he might engage in such a project is to show that these implications are such that we might need to reject the view on which they are founded. That is, if such a view cannot explain why Abraham, the father of faith, is held as exemplary, we might indeed need to reject such a view. This undermines a key part of Green's own approach, as we shall see later in this chapter.

HEGELIAN ETHICS

The same objection can be made to the interpretation in which Johannes' target is taken, more plausibly, to be Hegelian ethics. As we saw, Hegel's ethical 'universal' is that of the concrete public life of a people. Green suggests that *Fear and Trembling* can be read in two different ways as a critique of Hegelian ethics. (It is not clear to me that the difference here is particularly great.) In the first, the book is 'an *ethical* statement rejecting Hegel's nearly total subordination of the individual to the nation state and as a prophetic defense of the rights of the individual in the face of oppressive social collectivities'.[49] Read like this, the text offers 'an important corrective'[50] to the loss of self threatened by totalitarianism. (Recall the '*perestroika* era' reading mentioned at the start of this chapter.) Green's objection to this is again that to attempt to offer such an *ethical* justification of Abraham – perhaps reading Abraham's 'purely personal virtue' (FT 88) in terms of an 'ethics of individuality' of the kind often associated with existentialism – contradicts Johannes' 'repeated statements that Abraham cannot be ethically "mediated" or understood'.[51] Clearly, we can make the same response to this as we made above, as well as asking why the story of Abraham and Isaac specifically was needed to make this general point of individual protest against the collective.

Green makes precisely this objection to the second way of reading *Fear and Trembling* as a critique of Hegelian ethics, as a 'call for personal individuation'.[52] One proponent of this view is Jerome Gellman. For Gellman, *Fear and Trembling* is

> a 'call' out of the 'infinity' of the self, for self-definition as an individual, as opposed to self-definition from within the institutions of society, specifically the family ... The story is not about Abraham's daring to kill his son, but is about Abraham's having the courage to be willing to see himself not as a father, but as an individual ... The 'voice of God' ... is nothing other than the call for Abraham to be an individual in transcendence of the universal of ethics.[53]

Green seems entirely right to question why we need Genesis 22 in particular to give us this message. Indeed, Gellman's suggestion bears a strong family resemblance to Mooney's reading of *Fear and Trembling* as a 'call to selfhood' – and we already asked this question of Mooney. It is puzzling, though, that Green does not acknowledge that precisely the same question could be asked of the first of his 'anti-Hegelian' interpretations.

Neither of the two interpretations considered so far – the anti-Kantian and the anti-Hegelian – seems to pay sufficient attention to the specificity of the narrative that is at the heart of *Fear and Trembling*. Yet it is surely true that one point of *Fear and*

Trembling is indeed to place under scrutiny the idea that 'the ethical is the universal'. Neither the moral law nor the laws of any given society are divine: both assumptions, for Johannes (and Kierkegaard), are forms of idolatry.

DIVINE COMMAND ETHICS

This suggests the third of the possibilities discussed by Green that we shall also consider. According to this, *Fear and Trembling* is endorsing a form of 'divine command ethics'. Several interpreters offer a version of this reading, and in some ways it is the most natural 'surface' way to read the text. But in its simplest form, it clearly will not do. This simplest form suggests that the text's central message is that, faced with a command from God, one should always give that command precedence over what ethics demands. Thus Abraham's killing Isaac was unethical, but because God commanded it, he was obliged to do it.

There is an obvious problem with such a suggestion: it does not explain the four 'sub-Abrahams' of the 'Attunement'. What each of these figures has in common is that they are prepared to obey God's command. But Johannes is quite clear that none should be viewed as 'knights of faith' like the 'real' Abraham. This clearly implies that mere willingness to obey a divine command is not what makes Abraham the 'knight of faith'.[54] So what more subtle versions of the 'divine command ethics' reading are available?

We require a certain picture of God if the 'divine command' reading is to involve anything other than bending the knee to a divine tyrant. One's worries about the implications of such a reading could perhaps be partially assuaged if one accepts that 'God is love', as Green points out that Johannes does at one point in the text (FT 63). As Green puts it, 'Within the context of such a belief, unstinting obedience to God makes sense even when he appears to require horrific deeds or sacrifices'.[55] Evans takes a version of this line. What Abraham is prepared to do is often considered horrendous partially because he is supposed to have a concrete relation to Isaac, in contrast to which the voice of God may seem somewhat 'removed'; divine commands something of an abstraction. But Evans emphasises the point that in the Genesis narrative,

Abraham quite clearly has a 'special relationship' with God. In a relatively early essay, he glosses this relationship as follows:

> Abraham knows God as an individual; he knows God is good, and he loves and trusts God. Although he does not understand God's command in the sense that he understands why God has asked him to do this or what purpose it will serve, he does understand that it is indeed God who has asked him to do this. As a result of his special relationship, Abraham's trust in God is supreme. This trust expresses itself cognitively in an interpretative framework by which he concludes, all appearances to the contrary, that this act really is the right thing to do in this particular case. God would not in fact require Isaac of him ... or even if God did do this thing, he would nevertheless receive Isaac back ... Abraham's willingness to sacrifice Isaac might be compared with the confidence of a knife-thrower's assistant in the accuracy of a knife-thrower's aim.[56]

However, Green's objection to this is that *Fear and Trembling* hardly stresses the love of God. There is relatively little discussion of the features of God that would make the command more intelligible. One response available to Evans might be to point out that this could be because Johannes stands *outside* faith. But in response to that, we could add that love is hardly God's most obvious characteristic at this point in the Genesis narrative. For instance, recall that God has very recently destroyed Sodom and Gomorrah with fire and brimstone, despite Abraham's pleading with him to save the city. It might seem far from obvious, then, why God's love, rather than an awareness of his power, should be the feature uppermost in Abraham's mind.

Interestingly in this context, Jerome Gellman has noted that in recent Jewish thought, there has been disagreement over which of two images of Abraham – that of Genesis 18 or Genesis 22 – should be considered paradigmatic of Jewish spirituality. In other words, should we valorise the Abraham who argues with God over the fate of Sodom, apparently confident in his moral convictions? Or an Abraham who manifests unquestioning obedience to God in the face of the *akedah*?[57]

In the light of such debates, it is worth briefly considering Evans' more recent discussions of divine command theories of ethics in relation to Kierkegaard.[58] Here, it is *Works of Love* rather than *Fear and Trembling* that plays the major role, and Evans argues that *Fear and Trembling* is not the place to look for Kierkegaard's own ethical views.[59] Nevertheless, that text does play an important role, since Evans uses the *akedah* as a kind of 'test case' against which the divine command theory he has worked out in previous chapters might be tested. I have space here only to offer a sketch of Evans' view.[60] On this view, God issues commands through both general and special revelation, and these take the form of both universal duties applicable to all, and particular calls which take into account the distinctiveness of specific individuals, contexts and callings.[61] Such commands, which are rooted in a teleological conception of the good, are also directed towards the *human good*, central to which are relationships (the most important of which is our relation to God[62]) and the passions of faith and love.[63] Evans clearly shares the traditional view that Abraham's *obedience* to God is vital, reading Johannes' question about his motive ('Then why does Abraham do it? For God's sake, and what is exactly the same, for his own' [FT 88]) through this lens.[64] So what becomes of the *akedah* against the background of such a view?

In his final chapter, Evans aims to defend the following three claims:

> (1) It is indeed the case that a person ought to perform any action God commanded, and this implies that *if* God commanded someone to take the life of a child, that action would be right. (2) It is not possible for God to command an act that is unloving; if a being whom we thought to be God made such a command, that being would no longer warrant being thought of as divine, and its commands would not be moral obligations. (3) In our current epistemological situation, a person could not rationally believe that God has commanded an act of child sacrifice unless God supernaturally took control of the person's beliefs.[65]

In other words, what Evans is trying to preserve here is both the status of Abraham as 'father of faith' (at least in part in virtue of his willingness to obey divine commands), and the idea that if anyone now were to do likewise, we should have no hesitation in calling the police.[66] The questions of whether Abraham was a historical figure, and of whether God really did command him to do as Genesis 22 reports, seem to be less important to Evans' interpretation than the claim that we today can know, through both general and special revelation, that child sacrifice is condemned by God.[67] In so far as Evans is willing to speculate on why God might have issued such a command as described in Genesis 22, he sides with the majority view that it was to teach the Jewish people that – unlike the gods of the surrounding pagan culture – their God would not require human sacrifices.[68] This does give an answer to an important objection that arises for more simplistic 'divine command ethics' readings of the text. For readings which presuppose that what matters is that God's word should take precedence over the ethical leave mysterious why the sacrifice should not be carried out: they leave mysterious the significance of God's substituting the ram and 'calling off' the sacrifice. There are other readings that do offer an explanation of this, and to which we shall turn later. But note that Evans also stresses here the importance of 'the outcome': that God never intended Abraham to plunge the knife:

> Even though this feature of the story ... is not a factor in determining the rightness of Abraham's behaviour, since Abraham did not know in advance that God would in fact not require the action, and so his faith and trust in God was not based on such knowledge, it can rightly be a factor in our understanding why God would put Abraham to such a test.[69]

A key aspect of Evans' reading is that on his account, we must preserve the possibility that a divine command could challenge *Sittlichkeit*: the prevailing ethic of any given society. Evans takes this to be a vital part of the message of *Fear and Trembling*. So on this view, although we can now be confident (through revelation) that human sacrifice is forbidden – and so any 'voice' telling you to sacrifice your child is not the voice of God – there are other ways in which faith in God might require us to violate the norms of our society and thus be reviled by it.[70] It is in this sense that we can be called to emulate Abraham, and so it is in this sense that Abraham remains relevant to our contemporary religious situation.[71]

Interestingly, the scholar of Judaism Jon D. Levenson has argued along similar lines that no contemporary Jew, Christian or Muslim could reasonably assume that the overall message of Genesis 22 authorises child murder. Levenson notes such factors as the ban on human sacrifice in the Torah, and the restriction of sacrifice to the Temple in Jerusalem (destroyed in 70 CE and never subsequently rebuilt), concluding that 'Judaism quite forbids the act that some imagine Genesis 22 legitimates'.[72] Similarly, to hold the view against which he is arguing, Christians would have to believe that God's will could be known through the hearing of a voice one took unproblematically to be that of God, issuing a command contradictory to that of scripture and church tradition – and thus to ignore alternative sources of religious authority. While this might initially remind us of Kant's response, Levenson in fact castigates Kant for having abstracted his discussion of Abraham from the specificity of the patriarch's situation, as well as the larger context of biblical law and theology.[73] Thus Levenson criticises attempts (which he takes to include Kierkegaard[74]) to present Abraham as everyman, or attempts to present him as the archetypal abusive father.[75] While arguing that the case of Islam is more complex, Levenson notes that here too grounding justifications of murder in the Muslim version of the *akedah* are extremely forced.[76] Hence his overall conclusion that 'Abraham's literal deed is not presented as something to be duplicated by those who revere his memory'.[77] And yet – also like Evans – he claims that this does not render the story obsolete. Rather, it directs our attention on to other features of 'Abraham's absolute commitment to God': his obedience to, faith in and love of God.[78] I shall have more to say about these features, and their connections to hope and trust, shortly.

First, however, let us complete this survey of 'higher ethics' readings of *Fear and Trembling* by turning to aspects of Edward Mooney's interpretation that we have not so far considered.

MOONEY: ETHICS, DILEMMA AND SUBJECTIVITY

In this section, I want to go beyond Green's account to discuss two related aspects of Mooney's interpretation. The first focuses on the nature of dilemmas, and will lead us into a discussion of the nature of specifically tragic dilemmas. I shall argue that notwithstanding Johannes' attempted contrast of the knight of faith with the tragic hero, Abraham's situation is a tragic dilemma. The second issue relates to Mooney's claim that *Fear and Trembling* ultimately replaces a universal, 'objective' picture of ethics with a 'deeper', 'subjective' picture. While I shall challenge Mooney's position as being rather slippery, drawing attention to this dimension has a significant advantage: it highlights what might be at stake in Johannes' reference to Abraham's 'purely personal virtue' (FT 88).

In common with what I have already claimed, Mooney sees Johannes as questioning the idea that the ethical is the universal, and expanding or deepening the ethical's remit to include particular, subjective commitments. Such considerations play a central role in the infrastructure of the moral life. As we have noted, for Mooney *Fear and Trembling* is essentially a 'call to selfhood'. Moreover, part of its message is that any approach to dilemmas which supposes that a definitive 'right' answer can be given is untrue to the nature of such dilemmas. There *are* dilemmas which ethical theory cannot solve. So at least part of what is 'teleologically suspended' is the idea that, in moral dilemmas, ethics (understood as ethical theory) has the *power to decide* which is the 'right' option. So, faced with such a dilemma, how do we decide what to do? One option might appear to be Sartre's famous response to the student mentioned earlier in this chapter. 'You are free', Sartre said, 'therefore choose – that is to say, invent'.[79] But Mooney rightly insists that to emphasise freedom and choice can be misleading. This does not do justice to the 'anguish' of such dilemmas. If the young man really could just 'choose', that would amount to saying that the dilemma could be just made to disappear. But '[s]uch willing and casual adjustment would empty a self of substance, compromise its integrity, exact an impossible price in hypocrisy and self-deception'.[80] A self with any depth will find itself having to '*acknowledge*, *discover* or *testify* to values in some sense independent of its will'.[81] In other words, values are not just something we *create*. We find ourselves *receptive* to certain values, and dilemmas bring home to us both what the values we are beholden to actually are, and that they can often come into conflict. In this sense, 'receptivity' is at the heart of faith.

Part of the structure of 'ordeals of faith' is the clash between commitments that are defensible publicly and 'objectively' and 'subjective' commitments that are not. As we have seen, the 'tragic hero' can offer a justification for his decision, and so we can empathise with, and in this sense share, his tragedy. But the sense of feeling beholden to something that one cannot publicly articulate only adds to one's anguish. However, Mooney stresses that the recognition of the importance of subjective commitments in the moral life does not amount to the rejection of objectivity *per se*. Rather, Johannes' claim is that 'in some cases, objective universal considerations need not predominate'.[82]

SUSPENDING ETHICS

Mooney rejects, largely on textual grounds, the idea that the message of the teleological suspension is that obedience to God always has overriding force over competing ethical claims. (By now this will come as no surprise: recall once again that the four sub-Abrahams of the 'Attunement' all obey God.) He considers two alternative interpretations. The first, which he describes as an 'intermediate' interpretation, is what we have already been describing. The suspension of the ethical describes 'a *terrible deadlock* where inescapable requirements clash ... an ordeal of reason which leaves an individual without the comfort of moral assurance or definitive guidance'.[83] This is an 'ordeal of reason' in so far as there are reasons to do both: reasons are in deadlock. Thus 'what gets suspended for Abraham is the power of ethics to clearly guide or justify'.[84] Thus the teleological suspension is 'not a justifying principle', such as 'When commitments to God clash with ethical commitments, always obey God over ethics'. Rather, it 'describes a brutal fact. There *are* dilemmas and in such straits, ethics cannot guide, deliver us from wrong'.[85]

Mooney is here extrapolating from the specific story of Abraham a general point about tragic dilemmas. This enables him to offer a reading of the teleological suspension wherein 'faith' can be construed either in distinctively 'religious' or in 'secular' fashion. 'Faith', on this view, seems to be a category 'beyond' the ethical conceived as the universal. But what lies beyond the ethical thus conceived is not necessarily something distinctively 'religious'. Consider Abraham first. For him, commitment to his God has 'a compelling salience'.[86] But even for Abraham, the fact that he keeps his faith and trust in God to the point of drawing the knife does not mean that this faith provides, perhaps even to himself, 'an objective justification, an escape from the dark'.[87] (Hence, presumably, part of his 'anguish'.) Mooney makes the important point that it does not necessarily follow from the fact that Abraham obeys God that this must be because he takes faith (or obedience to God) to be an overwhelming good. As Mooney puts it, 'finding one's path confers no objective dominance on the alternative chosen'.[88] Nothing is justified either way by Abraham's action.

But Mooney's focus also takes us beyond Abraham. To our earlier question as to why, on Mooney's reading, we need the Abraham story specifically to make his point, we can now see a possible response available to him, for which there is some textual justification. Recall that, as well as Abraham, Johannes discusses more 'mundane' knights of faith. And this changes the emphasis: 'If the knight can be Abraham *or* a serving maid *or* a shopman, then we are forced *away* from reading the story as advocating sacrifice on demand'.[89] Rather, we should extrapolate from the *akedah* story a more general message: 'to be a knight of faith is to have had one's soul tempered through ordeals'.[90] The Abraham story illustrates, in a particularly graphic way, the horror of a tragic dilemma.[91] In so far as 'knight of faith' is a praiseworthy term, we can presumably infer that Johannes thinks that to come through such an ordeal deepens and strengthens one's character.

THE ETHICAL AS SUCH ISN'T THE UNIVERSAL

But Mooney thinks that it cannot be enough to stick with this 'intermediate interpretation'. It leaves mysterious why Johannes insists that 'the single individual is higher than the universal'. What justifies this claim? To see Mooney's answer to this question, we need to consider his second interpretation of the teleological suspension. On this reading, what *appears* to be a suspension of the ethical is not that. It appears to be so only to someone held captive by the picture that the ethical is – solely – the universal.

The 'teleological suspension' draws our attention to a 'moment of transitional conflict' in which a particular picture of the ethical is replaced by another, deeper, picture. What is suspended, or 'set aside', is not the ethical *per se*, but 'only a commonplace morality that absolutizes the claims of community, communication and reason'[92] – a view of the ethical that sounds essentially Hegelian. A deeper picture of the ethical must be understood if we are to understand the sense in which 'the single individual is higher than the universal'.

This deeper picture of the ethical, for Mooney, is one that takes agents or character, rather than acts or principles, as primary. Drawing on figures in recent moral philosophy such as Bernard Williams and Martha Nussbaum, Mooney argues that: 'An exclusive allegiance to "the universal", to the public, objective realm, can empty a person of substance.'[93] (Note the contrast between this view and the 'Hegelian' view, discussed in Chapter 4, that it is precisely such roles that give a person her identity.) For Williams, the moral life needs to include 'intuitive' private sentiments if it is to be 'that worthwhile kind of life which human beings lack unless they feel more than they can say, and grasp more than they can explain'.[94] Note that on this view, contrary to the 'Hegelian' position, one may have commitments for which a publicly available explanation cannot necessarily be given. Nussbaum argues that without the kind of conflicts integral to dilemmas, our lives would be less than fully human.[95] As Mooney puts it, 'Being shielded from moral struggle, exempt from ordeals of spirit, we would lack depth, dignity, the subtle if flawed beauty and strength of individual character.'[96]

The relative importance of character and principles is a massive topic, at the very heart of contemporary ethics, and we cannot possibly hope to do it justice, let alone settle it, here. Against a common but oversimplified picture of a dispute between Aristotelian (character-based) and Kantian (principle-based) moralities, some significant recent work has aimed to show that the gulf between these two thinkers is not as great as is often supposed,[97] and to draw other thinkers (amongst them Kierkegaard) into the debate. Suffice it to say that Mooney reads Johannes' claim about the single individual being higher than the universal as a preference for a character-based ethic. On this view, to read the teleological suspension in terms of a dispute about clashes of duties (duties to God versus ethical duties) is somewhat to miss the point. One advantage Mooney's reading has over such an approach is that this other approach does not address the centrality to the text of Johannes' being transfixed by Abraham. Whereas on Mooney's reading, we see this as an example of how a certain kind of virtuous agent can impress us as exemplary. 'And to the extent that our appraising faculties retain a grip, she alone, he alone, becomes the focus of our awe or pity, praise or condemnation.'[98] He or she alone, his or her *character*, that is, rather than his or her *actions*.

This focus on character, rather than prioritising conflicting duties or principles, moves the emphasis from not just *what* Abraham (or any exemplary agent) does, but *how* he does it. Indeed, though I shall not have the chance to pursue this here, Mooney goes so far as to suggest that a great deal of what Kierkegaard values about faith would be consistent with Abraham's *refusing* God's command.[99]

'GETTING ISAAC BACK': RECEPTIVITY

Abraham's faith that he will 'get Isaac back' draws our attention back to the importance of 'receptivity' in faith. But, as Alastair Hannay has argued, Abraham gets Isaac back under a new mode of valuation. For Mooney, the question that this highlights is: In virtue of what does *what* we value *have* value? No longer the 'possessor' of a son through whom he will be the father of nations, Abraham comes to see that 'worldly things have value not on his account, but, in Hannay's phrase, "on their own account and from God"'.[100] His trial enables him to accept things back 'on a new basis, their status clarified'.[101] Isaac is 'his' only as a gift from God.[102] Part of this recognition is that 'nothing in the world has value simply because one values it' – or, as Mooney glosses this, that 'anything that possesses *real* value will possess it regardless of our attitudes toward it'.[103] The recognition that the value of something is ultimately not a function of the fact that I value it – a function of my will – looks like one dimension of what it means to 'die to the self', a crucial phrase in the Kierkegaardian 'religious' outlook.[104]

But here Mooney's account seems to pull in opposite directions. Having said this, he then adds – plausibly enough – that neither is what I value dependent upon 'the universal' (in the Hegelian sense). If value is not a function of my will, then why suppose that it is a function of a social order's aggregation of wills? This line appears consistent with Johannes' scepticism about 'the universal'. But once Mooney turns his attention back to understanding the sense in which 'the single individual is higher than the universal', what he has used Hannay to draw upon above seems to be forgotten. He reads the Kierkegaardian category of 'becoming subjective' as 'in part renouncing the universal for the particular' and glosses what this means as follows:

> The structure of one's subjectivity, one's priceless worth, can be spelled out as a complex of virtues that provide standards for self-evaluation. To abjure the universal as the dominant seat of value is to see that individuals generally, and more especially, the particular individual you or I happen to be, become 'justified'. We acquire some ultimate, inalienable standing in the broadest scheme of things. This standing or worth is constituted by a triad of personal virtues: *freedom*, *integrity*, and trusting reception or *faith*. To move beyond the universal is to move toward freedom, integrity and faith.[105]

Apart from the rather vague reference to faith (which elsewhere Mooney sees as interpretable in secular, as well as religious, terms), God seems to have dropped out of the picture. It now looks as if justification and value stem not from God, but from our being virtuous agents. Mooney continues in the same vein:

> Faith is 'higher' than social, civic, or rational morality ... because for someone having weathered its ordeals, it can be felt, retrospectively, to have *transformed and completed* a moral outlook all-too-familiar yet finally *provisional*. Faith enscribes space for a new ethics. Conventional practices and codes are now complemented by a self-structure of inward virtues.[106]

There seems nothing outrageous about this in its own terms. It also serves as a useful gloss on what 'the single individual' being 'higher than the universal' could mean. But this seems to be a move in quite the opposite direction from what we had moments ago. The idea that I am somehow 'justified' because I have certain virtues seems to be at odds with the idea that value ultimately stems from God. (Unless 'virtue' is somehow mysteriously 'given': but which virtues are 'infused', and how; and which are available 'naturally', through training, practice and an effort of will?) Moreover, is this focus on the centrality of inward virtues supposed to eradicate the previous claim that nothing has value simply because I value it? Is that now *false* for the virtuous agent? Perhaps there are answers available to these questions. But there are, at the very least, certain *prima facie* tensions between these two parts of Mooney's account – and Mooney does not explain how they are compatible.

That said, I agree with Mooney that the importance of receptivity – 'getting Isaac back' – is of crucial importance to understanding *Fear and Trembling*. We shall return to it in the next section but one.

DERRIDA: SACRIFICING ETHICS

One final ethics-centred interpretation of *Fear and Trembling* that has attracted considerable attention is that of Jacques Derrida in *The Gift of Death*. A central issue in Derrida's text, taking its cue from a discussion of the Czech phenomenologist Jan Patočka, is the relationship between secrecy and responsibility. Thus Abraham's 'silence' is of central importance to Derrida's reading. As Marius Timmann Mjaaland puts it, on this account, 'there is a demand for secrecy in individual responsibility which expels the free self into absolute silence and solitude in the moment of decision'.[107] What is most striking about Derrida's reading is as follows. Contrary to Johannes' focus on the abnormal terror of Abraham's dilemma, Derrida claims that in fact '"the sacrifice of Isaac" illustrates ... the most common and everyday experience of responsibility'.[108] His basic idea – compare Lévinas here – is that whereas 'Duty or responsibility binds me to the other', we cannot come good on duties and responsibilities to *everyone*: 'I cannot respond to the call, the request, the obligation, or even the love of another without sacrificing the other other, the other others'.[109] That is, genuine responsibility to specific others requires us to make choices: to put their interests above the competing interests of possibly equally deserving cases. For instance, I sponsor a child in a third world country. But what about all those other children in third world countries that I do *not* sponsor? Apparently construing 'ethics' in terms of equal treatment for all deserving cases, Derrida suggests: 'As soon as I enter into a relation with the other ... I know that I can respond only by sacrificing ethics, that is, by sacrificing whatever obliges me to also respond, in the same way, in the same instant, to all the others'.[110] In so far as we simply cannot avoid this – I cannot sponsor *every* deserving child – Moriah is 'our habitat every second of every day',[111] in the sense that every time I give money to this particular child, I effectively 'sacrifice' all the other, equally deserving, children. Yet supporting this child rather than that one can never really be justified, according to Derrida. As he memorably (if rhetorically) puts it, 'How would you ever justify the fact that you sacrifice all the cats in the world to the cat that you feed at home every morning for years, whereas other cats die of hunger at every instant? Not to mention other people?'[112]

Prima facie, this is an interesting line, but as a reading of the message of *Fear and Trembling*, we might again wonder why we need the specific story of Abraham and Isaac to make this claim. Far more importantly, the apparent assumption that ethical responsibility inheres in treating all deserving cases equally can clearly be questioned. Indeed, as Davenport has argued in forceful detail, once one puts it under the microscope, Derrida seems committed to a breathtakingly extreme view, simply assuming 'that this is the right understanding of agapic duty, thus begging the question against all saner interpretations of the neighbor love commands, and against ... all moral theory in world history before him'.[113] Derrida's is, in short, an extreme version of an 'overdemanding' ethical theory, in which we are 'always in a moral dilemma, whatever we do, at all times, with respect to everyone'.[114] Moreover, there is a further objection that arises from Derrida's claim that 'the sacrifice of Isaac' is 'the most common and everyday experience of responsibility'. It is odd in this context that Derrida should draw attention to Johannes' remark about the 'terrible responsibility of solitude [*Eensomhed*]' (FT 138)[115] that Abraham faces. For to treat Abraham's situation as symptomatic of a situation we all face on a daily basis seems to rob this phrase of much of its force. If we, as well as Abraham, have to make such sacrifices daily, it is hard to see in what sense Abraham faces 'solitude', still less one of which the tragic hero 'knows nothing' (FT 138). Such an approach seriously downplays what Anthony Rudd has called the 'irreducible particularity of Abraham's situation';[116] his being 'God's confidant, the Lord's friend' (FT 105), someone who can speak to God in the second person familiar (to say 'You' [Du]), whereas we are explicitly told that the tragic hero can speak to God 'only ... in the third person' (FT 105). Amongst other flaws, Derrida seems to reduce the religious to the ethical in a highly problematic way. Mjaaland apparently agrees, accusing Derrida of levelling 'not only the distinction between every other and the wholly other but also between oneself (as another) and God'.[117] Nor – crucially – does the provision of the ram seem to be given much significance in Derrida's account (note again the reference to 'the sacrifice of Isaac' above).[118]

The above sections have focused upon *Fear and Trembling* as being, in some way or other, about ethics. However, Green has forcefully denied that the book is about ethics at all. (The title of one of his articles says it all: 'Enough is enough!: *Fear and Trembling* is *not* about ethics'.[119]) Before turning to the tradition of which Green's alternative reading is a part – the tradition that sees in *Fear and Trembling* a hidden Christian message – let us consider his reasons for rejecting what he calls 'ethical' readings of the book.

'IT'S NOT ABOUT ETHICS!' A DISSENTING VOICE

Green's chief objection to reading the book as a contribution to ethical debate is that doing so 'produces a serious tension and even a degree of incoherence in the text'.[120] This is because for Johannes, if there is to be any justification of Abraham, such justification must be external to the ethical. Abraham's behaviour 'lies entirely outside the sphere of universal concepts or values to which ethics belongs; it cannot be rationally explained and justified – "mediated" – in any way; and it cannot be expressed in language'.[121]

It should again be noted that this simply assumes that 'the ethical is the universal' is a position to which Johannes is unequivocally committed, rather than a dominant view of the ethical that he is placing under the microscope to test its adequacy. Our account of Mooney above is enough to show that at least some 'ethical' readings of the text read it as making space for an alternative conception of the ethical. Green mentions Mooney's reading in a footnote, but dismisses it on the grounds that it 'openly defies *Fear and Trembling*'s repeated assertion that Abraham's conduct does not reside within the ethical'.[122] But this will not do: Green is simply assuming, without argument, that 'the ethical is the universal' is Johannes' *actual view*. Moreover, Green seems to limit the possible range over which the term 'ethics' can be applied. In another footnote critical of Merold Westphal, he argues that the latter's claim that the conception of the ethical under scrutiny in *Fear and Trembling* is Hegelian can be countered by 'equally compelling evidence'[123] that the text has Kantian features. But from this Green concludes that this 'shows that it is not just the limits of one or other theory of ethics but the moral life in its most comprehensive sense that *Fear and Trembling* proposes to transcend'.[124] This is surely a *non sequitur*: Kant and Hegel hardly exhaust the range of possible views of ethics or 'the moral life'. In short, Green does not succeed in justifying his dismissal of all 'ethical' readings of the text: some, such as Mooney's, might be able to escape his objections.

However, a more powerful critique of 'higher ethical' readings has recently been made by John Davenport.[125] Davenport divides such readings into three camps: 'strong divine command' interpretations (according to which the sole source of moral obligation is God's power or status as creator); 'agapic command ethics', exemplified by Evans and Westphal, according to which 'our highest obligations' are derived from the commands of a *loving* God;[126] and 'aretaic love ethics', exemplified by Gellman and Mooney, according to which universal rules are rejected in favour of 'singular *phronetic* responses to unique situations'.[127] Recognising merits in the second and third camp, Davenport nevertheless finds them to lack something crucial: an account of 'how ethical motivation is preserved within faith',[128] key to which is his notion of faith as 'eschatological trust', which on Davenport's view is the main point of *Fear and Trembling*.[129] (More on this shortly.) Arguing that it is not only 'Hegelian' ethics that is suspended in faith,[130] Davenport points out that both forms of divine command ethics hold that Abraham must violate 'the social obligation to love Isaac in order to give highest priority to his love of God', where loving God amounts to obeying his general and specific commands as 'the highest source of moral obligation'.[131] (The difference being whether God's power or 'agapic goodness' is the source of this obligation.) Davenport notes the counter-example of the 'sub-Abrahams' (all willing to obey God's command, but none counting as true exemplars of faith). What distinguishes Abraham from them, he claims, 'is his trust in the ultimate fulfilment of God's promise, not his willingness to bow to divine commands – either as arbitrary expressions of absolute power, or as agapic expressions of absolute love'.[132]

FAITH, 'ESCHATOLOGICAL' TRUST AND 'RADICAL' HOPE

We have already noted the importance of trust in several of our discussions above, and this should come as no surprise, given how central trust is to biblical faith. Jacob Howland notes how in Genesis Abraham's faith is represented as 'a matter of personal trust in the particular individual to whom Scripture refers by the name of YHVH' and how *pistis* [trust] is 'the New Testament's favorite word for "faith"'.[133] Davenport acknowledges that his reading is 'not entirely "new", since it is indebted to past readings by Mooney, Evans, Hannay, Lippitt, and others'.[134] In the following section, I shall outline Davenport's 'eschatological trust' reading and – returning the favour – seek to complement it by putting more emphasis than is typical on the role of *hope* in Abraham's faith. (Although it plays a significant role in the eschatological trust interpretation, Davenport does not discuss hope in detail.) I aim to flesh this out by showing the relevance to *Fear and Trembling* of the 1843 discourse 'The Expectancy of Faith', one of the places in which Kierkegaard discusses the concept of hope in most detail. Then, after a brief outline of the 'eschatological trust' reading, I'll discuss two possible objections thereto, which arise from 'The Expectancy of Faith'. Both, I'll suggest, can be resisted. The second can be addressed by comparing Abraham's hope with the 'radical hope' discussed by Jonathan Lear in his book of that title. This reading will clarify the importance of hope in faith. It will also throw some light on what Johannes calls 'the courage of faith', and why he describes that courage as 'humble'.

Hope doesn't exactly leap off the page as an important theme in *Fear and Trembling*, and we already noted that at one point Johannes contrasts faith with a 'paltry [*usle*] hope' (FT 66).[135] The hope that plays a key role in Abraham's faith must be hope of a particular kind. I shall argue that it is akin to what Kierkegaard in the discourses calls 'expectancy' [*Forventning*] which, we also recall, Johannes mentioned at the start of the 'Speech in Praise'.

THE EXPECTANCY OF FAITH[136]

In *Works of Love*, in a deliberation entitled 'Love Hopes All Things', Kierkegaard claims that to hope is to relate oneself in expectancy to the possibility of the good (WL 249). The topic here is not merely 'episodic' hope, but rather a hopefulness that is, as Robert C. Roberts puts it, a 'formed disposition of the person of faith'.[137] This seems highly pertinent to Abraham.

Davenport briefly discusses this discourse.[138] But commenting on this connection, Hannay remarks that 'the faith that is the topic of the discourse is surely closer to Abraham's attitude or state of mind before he received God's command than to the pathos-filled way he saw matters after receiving it'.[139] I don't think this is true. Rather, on an 'eschatological trust' reading, Abraham could respond – even in the face of the *akedah* experience – in the way 'The Expectancy of Faith' discourse suggests. That is what I shall argue in this section.

Aside from the fact that this discourse was published on 16 May 1843 (precisely five months before *Fear and Trembling*), there are several points in its discussion of faith that invite comparison with the later text, as we shall see.[140]

What is faith's expectancy? Expectancy is clearly occupied with the future (EUD 17), and such occupation is 'a sign of the nobility of human beings; the struggle with the future is the most ennobling' (EUD 17). Our ability to project ourselves imaginatively into the future is one of the things that separate us from the animals. Faith has already been presented in this discourse as 'the only power that can conquer the future' (EUD 16), and make one's life 'strong and sound' (EUD 17). But this battle with the future is really a battle with oneself (EUD 18), in so far as the only power the future has over us is that which we give it. Kierkegaard describes the future – like the ethical in *Fear and Trembling* – in terms of temptation (EUD 16). The above passage also recalls the point where, in distinguishing the tragic hero from the knight of faith, Johannes says 'to struggle against the whole world is a comfort, to struggle with oneself is frightful' (FT 138, translation adjusted to Walsh's). The way to win this battle, the way to face the future, is compared to the tactic of the sailor who orients himself by looking up at the stars,

> because they are faithful; they have the same location now that they had for our ancestors and will have for generations to come. By what means does he conquer the changeable? By the eternal. By the eternal, one can conquer the future, because the eternal is the ground of the future, and therefore through it the future can be fathomed.
>
> (EUD 19)

So: one conquers the future, oneself, by means of something constant, 'the eternal'. But the 'eternal power in a human being' (EUD 19) is precisely faith. And faith expects 'victory', interpreted as that God is working all things together for good.[141] So is it this trusting expectancy which is at the heart of Abraham's faith?

Kierkegaard goes on to make several key comparisons that might remind us of the cast of characters in *Fear and Trembling*. First, we encounter a figure we might label *the naive hoper*. This person's default attitude of hope, which 'expects victory in everything' (EUD 20), is simply the result of inexperience. The naive hoper's real position, Kierkegaard suggests, is to expect 'to be victorious without a struggle' (EUD 20). Kierkegaard predicts that life will educate this person in the error of his ways, and he will learn that his expectancy, 'however beautiful, was not the expectancy of faith' (EUD 20). The naive hoper makes a brief walk-on appearance in *Fear and Trembling*, in the guise of those '[f]ools and young people' who make the mistake of chattering 'about everything being possible for a human being' (FT 72–3). Johannes warns that what they fail to recognise is that whereas '[e]verything is possible spiritually speaking ... in the finite world there is much that is not possible' (FT 73). What 'fools and young people' fail to recognise, like the naive hoper, is that it is only *with God* that all things are possible.[142]

Kierkegaard contrasts the naive hoper with *the troubled person* (EUD 20). This latter *lacks* hope: he 'expects no victory; he has all too sadly felt his loss, and even if it belongs to the past, he takes it along, expecting that the future will at least grant him the peace to be quietly occupied with his pain' (EUD 20). To the reader of *Fear and Trembling*, this character sounds like one dimension of Johannes' description of infinite resignation, in which 'there is peace and repose and consolation in the pain' (FT 74). As we noted in Chapter 3, Davenport argues that this person embodies not resignation *simpliciter*, but resignation explicitly combined with *the rejection of hope*. This is that variety of despair described in *The Sickness unto Death* as not wanting (and thus refusing) '[h]ope in the possibility of help, especially by virtue of the absurd, that for God everything is possible' (SUD 71).[143]

Both are frowned upon by *the man of experience*, the voice of 'common sense'. On this person's view, common sense suggests that one needs to take the rough with the smooth, such that neither naive hope nor the complete absence of hope is justified:

> If one has almost every good one could wish for, then one ought to be prepared to have the troubles of life visit also the home of the happy; if one has lost everything, then one ought to consider that time reserves many a priceless cure for the sick soul, that the future, like a fond mother, also hides good gifts: in happiness one ought to be prepared to a certain degree for unhappiness, in unhappiness, to a certain degree for happiness.
>
> (EUD 20)

Both the naive hoper and the troubled person are willing to 'lend an ear' to the man of experience, and to organise their lives accordingly. But such apparent common sense contains a threat. The man of experience's phrase 'to a certain degree' (EUD 21) 'ensnares' his hearers. The initially happy person is troubled by the thought this 'certain degree' of unhappiness could apply just as easily to that one thing she cannot bear to lose without becoming unhappy as it can apply to those things she can far more readily give up. In this way, Kierkegaard warns, experience engenders *doubt* (EUD 21).

Thus experience has the same potentially damaging effect as the words of *Fear and Trembling*'s 'frogs in life's swamp', who tell the young lad that his love for the princess is foolishness and that 'the rich brewer's widow is just as good and sound a match' (FT 71). Note how much courage and resolution even the 'knight of resignation' lad needs to resist their 'common sense' negativity. Recall how, having checked that the love really is 'the content of his life', and let it 'steal in upon his most secret, most hidden thoughts, to let it twine itself in countless coils around every ligament of his consciousness', he

> feels a blissful rapture when he lets it tingle through every nerve, and yet his soul is as solemn as his who has emptied the cup of poison ... – for this moment is life and death. Having thus imbibed all the love and absorbed himself in it, he does not lack the courage to attempt and risk everything. He reflects over his life circumstances, he summons the swift thoughts that like trained doves obey his every signal; he waves his wand [*Stave*] over them, and they rush off in all directions. But now when they all return as messengers of sorrow and explain to him that it is an impossibility, he becomes quiet, he dismisses them, he remains alone, and then he performs the movement.
>
> (FT 71, translation slightly adjusted)

All three figures – the naive hoper; the troubled person; and the man of experience – may be contrasted with *the person of faith* [*den Troende*], who says: 'I expect victory' (EUD 21). Yet against such a voice, enter now the voice of a cousin of the man of experience, 'the earnestness of life' (EUD 22), who teaches 'that your wishes would not be fulfilled, that your desires would not be gratified, your appetites would not be heeded, your cravings would not be satisfied ... it also taught you to come to people's aid with deceitful words, to suck faith and trust out of their hearts, and to do this in the sacred name of earnestness' (EUD 22). However, Kierkegaard says, life could have taught a very different lesson: faced with just the same experience, two people may draw very different conclusions. Kierkegaard's example is of two children being praised, reprimanded or punished, comparing their possible reactions of proper pride or haughtiness; humility or indignation; a willingness to be healed by suffering or resentment. Now: all this points forward to what Kierkegaard's *Works of Love* will go on to say about hope and despair; trust and mistrust. Both have access to the same evidence. When obliged to judge in the wake of ambiguous evidence, the existential choices that we tend to make reveal something important about our character (WL 231).

Similarly, Kierkegaard adds, in the manner typical of his discourses, 'so also with you' (EUD 22). We need to learn silence in the face of our doubts: 'We do not judge you for doubting, because doubt is a crafty passion, and it can certainly be difficult to tear oneself out of its snares. What we require of the doubter is that he be silent. He surely perceived that doubt did not make him happy – why then confide to others what will make them just as unhappy?' (EUD 23).

The key thing is that the expectancy of faith is able to triumph over this doubt. Doubt has a good go at unsettling the faithful person, attempting to convince her that 'an expectancy without a specified time and place is nothing but a deception' (EUD 23). And it is true that 'the person who expects something particular can be deceived in his expectancy'. But – Kierkegaard insists – 'this does not happen to the believer' (EUD 23). There is a sense in which genuine hope, open as it is to the future, cannot be disappointed.[144] Despite the challenges of life, the person of faith is able to say:

> There is an expectancy that the whole world cannot take from me; it is the expectancy of faith, and this is victory. I am not deceived, since I did not believe that the world would keep the promise it seemed to

be making to me; my expectancy was not in the world but in God. This expectancy is not deceived; even now I sense its victory more gloriously and more joyfully than I sense all the pain of loss.

(EUD 24)

Consider this in light of the 1844 discourse in which Kierkegaard glosses being victorious as *God* being victorious (in line with the Lutheran idea of one's 'centre of gravity' being transferred to God).[145] Is it not so with Abraham? *Pace* Hannay, I want to suggest that the Abraham of *Fear and Trembling* can hold precisely this view. What is crucial to the position Kierkegaard describes in this part of the discourse is the idea that *the only appropriate object of such faith is God*. He stresses that faith in human beings is always susceptible to disappointment (EUD 24) – though as *Works of Love* goes on to insist, this is no excuse for cynicism or mistrust. But God alone, that individual in whom Abraham rests his trust, is our rock.[146] We now read words that, once again, Abraham might very well have said to himself during his trial:

if you had faith in God, how then would your faith ever be changed into a beautiful fantasy you had better give up? Would he then be able to be changed, he in whom there is no change or shadow of variation? Would he not be faithful, he through whom every human being who is faithful is faithful; would he not be without guile, he through whom you yourself had faith? Would there ever be an explanation that could explain otherwise than that he is truthful and keeps his promises?[147]

(EUD 25)

Abraham's hope is hope in the steadfast love of a personal God. Kierkegaard then contrasts such a position with the 'fair weather' faithful, for whom 'When everything changes, when grief supersedes joy, then they fall away, then they lose faith, or, more correctly – let us not confuse the language – then they show that they have never had it' (EUD 25).[148] Again, the claim is that, like hope, genuine faith is not disappointed: 'Every time I catch my soul not expecting victory, I know that I do not have faith' (EUD 27).

So perhaps part of what is meant by *Fear and Trembling*'s repeated claims that 'Abraham did not doubt' and that 'Abraham had faith' is that Abraham was graced the ability to resist the snares of this 'crafty passion'.[149] What I want to stress is that one could hardly do so without *hope*. Importantly, Kierkegaard goes on to emphasise that such faith and its concomitant hope is compatible with grief and sorrow: he has the person of faith say that 'the hard times can surely bring tears to my eyes and grief to my mind, but they still cannot rob me of my faith' (EUD 26). Again *pace* Hannay, I cannot see why the same as Kierkegaard here says about grief and sorrow cannot be said of the 'pathos-filled' Abrahamic 'anguish' which Johannes stresses. Abraham's anguish is compatible with hope, which is a key weapon faith has against the dangers introduced by doubt.[150] But it is crucial to see that the hope at work here is not just a sunny optimism. Rather, I am suggesting – along with Paul in the epistle to the Romans – that to live in hope is not to be spared from 'groaning' along with the rest of creation.[151]

So: such hope is not mere wishing – it *expects* victory (construed as *God's* victory). For this reason, it differs from 'everyday' hope in that – although it is compatible with anguish – it is claimed to be ultimately unshakable against the snares of doubt.[152]

But finally, we should note that 'The Expectancy of Faith' goes on to outline two ways of *not* having faith. One is unsurprising: to expect absolutely nothing. But the other is both less obvious and more significant for our purposes: to expect *something particular* [*noget Enkelt*]. Kierkegaard claims: 'not only the person who expects absolutely nothing does not have faith, but also the person who expects something particular or who bases his expectancy on something particular' (EUD 27). Hence a key question: is Abraham's faith that he will 'get Isaac back' about 'something particular'? The discourse makes a claim that, at first glance, might seem to be in significant tension with *Fear and Trembling*: 'The person of faith demands no substantiation of his expectancy'; he says that 'it is not the case that the particular can substantiate or refute the expectancy of faith' (EUD 27). Precisely what does this claim amount to, and is it in tension with the *Fear and Trembling* portrayal of faith? We shall return to this shortly. First, as essential background to my answer to that question, I need, as long promised, to sketch an outline of the 'eschatological trust' reading argued for by Davenport.[153]

DAVENPORT ON FAITH AS 'ESCHATOLOGICAL TRUST'

Building on the widespread recognition that trust is, at the very least, a key aspect of faith,[154] Davenport's account takes the faith that Abraham embodies to be 'a type of eschatological hope. Eschatology in its most general sense refers to the final realization of the Good by divine power in this temporal order or its successor.'[155] Compare this to the interpretation of 'victory' in 'The Expectancy of Faith': God is working all things together for good.

On Davenport's reading, 'the *telos* toward which Abraham suspends his ethical duties to Isaac is the absurd possibility of Isaac's survival despite God's requirement that he be sacrificed'.[156] What ultimately matters about the story is Abraham's trust in God and his 'absurd' promise, based on this 'eschatological hope'.

The following key elements are involved:

1. An *ethical ideal* that must be recognised and willed; it is not rejected or transcended as a moral imperative. Abraham must continue to love Isaac 'with all his soul' (FT 101).
2. An *obstacle* thereto: 'the human agent is prevented from achieving his or her moral ideal' by some circumstances 'that make it practically impossible for the agent to secure it by his or her own powers'.[157] God commands Abraham to sacrifice Isaac.
3. *Infinite resignation*. Having concentrated his 'entire identity in commitment to' the ethical ideal, the agent accepts that it is 'humanly unattainable' because of the obstacle. So – as noted in Chapter 3 – the agent either stops pursuing the ideal by his own endeavours ('elegiac' resignation) or continues out of principle, without any hope of success ('Beowulfian' resignation).[158] On Davenport's view, Abraham is resigned in the first sense,[159] and 'he accepts that he cannot save Isaac if God demands him'.[160]
4. An *eschatological promise* (requiring revelation rather than natural reason alone[161]) that the ideal 'will be actualised by divine power within the created order of existence' within time.[162] God has promised Abraham that Isaac will become 'the father of a holy nation to bring the Word to all peoples'.[163]
5. *The absurd*: 'the content of the eschatological promise, which is only eschatologically possible given the obstacle (and thus

appears unintelligible outside of faith'.[164] The possibilities that, despite mounting evidence to the contrary, Isaac will not have to be killed, or that, despite being killed, he will somehow survive to fulfil his promised destiny.[165]

6. *Existential faith*: defined in terms of 1–5: 'the agent infinitely resigns [the ideal], yet trusting entirely in the eschatological promise, stakes his/her identity on the belief that [the ideal] will be actualized by God'.[166] Even at the point of willingness to sacrifice, Abraham believes that he will get Isaac back 'by virtue of the absurd'.[167]

Thus we can see more clearly what, on this view, the teleological suspension of the ethical amounts to. The *telos* to which the ethical is suspended is not God's command to sacrifice Isaac. Rather, that command is the obstacle.[168] It forces Abraham 'to rely on an eschatological telos toward which the ethical is "suspended" – a telos whose possibility depends on God's action'.[169] In other words, 'the telos to which the ethical is suspended is the eschatological good';[170] that God is working all things together for good. So the fulfilment of the ethical ideal no longer turns simply on the agent's own efforts, but 'depends on a more complex intention that involves faith that despite action that would be unethical by itself (without this further consideration), the harmful outcome that it would be unethical to intend or accept will not come about'.[171] This means that the *telos* is not a *telos* in the sense of being something for which we strive in action (à la Aristotle). Abraham does not target it as 'the goal of action, but rather by embracing its possibility with his whole being as the condition for the ultimate significance of all his cares and projects'.[172] That is, his volitions (to love Isaac; to hope that Isaac will become the father of many nations) remain the same, but their meaning is transfigured by the acceptance that 'successful pursuit of this good is conditional on the miraculous divine response in which he trusts absolutely'.[173]

In terms of hope specifically, this fits the thinking, in the 'Speech in Praise', that each becomes great in proportion to his expectancy, such that 'he who expected the [humanly] impossible became greater than all' (FT 50). As we saw, Abraham is great by 'that hope whose outward form is ["humanly" understood] insanity [*Vanvid*]' (FT 50).[174]

Let us consider two possible objections to such a reading.[175] First, Johannes' apparent distancing of himself, in Problema I, from the idea that the story of Abraham is about 'the outcome'. And second, that 'getting Isaac back' sounds like 'something particular' in the way criticised in 'The Expectancy of Faith'.

In his discussion of how 'the single individual' assures himself that he is 'justified' in standing 'in an absolute relation to the absolute' (FT 90), Johannes appears to criticise the view that one judges it 'according to the outcome'. This is what a 'hero who has become an offense or stumbling block to his age'[176] might cry to his contemporaries (though 'our age' allegedly produces no heroes). However, Johannes warns:

> Whenever nowadays we hear the words, 'That's to be judged according to the outcome', then it is clear right away with whom we have the honor of speaking. Those who speak thus are a populous tribe which, to give them a common name, I shall call the 'lecturers' [*Docenterne*]. They live in their thoughts, secure in life, they have a *permanent* position and *sure* prospects in a well-organised state ... *Their task in life is to judge the great men and to judge them according to the outcome.*
>
> (FT 91, translation slightly adjusted, final emphasis mine)

Is this a problem for the eschatological trust reading? When push comes to shove, is that reading not saying that Abraham is to be judged 'according to the outcome'? After all, in a brief discussion of Jewish readings of the *akedah*, Davenport explicitly sides with the view that it is about the 'happy ending', rather than the original command, or both of these aspects.[177]

Too much can be made of the significance of Johannes' comments here. As Davenport notes, Brand Blanshard errs in this way when he asserts that 'the fact that at the last moment [Abraham] was relieved of the need to strike is irrelevant [sic] in appraising him'.[178] Few put it as bluntly as this, but several seem to work on a similar assumption, talking of 'Abraham's sacrifice' as if the sacrifice had actually taken place.[179] In fact, I do not think that this passage is the problem for the eschatological trust reading that it might at first appear to be. For what Johannes is objecting to here about the 'outcome' is merely sitting in judgement on 'great men', and not applying anything learned about them, to our own lives. (Compare the contrast, at the very start of the 'Speech in Praise', between the hero (who does great things) and the poet (who just admires and praises greatness) [FT 49–50].) The passage quoted above continues: 'Such conduct towards the great betrays a strange mixture of arrogance and pitifulness, arrogance because they feel called to pass judgment, pitifulness because they feel their lives unrelated in even the remotest manner to those of the great' (FT 91).[180]

The eschatological trust reading thus has a response available to it here. I take it that Davenport's focus on faith as eschatological trust as a means through which 'the individual is singularized', coming as an 'essentially particularistic attitude toward God as Thou', is precisely an attempt to avoid the disinterested judgementalism Johannes condemns.[181] So what is it that we are to learn from Abraham? The short answer is: what it means to trust – and, I would add – to hope.[182] My further suggestion is that Abraham serves as a precursor of the love that *Works of Love* describes as 'believing all things' (a deliberation essentially about trust) and 'hoping all things'.[183] In the *Works of Love* deliberation 'Love builds up', which immediately precedes these deliberations on trust and hope, Kierkegaard famously argues that to love is to presuppose love in the one loved. If that is so, then for Abraham to love his God, he must presuppose God as loving. Imagine, then, a version of the discussion between mistrust and love (cf. WL 228) applied to the *akedah* case. Mistrust will say: 'All is lost! God is a deceiver!' But love will see God's apparent 'badness', the 'test', as mere 'appearance' (WL 228). (The companion discourse to 'The Expectancy of Faith', 'Every good and every perfect gift is from above', insists that the idea that God would tempt a person is a 'terribly mistaken belief' [EUD 33].) Love, we are told, knows all that experience knows – and yet trusts. If this loving trust is recommended for our relations to other people, how much more must it be so for our relation to God? It is the same with respect to hope. Kierkegaard puts these words into the mouth of the truly loving person:

'Hope all things: give up on no human being, since to give up on him is to give up your love for him' (WL 255). Again, if this is so of humans, how much more so of God? To give up on his trust and hope, then, would be for Abraham to give up his love for God.[184]

We turn to the second objection. Is faith in 'getting Isaac back' faith in 'something particular' in a way judged illegitimate in 'The Expectancy of Faith'? It certainly sounds like 'something particular' in one sense. After all, God has made Abraham a specific promise. But compare the 'tax collector' knight of faith whom Johannes imagines fantasising about a sumptuous meal. He hopes against the available evidence, yet if he doesn't get this particular something (the sumptuous dish, way beyond the family budget, about which he fantasises), then 'curiously enough he is exactly the same' (FT 69). Should we then extrapolate from this example? Is faith's hope a genuine trust in God in a more general sense, perhaps after the fashion of Julian of Norwich's 'all shall be well, and all manner of thing shall be well'?[185]

To show why faith in 'getting Isaac back' is not 'something particular' in a problematic sense, I think Davenport's reading can usefully be supplemented by Jonathan Lear's discussion of 'radical hope'.[186]

RADICAL HOPE

Lear's *Radical Hope* discusses the fate of the Native American Crow Nation, and the reaction of their last great Chief, Plenty Coups (or Many Achievements), to the collapse of their traditional way of life. But Lear is interested in extrapolating from this discussion some more general lessons about radical changes in a people's future. I want to argue that the 'radical hope' that Plenty Coups' attitude embodies, on Lear's account, contains some important lessons for understanding Abraham as an exemplar of faith. If, as I think is the case, Abraham's hope is 'radical' in something like Lear's sense, this dispels the worry that Abraham's faith manifests 'something particular' in the sense Kierkegaard is troubled by in 'The Expectancy of Faith'.

I'll first outline Lear's account of Plenty Coups' likely reasoning. We shall then see how this can be applied to Abraham's case, and the way in which this illustrates his faith.

Plenty Coups had to face up to the potential collapse of life as he knew it, in which changed circumstances threaten to render meaningless the shared conception of what it is to live an excellent Crow life (in terms of its norms, values, ceremonial customs, established social roles, etc.). Yet Lear speculates that his reaction would make sense if we suppose him reasoning as follows. He recognises that there is much about the future that we don't understand. Yet he considers himself to have a hopeful message (in his case from a dream vision) that purports to come from a divine source – and he further considers this to be 'something to hold on to in the face of overwhelming challenge'.[187] (A key part of the dream is to learn from the chickadee, 'least in strength but strongest of mind of his kind', who learns by listening (itself a kind of 'attunement'), and from whom Plenty Coups takes the message that 'It is the mind that leads a man to power, not strength of body'.[188])

To survive and possibly once again to flourish, the Crow needed to be willing to give up almost everything they had understood about what constituted the good life: 'not a choice that could be reasoned about in the pre-existing terms of the good life. One needed some conception of – or commitment to – a goodness that transcended one's current understanding of the good'.[189] (Here Lear makes an explicit, if passing, reference to the 'teleological suspension of the ethical'.) He reads Plenty Coups as 'someone who experienced himself as receiving a divine call to tolerate the collapse of ethical life. This would include even a collapse of the concepts with which ethical life had hitherto been understood.'[190]

(Note that it is this which makes such hope 'radical'. It is not simply that Plenty Coups hopes for a future that is not entirely within his own control. While the latter might be argued to be a feature of most 'mature' hope – and a certain *openness* is key to both – most such hope does *not* require us to abandon and then rebuild concepts such as the good with which we aim to orient ourselves in the world.[191])

Lear then sets out a detailed account of what might plausibly have been Plenty Coups' reasoning.[192] I focus here on key aspects of this that in important respects parallel the Abraham case:

WHAT IS *FEAR AND TREMBLING* REALLY ABOUT? 189

1. A divine source tells us that an accepted way of life is coming to an end.
2. Our conception of the good is tied up with that way of life – precisely the way of life that is about to disappear. Thus:
3. 'in an important sense we do not know what to hope for or what to aim for. Things are going to change in ways beyond which we can currently imagine.'[193] Still,
4. *'There is more to hope for than mere biological survival. ...* If I am going to go on living, I need to be able to see a genuine, positive and honourable way of going forward. So, on the one hand, I need to recognize the discontinuity that is upon me – like it or not there will be a radical shift in form of life. On the other, I need to preserve some integrity across that discontinuity.'[194] However, there are grounds for hope because:
5. 'God ... is good. My commitment to the genuine transcendence of God is manifest in my commitment to the goodness of the world transcending our necessarily limited attempt to understand it. My commitment to God's transcendence and goodness is manifested in my commitment to the idea that *something good will emerge even if it outstrips my present limited capacity for understanding what that good is.*'[195]
6. 'I am thus committed to the idea that while we Crow must abandon the goods associated with our way of life – and thus we must abandon the conception of the good life that our tribe has worked out over centuries.[196] *We shall get the good back*, though at the moment we can have no more than a glimmer of what that might mean.'[197]

My suggestion is that *mutatis mutandis*, this general schema seems to apply also to Abraham *qua* exemplar of existential faith. Regarding (1) and (2): With the *akedah* command, something radical has changed in Abraham's understanding of God's covenant and thus what the future holds. Consequently, we can imagine Abraham reasoning as in (3). It is in this sense that Abraham's situation is beyond all 'human calculation' (FT 65). Perhaps such reasoning is what lies behind his ambiguous 'final word' ('My son, God will himself provide a lamb for the burnt offering' [Genesis 22:8; cf. FT 139]). (4) does not map on precisely, but is relevant in the sense that more is at stake than the mere biological survival of Isaac, as the second to fourth sub-Abrahams illustrate. Recall that Isaac survives in all three stories, but none illustrate faith, since in the second case, Abraham 'saw joy no more' (FT 46) as a result of his ordeal; in the third, he blames himself for violating his duty to his son, considering himself to be beyond forgiveness; and in the fourth, Abraham draws his knife in despair and Isaac loses his faith (FT 47–8).

Point (5) seems a good description of the possible thinking behind Abraham's despair-annulling hope. It is this – especially the italicised passage – that enables Abraham to say, with a flexibility that looks the very opposite of 'something particular', 'Surely it will not happen, or if it does, the Lord will give me a new Isaac, namely by virtue of the absurd' (FT 139). This is indeed a statement of 'radical hope' in Lear's sense. And (6) is akin to the notion of 'getting Isaac back', which Davenport describes as 'an eschatological possibility in which we can only have faith'.[198] I think the overall line for which I am arguing here is also consistent with that of Evans, when he treats Abraham's trust in God as amounting to a confidence that 'God will keep his promises' – without knowing *how*.[199]

Lear concludes that Plenty Coups' hope was a remarkable achievement in no small part because it managed to enable him to avoid despair.[200] Likewise, we can add, Abraham. But, as we stressed earlier, what makes the hope radical 'is that it is directed toward a future goodness that transcends the current ability to understand what it is'.[201] Thus, Lear concludes, 'hope becomes crucial for an ethical enquiry into life at the horizons of one's understanding'.[202]

Now, if Abraham's hope is 'radical' in something like Lear's sense, then this enables us to see that hoping to 'get Isaac back' is not 'something particular' in the sense condemned in 'The Expectancy of Faith'. Lear discusses the way in which Plenty Coups was able to give his people 'a basis for hope at a time when it was systematically unclear what one could hope for. Plenty Coups' dream held out for the Crow the hope that if they followed the wisdom of the chickadee (whatever that would come to mean) they would survive (whatever that would come to mean) and hold on to their lands (whatever that would come to mean)'.[203]

Similarly, I suggest, Abraham's faith in God enables him to believe that all will be for the good (whatever that would come to mean) and that he will get Isaac back in this life (whatever that would come to mean). In this way, his faith is not in 'something particular' in the problematic sense.

On the other hand, nor is this the 'general, vague, deistic belief in divine providence' that Westphal seeks to distinguish from biblical faith, in a criticism of Krishek and Kellenberger.[204] Westphal claims that 'the promises of biblical faith for those who follow Abraham are concrete and specific, not by being addressed to a single individual, to be sure, but by having a quite determinate content, given through divine revelation through a God who speaks'.[205]

Our discussion above shows what is problematic about talking of these promises as having a 'quite determinate content'. The contrast that matters is not between 'biblical faith' as specific and 'general, deistic belief' as abstract or general. There is nothing unbiblical about the view that we have outlined of hope as radical. Indeed, John Macquarrie makes a similar point specifically about hope in both the Old and New Testaments. Discussing Abraham in particular, Macquarrie remarks that human promises tend to be 'sufficiently specific' to know whether or not they have been kept. However, he adds,

> no such simple criteria seem to operate when we are thinking of the promises of God. His basic promise is to give us more abundant life. But we cannot specify the conditions of such a life in advance. It is only in the unfolding of history and the actual deepening of human life that we can say whether the promise is being fulfilled. This could well mean that it is fulfilled differently from the way we had at one time expected, for our expectation could be framed only in terms of what we had experienced up to that point, whereas the fulfilling of the promise might bring with it something new.[206]

Westphal himself seems to recognise something like this earlier in his book, where he notes various uncertainties about the promises (and commands) given to Abraham. He mentions Abraham's 'confidence that God was up to *something good*'; the command to 'emigrate to somewhere *not yet specified*'; the fact that he 'doesn't even know what form this blessing [through Isaac] will take'; and Abraham's need 'to trust that God will fulfill that promise in God's own time and way, whenever and whatever that may be'.[207] These examples themselves hint at the truth of Macquarrie's claim. Kierkegaard's claim, in 'The Expectancy of Faith', that hope for 'something particular' is not faith is quite consistent with biblical faith, precisely because there is plenty that is unspecific about the promises of God.[208]

Let me return briefly to 'Love hopes all things' further to suggest how hope there seems to work at the same level of generality as does the eschatological trust reading. Love, we are told, takes upon itself the work of hope (WL 248); hope is nothing without love (WL 259). To 'hope all things' is the 'eternal' register of what is expressed temporally by talking of hoping 'always' (WL 249). But the help of 'the eternal' is further equated with the help of the possibility of the good (WL 250) – expressed at precisely the same level of generality as we drew on Davenport and Lear to describe.[209] Anything that does not deal with 'the eternal' – that is, the possibility of good – is not genuine hope (WL 251), and – expressed temporally – 'the whole of one's life should be the time of hope' (WL 252).[210] This is what Abraham embodies in so far as he does not fall into the snares of doubt.

Finally for this section, I want briefly to suggest some connections between Abraham's hope and both courage and humility, to try to shed some light on Abraham's 'paradoxical and humble courage' (FT 77).[211]

HOPE'S LINK WITH COURAGE

For Lear, radical hope plays a crucial role in a courageous life. But in line with what we have so far said, the Crow conception of courage had to change. Hence Lear's suggestion is of more general interest for our purposes:

> Might there be a certain plasticity deeply embedded in a culture's thick conception of courage? That is, are there ways in which a person brought up in a culture's traditional understanding of courage

might draw upon his own inner resources to broaden his understanding of what courage might be? In such a case, one would begin with a culture's thick understanding of courage; but one would somehow find ways to *thin it out*: find ways to face circumstances courageously that the older thick conception never envisaged.[212]

So it is, I suggest, with the hope Abraham manifests as part of his faith. That is, he finds ways to hope that go beyond his original understanding of God's promise. Abraham starts with a relatively clear idea of what God has promised him through Isaac. But his 'trial' challenges this expectation. One way of thinking about Abraham's situation is that he is faced with the following dilemma. Does he give up this hope (perhaps in the manner of some of the sub-Abrahams)? Or does he maintain his faith in God in a manner to which radical hope – as summarised above: a hope that transcends his understanding – is central? The fact that Abraham responds in the latter way is a key part of why Johannes presents him as exemplary of faith.

The connection with courage can best be approached by considering why we consider courage as a virtue. Lear's answer is because it is an excellent way of responding to the fact that we are finite erotic creatures: 'we reach out to the world in yearning, longing, admiration, and desire for that which (however mistakenly) we take to be valuable, beautiful and good'.[213] As such, 'we take risks just by being in the world'.[214] And here we should note what it means to inhabit a world:

a world is not merely the environment in which we move about; it is that over which we lack omnipotent control, that about which we may be mistaken in significant ways, *that which may intrude upon us, that which may outstrip the concepts with which we seek to understand it.* Thus living within a world has inherent and unavoidable risk.[215]

Surely this is something that Abraham learns, and as Johannes Climacus famously reminds us, without risk, no faith. Yet Kierkegaard's more positive spin on this is to say that 'in reliance on God, one dares to venture everything' (EUD 369). The relevance of all this to courage is that in its thinnest sense, Lear suggests, courage is 'the capacity for living *well* with the risks that inevitably attend human existence'.[216]

It is vital to stress that these risks are inextricably bound up with our finitude, and that this in turn impacts on a conception of the good life for creatures like us. In other words, goodness 'transcends our finite powers to grasp it'.[217] Indeed, 'it seems oddly inappropriate – lacking in understanding of oneself as a finite creature – to think that what is good about the world is exhausted by our current understanding of it.'[218] Recognition of this finitude and God-dependence – and embodying radical hope in the face of this recognition – is again a significant part of why Johannes presents Abraham as exemplary. In the discourse 'Against cowardliness', the 'courage of faith' is presented as being a recognition of one's total reliance upon God, in language that recalls *Fear and Trembling*'s references to 'knights' of faith: 'no one should fear to entrust himself to God with the idea that this relationship would deprive him of his power and make him cowardly. It is just the reverse. Anyone upon whom God does not confer knighthood with his powerful hand is and remains cowardly in his deepest soul' (EUD 352–3).[219]

HOPE'S LINK WITH HUMILITY

So why is Abraham's courage 'humble'? A full answer is beyond the scope of this discussion, but let me offer a provisional sketch. One preliminary answer might be that the link between courage and humility is what you would expect, given that in 'Against cowardliness', Kierkegaard equates cowardliness with pride: 'cowardliness and pride are one and the same' (EUD 354). In this discourse, the proud person is presented as one who is struggling with God and wanting to do this under his own power (EUD 354). But there is a falsity about this, since such a person needs the support of others. God, says Kierkegaard, will expose his solitariness as a mirage, and this he can't stand (EUD 355). But Abraham, by contrast, is for Johannes both *genuinely* solitary in his trial (unlike the 'tragic hero') *and* recognises his absolute dependence upon God. However, here too a further parallel between Abraham and Plenty Coups might help. In Plenty Coups' courage, 'There is no implication that one can glimpse what lies beyond the horizons of one's historically situated understanding. There is no claim to grasp ineffable truths. Indeed, this form of commitment is impressive in part because it acknowledges that no such grasp is possible.'[220] Yet both Plenty Coups and Abraham commit 'to a goodness that transcends his understanding'.[221] This is 'a peculiar form of hopefulness. ... the hope for *revival*: for coming back to life in a form that is not yet intelligible'.[222] This is a form of commitment far more akin to humility than arrogance – especially when combined with the dependence on God stressed above. In other words, what might appear as Abraham's arrogance – standing as a single individual above the universal; heading for Moriah without discussing the matter with Sarah – can be viewed differently if one sees this through the lens of his humility before God, and his openness and willingness to turn the whole situation over to God in faith, trust and hope.

Let us recap. In this section, I have argued that, read against the background of 'The Expectancy of Faith', one can find much support for a version of the 'faith as eschatological trust' reading of *Fear and Trembling* Davenport has developed out of earlier interpretations. Two likely objections to that position – those about 'the outcome' and about 'something particular' – can be resisted. I have also stressed the advantages of understanding how Abraham's hope is 'radical' in something like Lear's sense, a focus that also throws some light on why Johannes claims that Abraham manifests a 'humble courage'. The significance of Abraham's hope deserves more attention than it has typically been given, not least because Abraham serves as a striking illustration of Kierkegaard's claim that so long as there is a task, there is hope (UDVS 276–7).

Finally, we can add that the question about the importance of the specific narrative of Genesis 22, which we raised against several earlier interpretations, is addressed by this reading. As Davenport puts it, 'What distinguishes the *akedah* from other eschatological stories is the unusual nature of the element that makes fulfillment of the divine promise absurd, or inaccessible to human power and reason ... in the *akedah*, the obstacle that makes it humanly impossible to keep Isaac and to save Isaac's posterity is none other than God's own command to sacrifice Isaac'.[223] Citing Kierkegaard's observation that the terror of Abraham's predicament is the collision 'between God's command and God's command' (rather than 'God's command and man's command') (JP 1: 908), he reminds us that as well as the command to sacrifice, 'God also commands Abraham to love Isaac and to trust in His original promise'.[224] It is this 'special complication'[225] that gives the Genesis 22 narrative its importance and significance.

There is one final task for this chapter. Many scholars, Davenport and Westphal included, are resistant to readings that aim to 'Christianise' Abraham. I am with such scholars if by this they mean that there is *nothing more* to *Fear and Trembling* than seeing the *akedah* as a precursor to the Atonement (more of which in the next section).[226] But this does not mean that specifically Christian interpretations of the text are not worth considering, as one more of Green's 'levels' of reading the text. It is to that tradition of *Fear and Trembling* interpretation that we now turn.

FEAR AND TREMBLING'S HIDDEN CHRISTIANITY?

As we have already noted, Abraham holds a special status within the Christian tradition as a paradigm of righteousness as well as faith. Allied with Kierkegaard's own Christian commitments, it is therefore no surprise that several commentators have seen in *Fear and Trembling* a distinctly Christian message. It has been claimed that the book is really about Christian teachings on sin, grace and forgiveness. This claim is made in slightly different ways and in very varying degrees of detail. We shall consider three such commentators in what follows.

One commentator who makes this claim is Louis Mackey.[227] Mackey claims that a key part of the book's message is that 'whatever Johannes says about Abraham is to be understood obliquely of the Christian believer ... Abraham is the "father of faith" because he is a type or figure of faith, foreshadowing the faith of the New Covenant'.[228] Mackey reminds us of the long-standing Christian tradition that scripture can be interpreted on three different levels: the literal, the allegorical and the anagogical (whereby themes in the Old Testament foreshadow those in the New). We shall return, in the next chapter, to the possible significance of Johannes' perhaps excessive stress on the literal (recall here his condemnation of the preacher and discussion of the Luke passage about hating one's father and mother). Though Mackey does not himself note this criticism, we can say that on his reading, Johannes does not practice what he preaches, since his focus is actually what Mackey rather misleadingly calls the 'moral' dimension. It is an implicit assumption that 'Abraham's faith is the pattern after which the Christian must model his own belief ... Abraham is the paradigm of faith'.[229] Mackey makes the following claim:

> Abraham ... does explain, as a figure explains that of which it is a figure, the predicament of the man for whom the ethical is permanently suspended by sin and to whom is given, by virtue of the absurd, the promise of the grace of forgiveness. And in such a knight of faith — the Christian believer — the paradox of Abraham will repeat itself when he attempts to live the new life that is given to him beyond the extremity of guilt and condemnation.[230]

Exactly what does this mean, and how is it supposed to be so?

To flesh out an answer to this, I shall turn to two further commentators, Green and Stephen Mulhall, both of whom support, in different ways, the anagogical dimension of Johannes' treatment of the Abraham narrative. But before getting into their readings in any detail, it is worth pointing out one of Kierkegaard's central concerns.

One of Kierkegaard's fundamental problems with 'Christendom' — his term for the confused form of Christianity which he saw as being all around him — is its amnesia about its own concepts, such as sin, revelation and redemption. In *Philosophical Fragments*, Johannes Climacus aims to clarify the 'grammar' of the Christian concept of revelation, and how a world-view that has sin, redemption and revelation as its distinguishing features differs from various views Climacus labels 'Socratic'. Very basically, the distinction is as follows. On the 'Socratic' view, the truth we need is immanent 'within' us: whatever 'salvation' is available, we can achieve by and for ourselves. Whereas, on the Christian view, our state of sin separates us from God in a fundamental and radical way. Sin, thus understood, is a state characterised by disobedience to and estrangement from God. Owing to the radical nature of this separation, if salvation is to be possible, God must intervene in human history. This is what happened, Christians claim, when God the Father became incarnated in Jesus Christ, suffered death by crucifixion to redeem the sins of the world, and rose from the dead (the 'Christ event').

One of Kierkegaard's abiding themes is that much of what passes for Christianity (and thinks of itself as that) within 'Christendom' is really much closer to a form of Socratism. Christendom is rife with a forgetful religious confusion about Christianity's fundamental claims.[231] Moreover, Kierkegaard's Lutheran Protestant heritage means that his answer to the question of how the individual can be saved from sin is basically in terms of divine *grace*. We have already noted that there is a long tradition within Christianity of reading the story of Abraham by means of its analogy with the Christian gospel. On this reading, the first and most obvious point is the significance of the fact that Isaac is Abraham's *son*. This foreshadows the Christian atonement, in which God the Father is prepared to sacrifice God the Son (Christ) to redeem humanity. Hence according to this Christian reading the central message of *Fear and Trembling* is as follows. God transcends the ordinary standards of the ethical – what, as sinners, we *deserve* – and through making both a 'teleological suspension of the ethical' and a sacrifice of his son (or, more accurately, of himself as God the Son) redeems humanity. A 'natural' sense of justice would suggest that, if humanity is in a state of sin, then we do not *deserve* redemption. But just as Abraham teleologically suspends the ethical, so by this analogy God can teleologically suspend his justice (read: 'the ethical') in service of a higher *telos*: his love for humanity. The Christian claim is, in a nutshell, that this has happened.

On such a reading, Johannes is the messenger who does not understand the message that he conveys. Note that on such an interpretation, the teleological suspension of the ethical is, as on Davenport's reading, not what traditional readings assume (Abraham's willingness to sacrifice Isaac). Rather, what matters is the willingness of a loving God to 'suspend' the sense of justice according to which sinners deserve punishment for their sin. The Christian message is that a loving God can transcend such a 'natural' sense of justice.[232]

Moreover, this has an important implication for the believer's relation to ethical demands. Grace alters one's relation to the demands of the ethical in a subtle but important way. How one measures up to these demands is no longer the ultimate measure of one's self-acceptance. Living in grace involves what John Whittaker calls the 'setting aside of moral rules as standards of self-worth'.[233] This does not mean that the ethical ceases to matter – it is not an embrace of immorality or amorality – but that one's self-acceptance is ultimately a matter of being accepted by God, rather than the ultimate measure of acceptance being one's obeying the moral law. As one contributor to a recent discussion on *Fear and Trembling* allegedly put it, 'Maybe there is a teleological suspension of the ethical every time God forgives us. Grace is the possibility of seeing us in other than a merely ethical way.'[234] Evans describes this as 'morality in a new key', in which one is motivated not by 'autonomous striving to realize one's own ideals, but grateful expression of a self that has been received as a gift'.[235]

One obvious objection might be that on such a reading the 'anguish' of Abraham that we have seen Johannes so keen to stress drops out of the picture. But such an objection would be too quick. If Abraham stands for God the Father, and Abraham's anguish is central to the story, this actually reveals a second key feature of the Christian interpretation of *Fear and Trembling*. Abraham's (read: God the Father's) anguish draws attention to the Christian claim that God the Father *suffers* along with his creation – a view that has been thought by many to be part of any adequate answer to the 'problem of evil'.[236] Moreover, in this light, we can also see a hidden meaning in Johannes' claim that 'There is no higher expression of the ethical in Abraham's life than that the father shall love the son' (FT 88).

Are there good reasons to support this Christian reading of the text, aside from Kierkegaard's own Christian commitments and the long tradition of reading the Abraham story analogically? Is there anything in the text itself to direct us to divine grace and forgiveness as the book's 'secret message'?

Some have found a clue in the very title of the book. It might seem natural to understand 'fear and trembling' as being the state in which Abraham finds himself when told to sacrifice Isaac. But, as we noted in Chapter 1, the phrase is used as follows in Paul's letter to the Philippians: 'Wherefore, my beloved, as ye have always obeyed ... work out your salvation with fear and trembling. For it is God which worketh in you both to will and to do of his good pleasure'.[237]

Green draws attention to this, but we need to say more than he does.[238] 'Working out' one's salvation is normally taken, in the Protestant tradition, not to mean 'working for' it (which would seem to sponsor a doctrine of 'works' rather than 'grace'), but as *manifesting* or *expressing* the salvation that the Christian already possesses as a result of God's grace. In a famous journal entry, Kierkegaard refers to Christianity as being 'infinite humiliation [in the sense of "learning to be humbled"] and grace, and then *a striving born of gratitude*' (JP 1 993, my emphasis). The challenge is to live a life worthy of the Christian's new 'status'. To desire and to do God's will is a matter of 'fear and trembling' in part because many sacrifices may be necessary for one who has started along this path.[239] But the overall point of relevance here is this explicit connection of the phrase 'fear and trembling' with the Christian promise of salvation.

As we mentioned in Chapter 5, Green also draws attention to the explicit mention of sin in the discussion of Agnete and the merman in Problema III. We noted there his claim that 'Abraham [whose silence is "divine"] and the merman [whose silence is "demonic"] are counterparts, positive and negative expressions of the same problem. Both have suspended the ethical, one by obedience and one by sin, and both are saved only by a direct, supra-ethical relationship to God.'[240] In the light of Green's claim that this 'disquisition on sin is not a chance aside but a window into *Fear and Trembling*'s deepest concerns',[241] let us remind ourselves of what Johannes actually says at this point of the text.

In fact, it is worth quoting the whole passage on sin. Johannes is considering the possibility of the merman being 'saved in so far as he is disclosed', by marrying Agnete.

But he must still resort to the paradox. For when through his own guilt the individual has come out of the universal, he can only return to it on the strength of having come, as the particular, into an absolute relation to the absolute. Here I will insert a comment which takes us further than anything that has been said anywhere in the foregoing.*
Sin is not the first immediacy, sin is a later immediacy. In sin the individual is already in terms of the demonic paradox higher than the universal, because it is a contradiction on the part of the universal to want to impose itself on someone who lacks the *conditio sine qua non* [the necessary condition]. Should philosophy, along with its other conceits, imagine that someone might actually want to follow its precepts in practice, a curious comedy would emerge. An ethics that ignores sin is an altogether futile discipline, but once it postulates sin it has *eo ipso* [thereby] gone beyond itself.

* Up to this point I have carefully avoided all consideration of the question of sin and its reality. Everything has been centred on Abraham, and he can still be reached with the categories of immediacy, at least so far as I can understand him. But once sin makes its appearance ethics comes to grief precisely on the question of repentance. Repentance is the highest ethical expression but for that very reason the most profound ethical self-contradiction.

(FT 124)

What is going on here? Green makes some illuminating observations about this passage.[242] First, he sees the reference to sin as a second, not first, immediacy as a criticism of Hegel's association of sin with particularity. On the latter view, 'Sin is a "first immediacy" because it manifests itself with the fact of individuality ("isolated subjectivity") and is only remedied in an encounter with the ethical requirement.'[243] Whereas on Kierkegaard's view, sin is a 'second immediacy' in the sense that 'sin *follows* the moral law and presumes a full understanding of and engagement with it'.[244] Second, why would philosophy supposing 'someone might actually want to follow its precepts in practice' result in 'a curious comedy'? Green's answer is that 'the only result would be an awareness of sin'.[245] In other words, 'a rigorous understanding of the principles of morality only serves to highlight the enormous difficulty and perhaps the impossibility of an individual's ever fully acting on these principles'.[246] This helps us to understand the third and most significant point in the above passage: the sense in which an ethics that ignores sin is 'futile' – but also how, if it recognises sin, such an ethics necessarily 'goes beyond itself'. This two-pronged claim can be unpacked as follows. First, ignoring sin is 'futile' because of the impossibility of always following what the moral law demands.[247] (The ethical, we recall from Problema I, applies 'at all times'.) If always following such demands really is impossible, then we are 'lost'. That is, the problem of sin cannot be overcome so long as 'the moral law is the final and supreme arbiter of our spiritual destiny'.[248] But second, suppose there is 'a more ultimate possibility in which forgiveness and the suspension of our merited punishment by a source of moral judgment more authoritative than our own'.[249] That is, suppose there is an ethics that 'goes beyond itself'. Such is the Christian message of a loving God who, as we suggested above, suspends a 'natural' sense of justice, forgiving sin through divine grace.

Green points out that Climacus, commenting on *Fear and Trembling* in his 'Glance at a Contemporary Effort in Danish Literature' (his review of Kierkegaard's work in the *Postscript*), offers an interpretation of the text's significance that gestures towards the Christian reading. The following passage is indeed revealing:

> The teleological suspension of the ethical must have an even more definite religious expression. The ethical is then present at every moment with its infinite requirement, but the individual is not capable of fulfilling it. This powerlessness of the individual must not be seen as an imperfection in the continued endeavour to attain an ideal, for in that case the suspension is no more postulated than the man who administers his office in an ordinary way is suspended. The suspension consists in the individual's finding himself in a state exactly opposite to what the ethical requires.
>
> (CUP 266–7)

The echoes of what we have been discussing should be obvious. This 'state exactly opposite to what the ethical requires' is sin, which Climacus claims to be 'the crucial point of departure for the religious existence' (CUP 268). Moreover, sin 'is not a factor within another order of things, but is itself the beginning of the religious order of things' (CUP 268). This echoes the idea that an ethic with sin (and forgiveness) at its heart is a radical break with ethics as otherwise conceived: that such an ethic is an ethic that 'goes beyond itself'.

Green concludes that:

> *Fear and Trembling* is an introduction or propaedeutic to Kierkegaard's authorship as a whole. Read at all the levels of its meaning, *Fear and Trembling* contains the major themes of Christian faith and ethics that will emerge in the ensuing pseudonymous works and many of the religious discourses. *Fear and Trembling* deserves the fame that Kierkegaard predicted for it ... It is a profound theological treatise firmly rooted in the Pauline and Lutheran tradition to which Kierkegaard belonged.[250]

However, some commentators have been sceptical of this Christian allegorical reading. Gene Outka, for instance, in a reply to Green, suggests that Green is reading far too much into the sin and repentance passage in Problema III. Outka argues that Green gives no satisfactory answer to the questions of why the theme of sin is not explicitly mentioned until Problema III, or why it should be given such pivotal importance given Johannes' assertion that it does *not* explain Abraham.[251] *Prima facie*, this certainly seems a reasonable objection. If this brief passage were the only textual support one could find for a Christian reading, it would indeed be rather thin. However, as we shall now see, a rather more detailed, and in my view more intriguing case for a Christian reading of the text is provided by Stephen Mulhall.[252]

Mulhall also supports the anagogical reading, but in what I think is an improvement upon Green, also offers a fascinating interpretation of some additional aspects of the text. Consider first Mulhall's observation that Abraham's words, when he says 'God will provide a lamb for the burnt offering', have 'a prophetic dimension ... of which he is oblivious'.[253] Since God actually provides a ram rather than a lamb, Abraham's prediction turns out to be literally false, but prophetically true, since God eventually provides Christ, the 'Lamb of God'. Relatedly, 'Isaac's unquestioning submission to his father's will (his carrying of the wood of his own immolation to the place of sacrifice) prefigures Christ's submission to his own Father. In this sense, Isaac's receptive passivity represents the maturation of Abraham's activist conception of faith – a transition from an understanding of God as demanding the sacrifice of what is ours to an understanding of God as demanding the sacrifice of the self'.[254]

(The eschatological trust reading might balk at describing Abraham's faith as 'activist', in so far as there is already a strong dimension of passivity – receptive trust and hope – in Abraham's faith.)

But how exactly does this anagogical reading affect the question of what the 'teleological suspension of the ethical' means? Mulhall's intriguing suggestion is as follows:

> If the allegorical or analogical reading of Abraham's ordeal as a prefiguration of Christ's Atonement is correct, then we must reject the idea that God could conceivably require a form of worship that involves murder; for the maturation of faith that the ordeal symbolizes is precisely a shift towards a conception of God as willing to shed his own blood rather than eager to spill the blood of others – as concerned not only to transcend the primitive idea of human sacrifice by substituting a ram for Isaac, but also to transcend the idea of sacrificing one's possessions to God in favour of an idea of sacrificing oneself (the act and attitude by means of which one incarnates God by imitating his essential self-sacrificial nature).[255]

Thus faith requires not so much the *violation* of ethical duty, but its *transformation*. (This fits with Davenport's reading in so far as he is keen to emphasise the *cumulative* nature of progress through the existence-spheres.[256]) Mulhall seeks to root this in the text by noting Johannes' remarks on the importance of Abraham's *loving* Isaac. Johannes claims that if at the point of sacrifice Abraham *hates* Isaac, then 'he can be certain that God does not require this of him; for Cain and Abraham are not the same. Isaac he must love with all his soul. When God asks for Isaac, Abraham must if possible love him even more, and only then can he *sacrifice* him' (FT 101). That is, he can only genuinely give Isaac up – sacrifice him — if he genuinely considers him to be the most terrible loss. Mulhall reads this passage as saying that 'a voice in one's head inciting one to kill one's son can only be the voice of God if one's love for one's son is perfect'.[257] Any impurity in 'one's attachment to the Isaac in one's life'[258] make one a Cain rather than an Abraham, 'revealing the voice in one's head as an evil demon'.[259] (We might quibble about describing loving someone 'with [one's] whole soul' in terms of one's love being 'perfect', but Mulhall makes clear that by an 'ethically perfect being' he means 'one who lives out the demands of the ethical without exception, one whose soul is permeated and informed by the ethical',[260] showing that he is glossing ethical perfection in the same terms.)

All this means that if Isaac represents the demands of the ethical, then 'only an ethically perfect being' (as glossed above) 'could ever be in a position to judge that an impulse to suspend the demands of the ethical might be the manifestation of a divine command'.[261] But who meets this criterion? This question leads Mulhall into his own discussion of Agnete and the merman and the sin passage. Unsurprisingly given what we have already said in our discussion of this passage above, Mulhall points out that if we think of ourselves in terms of sin, then 'the idea of ethical perfection is utterly lost': repentance for our sin cannot 'entirely eradicat[e] the stain of past wrongdoing because even the smallest past misdemeanour reveals our absolute difference from Absolute Goodness, and hence our inability to save ourselves by our own powers'.[262] For salvation to be possible at all, then, divine grace is necessary. And the 'ethically perfect being' who alone is able to suspend the ethical is God himself.

So on this reading, as with Green's, the real 'secret message' of the teleological suspension of the ethical is to make space for a conception of the ethical that includes grace: 'Acknowledging our sinfulness means acknowledging our inability to live up to the demands of the ethical realm; acknowledging Christ means acknowledging that those demands must nevertheless be met, with help from a power greater than our own.'[263]

There is one especially important feature of Mulhall's version of the Christian reading to which we should draw attention. In our criticism earlier in the chapter of some 'divine command ethics' readings of *Fear and Trembling*, we pointed out that if what matters is that God's word should take precedence over the ethical, there seems no obvious reason why Abraham should not have to go through with sacrificing Isaac. In other words, some such readings leave mysterious the significance of God's substituting the ram and 'calling off' the sacrifice. One of the advantages of Mulhall's version of the Christian reading over that of Green, for instance, is that it clearly explains the significance of this. As we saw Mulhall claim earlier, essential to the Christian vision is a move away from one picture of sacrifice and towards an alternative. The idea that gets replaced is the idea that one should sacrifice to God one's possessions – and, perhaps especially, the idea that one could legitimately view another human being as such a possession. This is replaced with the idea that the sacrifice God requires is a sacrifice of one's self – the idea of 'dying to the self'. God's 'calling off' the 'blood' sacrifice of Isaac, when allied to Abraham's realisation that he 'gets Isaac back' under a new mode of valuation – not as his property, but as a 'gift' that is not to be viewed as a possession – draws attention to this important feature.

CONCLUSION

Which of these interpretations should we support? I do not wish to deny that the text contains a 'hidden message' to Regine. But as we said, its relevance to the sad romance of a couple who lived in the 1840s can hardly exhaust the text's significance, or explain why it has fascinated commentators for so long. For what it is worth, my own view is now that in broad outline, the reading Davenport has sought to build out of earlier readings has the most going for it, and I have sought to build on this further with the above discussion of hope. In an important journal entry (part of a response to 'Theophilus Nicolaus'), Kierkegaard remarks, 'Abraham is called the father of faith because he has the formal qualifications of faith, believing against the understanding, although it has never occurred to the Christian Church that Abraham's faith had the content of Christian faith which relates essentially to a later historical event' (JP 6: 6598 [p. 300]). This fits with the strategy, which Davenport exemplifies, to sketch a wider account of 'existential faith' of which specifically Christian faith would be a sub-category. Central to both Abraham's faith and that of the Christian is expectancy that the good will prevail thanks to the actions of a loving God.[264]

However, I still think that Christian anagogical readings add an important additional 'level': Kierkegaard was surely aware of the tradition of reading the Abraham story anagogically, and it seems plausible that this would have struck him as the most important 'hidden message'. I do not think that noting this, in the qualified light of the above, involves 'Christianising' Abraham in any problematic way.

It is a common feature of great philosophical texts that they can be read on more than one level. And the diversity of interpretations to which a text gets put is often a sign of its richness. In Chapter 1, we noted how Kierkegaard claimed in his journal that 'once I am dead, *Fear and Trembling* alone will be enough for an imperishable name as an author. Then it will be read, translated into foreign languages as well. The reader will almost shrink from the frightful pathos in the book' (JP 6: 6491). In so far as *Fear and Trembling* is not only probably Kierkegaard's best-known and most commonly taught text, but also continues to be the subject of a plethora of readings, this claim seems to have been remarkably prophetic.

NOTES

1. John Davenport characterises as such those readings according to which saying that Abraham's faith goes beyond the ethical 'means that Abraham obeys a higher duty, calling or type of obligation that is contrasted with Hegelian social morality or (more broadly) with moral laws or universal precepts derived from any rational ground of understanding (Aristotelian, Kantian, utilitarian, moral sense, etc.)' (2008b: 169).
2. Notes from the Munch Archives, cited in Grelland 2013: 183.
3. Lukács 1982: 281, cited in Nagy 2009: 165.
4. Letter to Paul Ernst, 4 May 1915, in Fekete and Karádi 1981: 595, cited in Nagy 2009: 165.
5. Nagy 2009: 165.
6. See Loungina 2009: 271.
7. Cited in Goulet 1957: 177.
8. See Stewart 2013, Tomes II and III.

9 See the relevant articles in Stewart 2013, Tomes I, IV and V.
10 Irina 2013: 123. On the centrality of tests and trials in Kafka's narratives, see Danta 2011, especially pp. 1–25, 76.
11 Kafka 1977: 199–200, cited in Irina 2013: 123.
12 For instance, in a 1921 letter to Robert Klopstock, Kafka reports that he has been 'meditating a good deal' on Kierkegaard's Abraham, yet adds: 'but these are old stories, no longer worth discussing; especially not the real Abraham' (Kafka 1977: 285; cited in Irina 2013: 126). For a more detailed comparison of Kierkegaard's and Kafka's readings of Genesis 22, see Danta 2011. See also Blanchot 1982 and Rose 1992. Heiko Schulz describes *Fear and Trembling* as a 'constant source of inspiration' for Kafka (Schulz 2009: 333), noting, for instance, Brod's (admittedly contentious) claim that the Sortini episode in *The Castle* was inspired by it.
13 Essays on each of these figures can be found in the relevant volumes of the series *Kierkegaard Research: Sources, Reception and Resources*, edited by Jon Stewart (see Bibliography).
14 Irina 2013: 115. Irina adds that even within the world of Danish letters, interest in Kierkegaard was stimulated by early translations of Kafka (2013: 115).
15 See Green and Green 2011: 6.
16 Sartre was apparently reading Kierkegaard's and Kafka's journals and diaries alongside *Fear and Trembling*: see Hackel 2011: 338.
17 Sartre 1948: 30.
18 Sartre 1948: 31.
19 Sartre 1948: 34.
20 Sartre 1948: 35.
21 For de Beauvoir's related but distinct take on Kierkegaard's Abraham in *The Ethics of Ambiguity*, see Stewart 2009b: 446–7.
22 Hackel 2011: 346.
23 Hanson 2012: 174.
24 Lévinas 1998: 31.
25 Lévinas 1998: 34.
26 Lévinas 1998: 34. To put these remarks in context, it is perhaps not too much to say that for Lévinas the mainstream Western philosophical tradition is inherently 'violent'. For more on the wider context of these remarks, see Hanson 2012. For more detailed accounts of the Kierkegaard–Lévinas relationship, see, for instance, Sheil 2010, Simmons and Wood 2008 and Westphal 2008.
27 Lévinas 1998: 34.
28 Lévinas 1998: 34.
29 Compare here Martin Buber's question as to whether we can legitimately take the first voice (the demand of sacrifice) to be God's at all (Buber 1975: 226).
30 On this point, see Davenport 2008b: 176–7.
31 For more on the category of 'humour' in Kierkegaard, see Lippitt 2000.
32 Cf. Evans 2004: 63–4.
33 See Green 1998.

34 Note that a version of this passage appears in a journal entry of 1843, after which Kierkegaard remarks, 'The person who explains this mystery has explained my life' (KJN 2: JJ 87 [cf. JP 5: 5640]). See also JP 6: 6473, 6491 and 6843.
35 Hannay 2001: 191.
36 Hannay 2001: 191.
37 Green 1998: 274. Note in passing the number of uses of the phrase 'fear and trembling' in the autobiographical passages in KJN 3 Not. 15: 15.
38 Malantschuk 1971: 236. For more on Malantschuk's reasons here, see especially pp. 236–9.
39 There might be additional reasons not to put too much weight on such biographical readings of Kierkegaard's works. Habib C. Malik suggests that such a 'biographical-psychological approach' (the most prominent early practitioner of which was the Danish critic George Brandes), which focuses on the 'sensational aspects of Kierkegaard's personal life and the inner workings of his mind, as delineated in his journals, became [a] convenient tool in the hands of those who wished to deflect attention from the substantive significance of his works, thereby undermining their potential intellectual and spiritual significance' (1997: 217).
40 Green 1998: 258.
41 Green 1998: 258. The phrase is Paul Dietrichson's (1965: 2).
42 Green 1998: 261.
43 Green 1998: 262.
44 Green 1998: 262.
45 Green 1998: 263.
46 Green 1998: 264.
47 Green 1998: 264.
48 Green 1998: 264.
49 Green 1998: 265.
50 Green 1998: 266.
51 Green 1998: 266.
52 Green 1998: 266.
53 Gellman 1990: 297, 299.
54 On the sense in which Johannes departs from both Luther and Kant on this point, see Carlisle 2015: 56–7.
55 Green 1998: 267.
56 Evans 1981: 145. For more along these lines, see Evans 2004: 315–16.
57 Gellman discusses Yeshayahu Leibowitz as a representative of the first tradition and David Hartman as a representative of the second. On the former view – according to which the *akedah* is an aberration – the assumption is that God 'would never violate your fundamental moral intuitions of justice and love' (Hartman 1999: 13). Gellman finds both views wanting, arguing that what Abraham learns through the *akedah* is not a new paradigm, but 'to transcend paradigmatic thinking altogether' (Gellman 2003: 113), being open to a new future. While it is so briefly sketched that I cannot be sure, I believe that the

view Gellman outlines here has some similarities with the 'eschatological trust and radical hope' reading I shall outline later in this chapter. George Pattison notes that in one of the upbuilding discourses of October 1843, Kierkegaard makes more of the first Abraham than does Johannes: see EUD 66, Pattison 2002: 201 and note 136 below.

58 See especially Evans 2004.
59 Evans 2004: 62–3.
60 This work deserves a more detailed treatment than I have space for here: nevertheless, even a brief treatment may be of value.
61 See especially Evans 2004: Chapter 7.
62 Evans 2004: 12–14.
63 Evans 2004: 28–9.
64 Evans 2004: 21. In this way, Evans seeks to show how a divine-command theory can both incorporate and build upon a 'human nature' theory of ethics (see especially his Chapter 6), such that 'human happiness is best found by living in accord with the command' (2004: 113). Though one's own happiness cannot be the primary motive for one's obedience, this quote from Johannes, as Evans reads it, does suggest that it can supervene. 'God's commands are linked with human happiness, though that link may be one that can be discerned in this life only through faith and hope' (2004: 113).
65 Evans 2004: 305–6.
66 For an extension of this argument, see Evans 2015.
67 Evans 2004: 308.
68 Why issue the command to sacrifice, then? Evans emphasises 'God's successful revelation of his commands *and character*' (2004: 318, my emphasis), including (and perhaps especially) to Abraham, I suppose. So perhaps his answer to the 'power not love' objection considered above is that this point could be made dramatically to those who followed Abraham by putting to the test Abraham, who had as intimate a knowledge as it is possible to have of God's character. This raises the interesting possibility that the *akedah* events show something about God's trust in Abraham, as well as Abraham's trust in God.
69 Evans 2004: 311.
70 Evans discusses three such examples at 2015: 70–6.
71 Evans 2015: 76–8.
72 Levenson 2012: 109.
73 Levenson 2012: 107.
74 It should be admitted that Levenson's reading of *Fear and Trembling* (which is limited to one footnote) is not especially nuanced: see 2012: 223n59.
75 See, for instance, Delaney 1998, which Levenson considers to be the 'prime example' of this genre (2012: 223n60). See also Nørager 2008.
76 Levenson 2012: 110–11.
77 Levenson 2012: 112.
78 Levenson 2012: 112.
79 Sartre 1948: 38.

WHAT IS *FEAR AND TREMBLING* REALLY ABOUT? 211

80 Mooney 1991: 68. This reference to 'casual adjustment' seems slightly unfair to Sartre, given his emphasis on the anxiety that accompanies a genuine realisation of our freedom. However, I agree with Mooney that Sartre puts an excessive emphasis on choice.
81 Mooney 1991: 68.
82 Mooney 1991: 78.
83 Mooney 1991: 80.
84 Mooney 1991: 80.
85 Mooney 1991: 81.
86 Mooney 1991: 81.
87 Mooney 1991: 81.
88 Mooney 1991: 81. For a famous defence of essentially this view in the case of another moral dilemma, see Winch 1972.
89 Mooney 1991: 84.
90 Mooney 1991: 84.
91 For another important reading of the *akedah* as a kind of 'religious tragedy', see Quinn 1990.
92 Mooney 1991: 80.
93 Mooney 1991: 80.
94 Williams 1981: 82, cited in Mooney 1991: 84.
95 See for instance Nussbaum 1986.
96 Mooney 1991: 85.
97 See, for instance, Engstrom and Whiting 1996.
98 Mooney 1991: 85.
99 See the discussion of Maharba – Mooney's imagined 'Abraham backwards' (1991: 87).
100 Mooney 1991: 93.
101 Mooney 1991: 93.
102 As Hannay suggests in a recent essay, 'Isaac's true father is God' (2015: 14).
103 Mooney 1991: 92.
104 For more on the themes of self-denial and self-love in Kierkegaard's thought, see Lippitt 2013.
105 Mooney 1991: 94.
106 Mooney 1991: 94.
107 Mjaaland 2012: 118.
108 Derrida 1995: 67.
109 Derrida 1995: 68.
110 Derrida 1995: 68. Davenport argues that 'Derrida's whole analysis depends on this one claim' (2008b: 184).
111 Derrida 1995: 69.
112 Derrida 1995: 71.
113 Davenport 2008b: 185. For Davenport's full critique of Derrida's reading, which he judges as 'comical', 'arrogant' and 'frightening', see 2008b: 180–8.
114 Davenport 2008b: 184–5. Elsewhere (Lippitt 2013), I have argued that we need – and that Kierkegaard in *Works of Love* and elsewhere also thinks that

we need – an account of 'proper self-love' that recognises, *inter alia*, the importance of care of (and duties to) the self that are not only instrumental routes to love of God and neighbour. Anyone familiar with this argument will grasp why I side with Davenport over Derrida on this point.

115 I have substituted Hannay's translation. Derrida's translator uses the Hongs' phrase 'the dreadful responsibility of loneliness'.
116 Rudd 2015: 202.
117 Mjaaland 2012: 122; cf. also p. 121.
118 On this point, see also Danta 2011: 43.
119 Green 1993.
120 Green 1993: 193.
121 Green 1993: 193–4.
122 Green 1993: 195n.
123 Green 1993: 195n.
124 Green 1993: 195n.
125 Davenport 2008a: 206–15.
126 For Davenport, the key difference between the first and second camp is that for the latter, the concept of agapic love has 'some content that is understandable by us, however imperfectly, prior to accepting the authority of God's will as the highest (or even sole) source of moral normativity' (2008b: 171).
127 Davenport 2008a: 207. As we saw above, Mooney does not outright reject universal rules, which is perhaps why Davenport describes his as the 'mildest version' of such an approach. For more on his reasons for locating Mooney here, see Davenport 2008a: 208.
128 Davenport 2008a: 209.
129 See Davenport 2008a, 2008b, 2008c and 2015 (especially the first).
130 Davenport 2008a: 208–12.
131 Davenport 2008a: 212.
132 Davenport 2008a: 212.
133 Howland 2015: 35.
134 Davenport 2008c: 885n8.
135 Here I prefer Walsh's 'paltry' to Hannay's 'miserable'.
136 Several scholars have noticed the intriguing prospects for reading Kierkegaard's pseudonymous texts against the background of one or more of the *Upbuilding Discourses*. Here I focus on one of the two discourses of May 1843, but see also Pattison 2002: 192–202 for a reading of *Fear and Trembling* in light of the two 'Love will hide a multitude of sins' discourses from October of that year.
137 Roberts 2003: 187. On the importance of hope at times of spiritual trial, in the face of anxiety and potential despair, see Kierkegaard's early sermon at JP 4: 3915.
138 Davenport 2008a: 199–200.
139 Hannay 2008: 242.
140 Kierkegaard says that he intended for Regine the preface to the Two Upbuilding Discourses of which 'The Expectancy of Faith' is the first (KJN 3 Not. 15: 4 [p. 436]).

141 Kierkegaard's text here glosses victory as 'that all things must serve for good those who love God' (EUD 19), an echo of Romans 8:28.
142 Similarly, compare Kierkegaard's contrast between youthful and Christian hope at CUP 2: 70 (JP 2: 1668); also EUD 437–8 and SUD 58.
143 Cf. Davenport 2008a: 226.
144 Kierkegaard reaches the same point from a different angle in the *Works of Love* deliberation 'Love hopes all things', with his claim that hoping for something for which it is shameful to hope amounts to not really hoping, as genuine hope 'relates essentially and eternally to the good' (WL 261). Wishing, craving and merely temporal expecting (that is, an expectancy which is not that of faith) can all be 'put to shame', but true hope cannot (WL 262). It seems clear, therefore, that the hope described at the opening of *Repetition*, for instance – which is associated with youthfulness, cowardice and superficiality, and which is described as 'a beckoning fruit that does not satisfy' (R 132) – is not genuine hope as Kierkegaard understands it. Perhaps this is another version of the hope that *Fear and Trembling* judges as paltry? (I am grateful to Frances Maughan-Brown for pressing me on this point.) Compare also the contrast between hoping and wishing in 'An Occasional Discourse' (UDVS 100–1). On openness to the future, see Gellman 2003: Chapter 8.
145 'One who prays aright struggles in prayer and is victorious – in that God is victorious', the last of the *Eighteen Upbuilding Discourses*. On the 'centre of gravity' point, see Hampson 2013: 22.
146 Thus, I think Kierkegaard would view Carlisle as fudging the issue somewhat when she describes the 'courage that belongs to faith' as consisting in part in 'accept[ing] the beloved back in the form of a gift – a gift from God, a gift from life, a gift from death, or a gift from love as it is incarnated in each living being' (2010: 195). On this point, I agree with Westphal that it is important that this is trust in a personal God who makes, and keeps, promises (2014: 26). On the distinction between faith in a broad and in a strictly Christian sense, see, for instance, FSE 81–2.
147 As should hopefully be clear by now, to speculate that Abraham could utter such words is not inconsistent with Abraham's 'silence'. To say that Abraham cannot justify himself is not to say that he could not formulate meaningful utterances, but rather that these utterances would not be comprehensible as reasons to those lacking Abraham's second-person relationship to God (or something sufficiently like it).
148 On this point, compare the discussion of loss of hope at EUD 94–5.
149 Kierkegaard explicitly discusses the possibility of someone's thinking that 'something in particular' has robbed them of their faith (EUD 26). A divine command to sacrifice one's son, for instance? Again we might recall some of the Attunement's sub-Abrahams.
150 Further light is shed on this by an 1850 journal entry in which Kierkegaard discusses how a person who lacks a concrete impression of God's love can nevertheless cling on to the *thought* that God is love, and that this is part of a 'rigorous upbringing' in faith that will eventuate in a concrete God-relationship

(CA Suppl. 172–3 [JP 2: 1401]). For a similar thought inspired by C. S. Lewis, see Roberts 2007: 29.
151 Romans 8:22–7.
152 Though perhaps 'everyday' hope sometimes has more resilience and greater flexibility than Kierkegaard here gives it credit for. One form of this flexibility is hope's ability to engender new constitutive hopes, as Luc Bovens puts it. For a discussion of this, see Lippitt 2013: 136–55, especially pp. 152–4.
153 For the full picture, see Davenport 2008a, 2008b, 2008c and 2015.
154 See, for instance, Adams 1990.
155 Davenport 2008b: 174; cf. 2008a: 200. Westphal raises an objection to the language of eschatology here (2014: 37–9), which I think Davenport ably rebuts (2015: 85–92). That said, with regard to my own support for the general line of Davenport's reading, nothing much hangs on the specific language of eschatology.
156 Davenport 2008b: 173.
157 Davenport 2008b: 173.
158 For more on these two types of resignation, see Davenport 2008a: 228–9.
159 Davenport 2008a: 229.
160 Davenport 2008b: 174.
161 Davenport 2008a: 203.
162 Davenport considers a second possibility ('either within time, or in the hereafter as a new temporal series [rather than as a Platonic *aeternitas*])' (2008b: 174) that need not concern us here.
163 Davenport 2008b: 174.
164 Davenport 2008b: 174.
165 In the summary of his position in 2008b (and, as I read it, in 2015: 103), Davenport stresses only the second possibility (which is that apparently envisaged in Hebrews 11:19). But much of *Fear and Trembling* (and several of Davenport's comments thereon: see for instance 2008a: 201) are also compatible with the first. It seems to me just as important to keep this open as a live option. On this point, see also Chapter 7, note 91.
166 Davenport 2008b: 174.
167 To grasp his position in more detail, see Davenport's gloss on Tolkien's notion of eucatastrophe (2008a: 203–5). To the first five points above, Davenport has now added another, namely *authority*, in which one is commanded to believe the promise revealed by a personal God such that 'the authority of this commanded trust in the promise transcends that of the ethical ideal' (2015: 83).
168 Davenport 2008a: 212.
169 Davenport 2008a: 212.
170 Davenport 2008a: 93. For more detail on kinds of 'suspension', see 2008a: 215–21.
171 Confirmed by Davenport in personal correspondence.
172 Davenport 2008a: 213–14.
173 Davenport 2008a: 214.

174 Compare such hope to that specifically Christian hope which Kierkegaard describes, from the perspective of our natural understanding, as 'lunacy [*Galskab*]' (FSE 83).

175 As well as those I will consider below, note that Westphal has objected that Davenport's reading (along with other associated readings by Mooney and Krishek [Westphal 2014: Chapter 4]) mistakes what is a 'preliminary' discussion (the distinction between faith and infinite resignation) for what according to Westphal is the 'main point' (the contrast between knight of faith and tragic hero). In pressing this objection, Westphal leans heavily on the idea that the former distinction occurs in one of the four 'introductions', which he distinguishes sharply from the problemata, seeming to take the latter as being the real meat of the text. (He cites the first edition of the present book for the 'four introductions' idea [2014: 27n4].) This is not a reversion to the bad old days of ignoring pretty much everything before the problemata: Westphal is far too astute a reader for that, and he recognises the importance of 'faith as trust in divine promises' and the faith-resignation contrast as vital to that (2014: Chapter 2). He does, however, set up what is to my mind an unnecessary choice between the problemata and the rest of the book as the places where one must look for its 'main point'. (This is slightly ironic, given that he seems to be accusing Davenport – and myself? – of doing precisely this [Westphal 2014: 73].) Hence the (in my view unnecessary) insistence that one must decide between whether it is the knight of infinite resignation or the tragic hero's contrast with the knight of faith that is the 'main point' of the book. Davenport offers an effective rebuttal of Westphal's critique (2015: 92–8). To this I would add that since the 'Preamble from the Heart' is a preamble *specifically to the Problemata*, this particular 'introduction' has an ambiguous status, at the very least, even by Westphal's own lights. One issue on which I differ from Davenport is that there seems to me simply no need to take Westphal's bait of insisting that either the faith–resignation or knight of faith–tragic hero distinction is primary (Davenport argues for the former). Why assume that there is *a* main point, *a* main contrast? Rather, it seems to me, *Fear and Trembling* presents us (as we have already noted) with a series of portraits of figures that superficially resemble faith but turn out not to be: the sub-Abrahams of the Attunement, the knight of infinite resignation, the tragic hero, the various 'aesthetic heroes' of Problema III. Each plays an important role, and I do not feel the force of the insistence that precisely *one* of these must be primary.

176 Walsh notes the resonance with 1 Corinthians 1:23 here.

177 Davenport 2008a: 198–9.

178 Blanshard 1969: 116, cited in Davenport 2008a: 213.

179 See, for instance, Agacinski 1998: 129–50, especially p. 139.

180 Compare also Johannes' distaste at 'flirt[ing] with the outcome aesthetically': 'no robber of temples hard-labouring in chains is so base a criminal as he who plunders the holy in this way, and not even Judas ... is more contemptible than the person who would thus offer greatness for sale' (FT 92).

181 Davenport 2008a: 217. 'This singularising relation is existential faith: the absolute duty to love God singles us out because it includes a "duty" to *have faith* in God as the ultimate person' (Davenport 2008a: 217). In a later article, Davenport further underlines that what justifies Abraham is not the outcome per se, but his *'obedient and loving trust* that God will bring about the good outcome, one way or the other' (2015: 103, emphasis in original). Davenport is responding (2015: 101–5) to a version of the objection about 'the outcome' in Tilley 2012. On this general point, see also Evans 2004: 311.

182 As we noted in Chapter 2, the sub-Abrahams of 'Attunement' demonstrate that mere obedience to God cannot be what makes Abraham exemplary. On the theological importance of this emphasis on faith as trust as opposed to other possible emphases, see Levenson 2012: 81–2.

183 This seems consistent with Davenport's general treatment of existential faith as the broader category of which Christian faith is a sub-category (2008a: 233).

184 A propos of our earlier discussion, this shows one way in which Evans could be right that while the specific command to Abraham in no way applies to us, Abraham is not thereby rendered irrelevant to us.

185 This possibility is touched upon by Pattison and Jensen 2012: 9. Cf. also Kellenberger 1997: 48–9; Krishek 2009: 98–9.

186 Lear 2006. Aside from a brief mention in Malesic (2013: 226), the only other attempt I know of in the secondary literature to bring *Fear and Trembling* into dialogue with Lear on radical hope is towards the end of Carlisle 2010. However, the primary focus of Carlisle's discussion is the link between faith and courage, whereas I want to explore the link between the two texts specifically through a more detailed exploration of what Lear means by 'radical hope'.

187 Lear 2006: 91.

188 Lear 2006: 70–1.

189 Lear 2006: 92.

190 Lear 2006: 92.

191 I am grateful to Daniel Conway for pressing me to clarify this point.

192 Lear 2006: 92–4.

193 Lear 2006: 93.

194 Lear 2006: 93–4, my emphasis.

195 Lear 2006: 94, my emphasis.

196 A form of infinite resignation?

197 Lear 2006: 94.

198 Davenport 2008a: 220.

199 See Evans 2006: xviii. Note that such a reading does not commit us to the idea that Abraham holds contradictory beliefs (that he both will and won't sacrifice Isaac) – an interpretation that I was at pains to avoid in Chapter 3. Nor does it present Abraham as having sussed God's real intentions and called his bluff. Rather, as Evans puts it, 'Abraham simply rests unwaveringly in his trust in God's goodness; he believes that God will keep his promises, *even though he does not know exactly how God will do this*, and realizes that from the perspective of human experience, it looks impossible' (2006: xix, my

emphasis). What I am suggesting is that drawing on Lear can enable us not only to gloss the italicised phrase but also to show that Abraham's hope is more radical than this way of putting it may at first make it appear.

200 Lear 2006: 100.
201 Lear 2006: 103.
202 Lear 2006: 105.
203 Lear 2006: 141.
204 Westphal 2014: 77.
205 Westphal 2014: 77.
206 Macquarrie 1978: 53. For more detail on how this might be seen as operating in the case of the *akedah*, see Levenson 2012: 84–5.
207 Westphal 2014: 28–9, my emphases.
208 Added to which, note that Julian of Norwich's famous phrase ('all shall be well. All shall be well, and all manner of thing shall be well') occurs in what is claimed to be a specific Showing of Christ (Julian of Norwich 1996: 48).
209 One can see something of the 'infinite frailty' (WL 251) of possibility that Kierkegaard talks about here by trying to imagine oneself in Abraham's situation. The dialogue between hope and despair (WL 254) is also worth reading with the *akedah* in mind. Perhaps the fourth sub-Abraham – and also the second? – has listened too much to despair.
210 This is also illustrated in the case of the prophet Anna, discussed at length in the discourse 'Patience in Expectancy'.
211 Only the courage of faith is humble, Johannes claims here. For a later discussion of 'humble courage', see SUD 85–6.
212 Lear 2006: 65.
213 Lear 2006: 119–20.
214 Lear 2006: 120.
215 Lear 2006: 120.
216 Lear 2006: 121.
217 Lear 2006: 121.
218 Lear 2006: 122.
219 I am grateful to Adam Pelser for this point. On the courage of faith as receptive, passive (in a sense), open-hearted and feminine, see Carlisle 2010: 198–9.
220 Lear 2006: 95. Compare here Kierkegaard's 1850 journal remark that 'the concept of the absurd is precisely to grasp the fact that it cannot and must not be grasped' (JP 1: 7).
221 Lear 2006: 95.
222 Lear 2006: 95.
223 Davenport 2008a: 206.
224 Davenport 2008a: 207.
225 Davenport 2008a: 207.
226 This is probably Westphal's and certainly Davenport's target. The latter's objection to Green is that Green is said 'implausibly' to add that 'Christian redemption is the *only* kind of soteriology that Kierkegaard intended to include within his conception of existential faith' (2008a: 222, my emphasis).

227 Mackey 1972.
228 Mackey 1972: 421–2.
229 Mackey 1972: 423.
230 Mackey 1972: 426.
231 Such confusion is not, of course, confined to Kierkegaard's age. One relatively recent example in Britain concerns the furore surrounding the resignation of the England football manager, Glenn Hoddle, in 1999. Hoddle, a self-proclaimed 'born-again Christian', was effectively forced to resign following the negative publicity surrounding some unwise comments he made to the effect that people with disabilities were paying for sins they had committed in a previous life. It was notable that, in all the massive press coverage surrounding this controversy, nobody seemed to point out the confusion inherent in a 'born-again' Christian apparently professing a belief in reincarnation. The mention of football in connection with religious confusion makes it irresistable also to mention David Beckham's comment, following the birth of his son Brooklyn, that he wanted to have the boy christened, but 'I'm not sure into what religion yet'.
232 Green suggests that this alters the significance of the biographical dimension of *Fear and Trembling*. If this traditional Christian message of divine grace and forgiveness is the book's real message, then instead of the intended recipient of the 'secret message' being Regine, it is the spirit of Kierkegaard's dead father 'and all those who, like him, are tormented by the problem of sin' (Green 1993: 203). For more on this unusual 'biographical' reading (some of which I find rather fanciful), see Green 1992: 198–200.
233 Whittaker 2000: 201.
234 Phillips 2000: 126. The contributor to whom this particular 'voice' belongs is unnamed.
235 Evans 1993: 26.
236 On this see, for instance, Moltmann 1974.
237 Philippians 2:12–13.
238 Green 1993: 200–1.
239 In his late writings, Kierkegaard goes to great lengths to emphasise the suffering involved in the Christian life. See, for instance, *Judge for Yourself!* and many of the journal entries under 'Imitation' (JP 2: 1833–1940).
240 Green 1993: 202.
241 Green 1993: 202.
242 Green's treatment of this issue is set in the context of his attempt to argue that Kant was a far greater influence on Kierkegaard than is normally recognised. See Green 1992: 190–7 for the full discussion.
243 Green 1993: 193.
244 Green 1993: 193.
245 Green 1993: 194.
246 Green 1993: 194.
247 John Hare talks here of the 'moral gap' (1996).
248 Green 1992: 195.
249 Green 1992: 196.

250 Green 1998: 278.
251 Outka 1993: 212.
252 Mulhall 2001: 354–88.
253 Mulhall 2001: 379.
254 Mulhall 2001: 379–80. On the significance of Isaac's carrying the wood, compare Tertullian: 'Isaac when delivered up by his father for sacrifice, himself carried the wood ... and did at that early date set forth the death of Christ, who when surrendered as a victim by his Father carried the wood of his own passion' (Tertullian 1972: 3.18, 225, cited in Lee 2000: 383).
255 Mulhall 2001: 383.
256 Davenport 2008a: 209–10.
257 Mulhall 2001: 384.
258 Mulhall 2001: 384.
259 Mulhall 2001: 384.
260 Mulhall 2001: 384.
261 Mulhall 2001: 384–5.
262 Mulhall 2001: 386.
263 Mulhall 2001: 386.
264 On this point, cf. Carlisle 2010: 167.

7

HOW RELIABLE IS JOHANNES DE SILENTIO?

There is one final important question we need to consider. We mentioned in Chapter 1 Kierkegaard's famous 'wish' and 'prayer' that his readers respect the distinctiveness of his pseudonyms. In the case of *Fear and Trembling*, this leads to the question of precisely what we should make of the point of view of Johannes de silentio. To what extent is he a reliable guide to the topic of faith? What degree of critical distance exists between Kierkegaard and Johannes? Bearing in mind the epigraph from Hamann with which *Fear and Trembling* begins, we have already suggested in the previous chapter that Johannes may be a messenger who does not fully understand the message that he delivers. So my reason for asking this question is not to speculate, for the sake of it, on what Kierkegaard's view of Johannes might be. Rather, I want to consider some important lines of criticism of Johannes that stem from the assumption that such a critical distance exists.[1] We can see this problem most clearly if we take seriously the fact that *Fear and Trembling* is less a book about Abraham than it is about its pseudonymous author's attempt to *relate himself to* Abraham, understood as a putative exemplary other – a paradigm exemplar of faith. The degree of reliability of the observations and analysis of the relater therefore matters. In this chapter, I consider three commentators who, for slightly different but related reasons, consider both that Johannes is unreliable, and that this is important to how we read the text. These commentators are Daniel Conway, Andrew Cross and Stephen Mulhall.[2] I shall conclude that Johannes is indeed a less than fully reliable guide to faith, but that while this is indeed significant for what we can and cannot learn from him, it is nowhere near as serious a concern as some have alleged. Indeed, much of Johannes' view of faith (in the 'formal' sense mentioned at the end of Chapter 6) stands up to scrutiny.

Numerous commentators have understood the critical distance between Kierkegaard and his pseudonyms in terms of the overall intelligence behind the pseudonyms setting up one or other of them for a fall. Apart from A in *Either/Or*, the pseudonymous work most commonly given this treatment is Climacus' *Postscript*. A relatively early such treatment is Henry Allison's classic article, though this way of reading Climacus was later developed by James Conant.[3] More recently, Stephen Mulhall has extended the Conant line of reading from the *Postscript* to its predecessor work, *Philosophical Fragments*, and also to *Fear and Trembling* and *Repetition*.[4] A similar suspicion to this seems to inform Daniel Conway's claim that in *Fear and Trembling*, Kierkegaard sets up Johannes de silentio – a representative of 'the spiritual crisis of the modern age'[5] – for failure.

DANIEL CONWAY AND ANDREW CROSS: JOHANNES' EVASION

According to Conway, we are intended to see Kierkegaard as a critic of the 'passional statis'[6] with which Johannes contents himself. Conway notes that Johannes' tone is 'confessional', suggesting that he needs to acquaint his readers with his own spiritual crisis. In other words, the book is ultimately about *Johannes*: 'he proffers his diagnosis of his impoverished generation as a means of directing our attention towards *him*'.[7]

Conway is surely right to claim that the book is 'about Johannes' in the sense that it is about his attempt to relate himself to Abraham as an exemplar of faith. But there is no need to conclude that there is necessarily anything fishy about this. The fact that Johannes acknowledges his limitations does not mean that what he has to say along the way can or should be discounted. Moreover, the first person nature of his 'confession' is far from unusual. Many other Kierkegaardian voices proceed in such a manner. We have noted more than once that Climacus – whose motivating question in the *Postscript* is 'How may I become a Christian?' – continually insists upon the importance of relating to ethical and religious matters in an engaged, first person manner, rather than in 'objective' abstraction. Moreover, in so far as this seems to be a view central to Kierkegaard, it cannot be used to argue for the existence of a critical distance between Kierkegaard and any one of his pseudonyms.

I think that Conway is being excessively suspicious in the following judgement of Johannes. He claims that Johannes aims to persuade us to 'honour his confession and not exhort him to "go further"'[8] than to 'fear and tremble' before the figure of Abraham. But this interpretation supposes that his attempts to understand Abraham are less than genuine, and I shall shortly suggest that there is good reason to resist this conclusion. Further, Conway alleges that Johannes' procedure manifests a deep spiritual laziness: it masks the 'unconfessed failing ... that he has neither the desire nor the wish nor the motivation to go any further'.[9] Despite the vast gulf between himself and Abraham, he wants us 'to allow him to remain content, to affirm him in his chosen stasis'.[10] But Conway acknowledges that this rests on the 'interpretative hunch' that what Johannes needs more than anything else is '*not* to look at himself'.[11] According to Conway, this is why he 'focuses his attention elsewhere – on Abraham [...] on his contemporaries, and on his readers'.[12] Again, I shall argue that this is a somewhat bowdlerised version of events, depending as it does upon overlooking or denying the genuineness of Johannes' continued attempt to *relate himself* to Abraham. Conway alleges that Johannes' 'disarming gesture of confessional self-disclosure thus diverts our attention (and his own) from the pressing question of *his own* interiority'.[13] We become distracted from the fact that he no longer aspires to Abrahamic faith.

I want to concentrate on this underlying assumption. I think that Conway's judgement is unfair to Johannes, but in order to show why, it will be profitable first to consider our second critic, Andrew Cross. Cross provides some interesting reasons, rooted in Kierkegaard's writing, for bringing against Johannes essentially the same charge of ethical and spiritual evasion and laziness. Let us turn, then, to Cross's criticism of Johannes.

ADMIRATION AND IMITATION

Cross draws attention to an important passage in *Practice in Christianity*, in which the Christian pseudonym Anti-Climacus demarcates two ways of relating oneself to an exemplary other. (The context of Anti-Climacus's discussion is what it means to imitate Christ, but as I have suggested elsewhere,[14] the passage is also of more general interest in relation to the question of relating oneself to an exemplar.) Anti-Climacus labels these two modes of relation 'admiration' and 'imitation', and he contrasts them thus:

> the admirer ... keeps himself personally detached; he forgets himself, forgets that what he admires in the other person is denied to him, and precisely this is what is beautiful, that he forgets himself in this way in order to admire. In the other situation [i.e. 'imitation'], I promptly begin to think about myself, simply and solely to think about myself. When I am aware of the other person, this unselfish, magnanimous person, I promptly begin to say to myself: Are you such as he is? I forget him completely in my self-concentration. And when I unfortunately discover that I am not like him at all, I have so much to do in and with myself that now, yes, now I have forgotten him completely – but, no, forgotten him I have not, but for me he has become a *requirement* upon my life, like a sting in my soul that propels me forward, like an arrow that wounds me. In the one case [i.e. 'admiration'], I vanish more and more, losing myself in what I admire, which becomes larger and larger; what I admire swallows me. In the other case ['imitation', or relating oneself to an exemplar], the other person vanishes more and more as he is assimilated into me or as I

> take him as one takes medicine, swallow him – but please note, because he is indeed a requirement upon me to give him back in replica, and I am the one who becomes larger and larger by coming more and more to resemble him.
>
> (PC 242–3)

On this view, it seems that the only appropriate relation to an exemplary other is one of apparently straightforward, immediate *emulation*. The exemplar discloses to me something about the 'higher self' that I have the capacity to become. This is what is lacking from 'admiration': the admired one makes such an impression on me that I 'forget' myself and my ethical or religious task. Such 'admiration' is thus ethically and religiously impotent, and thus the 'admirer' is ethically and religiously blameworthy.

Cross's criticism of Johannes is that his mode of relation to Abraham is an instance of precisely this form of impotent admiration. This is most clear, according to Cross, at the beginning of the 'Speech in Praise', where, as we recall, Johannes discusses the relation between a 'poet or speech-maker' and his 'hero'. The poet, we are told, 'has none of the skills of [his admired hero], he can only take pleasure in the hero. Yet he, too, no less than the hero, is happy; for the hero is so to speak that better nature of his in which he is enamoured, *though happy that it is not himself, that his love can indeed be admiration*' (FT 49, my emphasis). Moreover, 'he wanders round to everyone's door with his song and his speech, so that all can admire the hero as he does, be proud of the hero as he is' (FT 49). But, Cross argues, this is precisely the kind of relation to an exemplar that we saw Anti-Climacus criticise. If Johannes is such a poet, then he exemplifies, and aims to encourage in others, precisely this impotent form of admiration. And this is a wholly inappropriate way to relate oneself to an exemplar. Cross suggests that Kierkegaard is here indirectly exposing 'the wrongheadness of de silentio's stance toward his beloved Abraham'.[15] In support of this, he points us towards, as well as Anti-Climacus' distinction outlined above, the following slightly earlier passage:

> admiration is totally inappropriate and ordinarily is deceit, a cunning that seeks evasion and excuse. If I know a man whom I must esteem

because of his unselfishness, self-sacrifice, magnanimity, etc., then I am not to admire but am supposed to be like him; I am not to deceive and fool myself into thinking that it is something meritorious on my part, but on the contrary I am to understand that it is merely the invention of my sloth and spinelessness; I am to resemble him and *immediately begin* my effort to resemble him.

(PC 242, my emphasis)

To see the wider significance of this line of criticism, note that a similar criticism has been raised about a different tradition of writing on ethics, a tradition influenced by Wittgenstein. Onora O'Neill has complained about the use of examples made in 'Wittgensteinian' ethics. She complains that such ethical writing 'draws predominantly on literary examples', and that this has 'important implications'.[16] (Her discussion revolves largely around Peter Winch's discussion of Melville's Billy Budd, in which Captain Vere faces the dilemma of whether or not he must order Billy's execution for his violation of naval law.[17]) The 'important implication' relevant to our concerns here is O'Neill's allegation that literary examples 'impose a spectator perspective'.[18] The problem with this, she alleges, is that this means 'we do not have to do anything, beyond "deciding what we do want to say" [the phrase is Winch's] about the example and making sense of it. We do not have to decide whether to turn Raskolnikov in or whether to find Billy Budd guilty.'[19] Thus the 'atmosphere of moral seriousness and closeness to moral life' which surrounds Wittgensteinian writing on ethics is 'in some ways illusory'.[20] Ethics, for O'Neill, needs to be action-guiding in a way that focusing on literary examples cannot be. Hence her conclusion that 'the Wittgensteinian claim that moral thought can be reduced to "looking at particular examples and seeing what we do want to say about them" [Winch again] excludes elements that are indispensable if moral thought is to be not just a spectator sport but a guide to action'.[21] Somewhat like Cross, O'Neill would presumably condemn Johannes' intense focus on the Abraham example on the same grounds: its 'spectator perspective'.

A RESPONSE ON BEHALF OF JOHANNES

So is Cross's criticism fair? If so, this would have important ramifications for our reading of *Fear and Trembling*. But I want to argue that the hard and fast distinction between admiration and imitation apparently supported by Cross is untenable; that it is important to recognise an ethically and religiously significant middle ground; and that a large part of Johannes' procedure shows his tacit recognition of this middle ground. Johannes – who at one point explicitly *denies* being a poet (FT 116) – is certainly *not* the kind of *mere* 'poet and speech-maker' who wanders the country peddling his ethically and spiritually impotent admiration of Abraham. Even if he stands as an observer in relation to Abraham, he is an *engaged* observer. He has what Kierkegaard, in a journal note on *Fear and Trembling*, calls 'a passionate concentration'.[22] I want to suggest that one form the middle ground we are looking for could take is the Aristotelian 'perception' and attention discussed by Martha Nussbaum in her work on the ethical salience of literature (especially in *Love's Knowledge*[23]). A similar perception and attention, I suggest, is attainable from a sustained attention to exemplars, and this is what Johannes, in his sustained attention to Abraham, tacitly recognises. Further, I want to suggest that Johannes exhibits some key features of this perception.

Before coming to this, however, let me trail another possible response to Cross. Attention to the wider context of the second passage we quoted above shows that Anti-Climacus is criticising 'admiration' in relation to 'the universally human or that which every human being is capable of' (PC 242). This is further glossed as 'that which is not linked to any condition save that which is in everyone's power, the *universally human, that is, the ethical*, that which every being shall and therefore also presumably can do' (PC 242, my emphasis). The point at issue here is thus whether the 'faith' of an Abraham comes into this category. There are at least three reasons to suppose not. First, the project of *Fear and Trembling* makes very little sense other than against the background assumption that there is something *exceptional* about Abraham's faith. (Notwithstanding the relevance of Abraham as an exemplar of trust and hope, we noted in Chapter 6 – in our discussion of Evans — the stark differences between Abraham's situation and our contemporary situation.) Second, a key theme of the book is clearly that 'the ethical' and 'faith' can come into serious *prima facie* conflict — so any attempt to *assimilate* faith to 'the ethical' (understood as the 'universally human'), looks suspect. Third, faith is supposed to be a gift of divine grace. Bearing these points in mind, I suggest that if the exceptional faith of an Abraham is a gift, then far from being something 'which every being shall and therefore also presumably can do', it rather fits the following description, of that which one should not envy. Anti-Climacus insists: 'you shall not covet that which is denied to you; if it is given to someone else, rejoice that it was granted to him, and if what is given is of such a nature that it can become the object of admiration, then you shall admire it' (PC 241–2). More could be said about each of these three points. But I suggest that, in the light of them, it is far from obvious that Johannes would attract Anti-Climacus' censure.

Nevertheless, isn't there something objectionable about mere 'admiration' in relation to Abraham? After all, Anti-Climacus criticises those 'weak people' who are 'related to the admired one only through the imagination' and 'make the same demands that are made in the theater: to sit safe and calm oneself, detached from any actual relation to danger' (PC 244). Surely, if this is what admiration is, we cannot commend such a relation to Abraham as this?

The worry here, I think, is that, even if faith is a gift, and even if Abraham is exceptional, any proper relating of oneself to an exemplar must involve, in some sense, ethical or religious work on oneself. Perhaps, then, Johannes should be aiming to get closer to imitation of Abraham than admiration after all? The answer to this, I want to suggest, is yes: but with the emphasis on the 'closer'.

Let me explain by considering a second line of response to Cross. Consider Nussbaum's claim that ethics involves, as an essential element, appropriate *perception*, of the kind we get from sustained attention to the 'right' kind of literature. Indeed, it seems to be Nussbaum's view that this (Aristotelian) conception of ethics *requires* a literary embodiment. The basic idea here is that, in a novel or play, we are emotionally involved with the characters, seeing the world from their points of view through our active engagement with their thoughts, feelings and perceptions. There are two relevant points here. First, this is pretty much what Johannes is trying to do in relation to Abraham: imaginative identification, and with a character (viewed as an exemplar) in a particular narrative. Second, it is significant for Nussbaum that this engagement of our emotional and imaginative faculties takes place *outside our practical engagement in our own lives*. This is significant because such practical engagement can give rise to certain major 'sources of distortion that frequently impede our personal jealousies or angers or ... the sometimes blinding violence of our loves'.[24] Such sources of distortion are 'obstacles to correct vision'.[25] Engagement with a novel enables us to avoid them, and thus we find and experience 'love without possessiveness, attention without bias, involvement without panic'.[26] And this is itself an ethically valuable form of experience.

It is worth noting that Kierkegaard himself expresses a similar view in *Two Ages*. For literary 'persuasion' to be possible, he suggests, is needed 'the inviting intimacy of the cozy inner sanctum from which heated emotions and critical, dangerous decisions and extreme exertions are excluded, because there is no room or forbearance for such things' (TA 19). David Gouwens, citing Martin Thust, adds: 'Kierkegaard understands the virtue of literature to be that it operates first to lead one away from oneself: the aesthetic distancing functions positively as a mirror of possibilities ... And this objectivity is preparatory to a possible return to concrete actuality in subjective passion'.[27]

So, to repeat: this suggests that there could be an important middle ground between 'imitation' and 'admiration'. In the appropriate kind of engagement with the characters in a novel, I am able to be emotionally involved – thus I don't, unlike in 'admiration', 'vanish'. Yet my relation to the characters is not primarily and immediately to ask 'How does this impact on *my* life?', so it is not 'imitation' as Anti-Climacus characterises it. (Indeed, such a relation to a novel would typically look like a form of self-obsession.) Thus this is indeed a kind of middle ground. And if Nussbaum is right that this middle ground is an ethically (or, we might add, religiously) valuable form of experience, then it does not follow from the fact that Johannes does not 'immediately begin [his] effort to resemble' Abraham that he is ethically or religiously blameworthy for not doing so. My case rests, it would seem, on two things. First, the plausibility of the claim that something short of imitation can be an ethically valuable form of experience. (Cross, in his support of Anti-Climacus' distinction, simply seems to *assume* that this claim is false.) Second, whether Johannes' imaginative identification with Abraham has enough in common with Nussbaum's Aristotelian 'moral perception' to enable us to value it for the same reasons.

NUSSBAUM, MORAL PERCEPTION AND JOHANNES DE SILENTIO

What then are the salient features of the moral perception that Nussbaum commends? Perhaps her fullest response to this is in 'The Discernment of Perception: An Aristotelian Conception of Private and Public Rationality'.[28] Nussbaum aims to explain what Aristotle means by claiming that in practical reasoning, the 'discernment' of the correct choice lies in what he calls 'perception'. This involves 'some sort of complex responsiveness to the salient features of one's concrete situation'.[29] In fleshing out what this means, Nussbaum argues that there are three key interrelated dimensions of Aristotle's account: first, 'an attack on the claim that all valuable things are commensurable'; second, 'an argument for the priority of particular judgments to universals'; and third, 'a defense of the emotions and the imagination to rational choice'.[30] The latter two features play a significant role in *Fear and Trembling*. (The first has a more complicated role to play, as we shall later see.)

What are these roles? Johannes seems to agree with the Aristotelian rejection of the idea that 'rational choice can be captured in a system of general rules or principles which can then simply be applied to each new case'.[31] To see this, consider the following two claims made by Nussbaum for the Aristotelian position. 'The subtleties of a complex ethical situation must be seized in a confrontation with the situation itself ... Prior general formulations lack both the concreteness and the flexibility that is required.'[32] Relatedly, 'excellent choice cannot be captured in general rules, because it is a matter of fitting one's choice to the complex requirements of a concrete situation, taking all of its contextual features into account'.[33] This sensitivity to context is surely important and, as I shall shortly try to show, it appears to reflect the view that Johannes brings to the Abraham story.

Neither does Johannes overlook the importance to practical reason of emotion and imagination. (Nussbaum's opponents here are those who think of emotion and imagination as being *opposed* to reason; who place the emotions and the imagination within, as it were, the irrational part of the soul. She makes this charge, rightly or wrongly, against Platonists, Kantians and utilitarians.[34]) It should be quite clear that Johannes hardly falls into this camp. Recall the importance he attaches to the often overlooked 'anguish' of Abraham, and the centrality of imagination to his own attempt to engage with and 'understand' Abraham.

So I want to provide some textual evidence for the claim that Johannes' attention to the Abraham narrative involves an appropriate form of perception, involving due attention to particularity, and giving an appropriate role to emotion and the imagination. Doing so casts serious doubt on the claim that Johannes represents ethically impotent admiration.

As we have seen, it is clear from the Preface that what motivates Johannes is a passionate commitment to the idea that faith should be taken seriously and given its due. In the 'Attunement', we encountered the man who, from childhood onwards, has been returning to the story of Abraham, 'his enthusiasm' for it becoming 'stronger and stronger' the older he gets (FT 44). As we pointed out, it is reasonable to assume that this man is Johannes himself. And we saw his attempts to understand Abraham continuing in the four 'sub-Abrahams' – versions of the story that fall short of Abraham – of which the bulk of the 'Attunement' consists. That section ends with the following portrait: 'In these and similar ways this man of whom we speak thought about these events. Every time he came home from a journey to the mountain in Moriah he collapsed in weariness, clasped his hands, and said: "Yet no one was as great as Abraham; who is able to understand him?"' (FT 48). So note that even if this man is an observer, he is an *engaged* observer: someone trying to understand Abraham.

This becomes more explicit in the 'Speech in Praise of Abraham'. Johannes attempts to imagine himself into Abraham's situation ('All was now lost! ... That glorious treasure, as old as the faith in Abraham's heart, many many years older than Isaac, the fruit of Abraham's life, hallowed with prayers, ripened in struggle – the blessing on Abraham's lips, this fruit was now to be plucked out of season and have no meaning; for what meaning could there be in it if Isaac was to be sacrificed!' (FT 53). And so on.) Moreover, he aims to get his reader to do likewise, specifically, to compare himself to Abraham. (When God speaks to Abraham, Abraham boldly answers: 'Here I am'. Johannes asks us whether we would have had such courage, or whether we would have scarpered. 'When you saw, far off, the heavy fate approaching, did you not say to the mountains, "hide me", to the hills "fall on me"? Or, if you were stronger, did your feet nevertheless drag along the way?' [FT 54–5].)

Moreover, this attempted imaginative identification includes attention to the *particularities* of Abraham's situation. A large part of Johannes' method involves contrasting Abraham's apparently forthcoming loss of his son with superficially similar instances of such loss (for instance, the fact that Abraham is – unlike Agamemnon, for example – called upon to make the sacrifice himself [FT 55]). This results from his commitment to the idea that it is rare to find someone who 'can tell the story and give it its due' (FT 55). 'Giving the story its due', I take it, includes not conflating it with superficially similar stories. This attention to the particular continues throughout the book, and underpins Johannes' repeated attempts to get closer to understanding Abraham by comparisons with figures who might at first sight be analogous, but according to Johannes turn out on closer inspection not to be: the knight of infinite resignation (Preamble); the tragic hero (Problema I); and the instances of aesthetic rather than religious concealment (Problema III). It is precisely such nuanced differences that are likely to be overlooked by an overly generalist approach – and that is why Johannes avoids such an approach.

Moreover, the charge of impotent admiration seems to be at odds with Johannes' insistence that the Abraham story will only be 'glorious' if we are willing 'to "labour and be heavy laden"'

(FT 58) in our attempts to understand it. Part of what this amounts to, he implies, is recognising the 'anguish' of the story: precisely that 'anguish' that the spiritually 'squeamish' try to 'forget' (FT 58). Relatedly, in Problema I he criticises 'flirt[ing] with the outcome aesthetically', wanting 'nothing of the fear, the distress, the paradox' (FT 92). Moreover, he explicitly condemns the 'mindless praise' that effectively says that 'because Abraham has acquired proprietary rights to the title of great man, ... whatever he does is great, [yet] if anyone else does the same it is a sin, a crying sin' (FT 60). That is, he is critical precisely of those who want to evade the tough questions raised by the Abraham story: whether Abraham's action is justifiable; whether, and by what account, he stands as exemplary; and so on. Johannes' praise of Abraham needs to be set against this background, and the related assertion that 'If one hasn't the courage to think this thought through, to say that Abraham was a murderer, then surely it is better to acquire that courage than to waste time on undeserved speeches in his praise ... For my own part I don't lack the courage to think a thought whole' (FT 60). Further, and most importantly, Johannes stresses the significance of whether and how Abraham should impact upon *us*: 'for why bother remembering a past that cannot be made into a present?' (FT 60).

It seems, then, that Johannes, far from being set up by Kierkegaard to take a fall, is well aware of Cross's worry. In 'speaking of Abraham', Johannes does *not* mean heaping upon him 'mindless praise', nor is this what he does. The above concerns have to be considered before Johannes can conclude, almost a quarter of the way into the book, that 'It should be all right ... to speak about Abraham' (FT 61). It is 'all right' because Johannes has finally convinced himself that we can do so without the result being impotent admiration.

Consider a possible objection at this point. Johannes does talk of his being 'virtually annihilated' (FT 62) by the thought of Abraham: that is, of his inability to 'go further' in his relation to this exemplar. Might this be the ethical evasion that 'admiration' sponsors? I don't see any need to jump to this suspicious conclusion. Johannes insists that the 'monstrous paradox that is the content of Abraham's life' makes him (Johannes) 'constantly repulsed, and my thought, *for all its passion*, is unable to enter into it ... I strain every muscle to catch sight of it, but the same instant I become paralysed' (FT 62–3). That is, I see no conclusive reason to suppose that Johannes' limits in relation to Abraham *precede* his attempt to compare himself with Abraham. Such a comparison is integral to relating oneself to an exemplary other, and if Johannes were ducking this, he would indeed be culpable. But we cannot infer from the fact that Johannes cannot 'go on' beyond a certain point that he has made no genuine effort to try. It is what he sees as Abraham's sheer incomprehensibility that causes Johannes' problem – not his unwillingness to try to relate himself to him. Consider here Johannes' assertion that he would love to know where to find a knight of faith, and the claim that if he ever did find one, he would 'watch every minute how he makes the movements', for 'this marvel concerns me absolutely' (FT 68). Is this evasive 'admiration' speaking? Again, I think not. Although Johannes does describe himself as 'admiring', he insists that he would 'divide [his] time between looking at him [the knight of faith he discovers] *and practicing the movements myself*' (FT 68, my emphasis).

I suppose it is possible for my opponent simply to suggest that Johannes is just lying, or is self-deceived, in claiming all this. It is in the nature of such a hermeneutics of suspicion that it is difficult to answer (though that doesn't make it correct!). One of Conway's suggestions is a rather sophisticated version of such suspicion: that it is precisely by picking as his exemplar someone as impenetrable as Abraham (as Johannes presents him), that Johannes lets himself off the ethical and religious hook. The 'potentially solvable riddle of his own interiority' gets perpetually deferred by his focus on 'the unsolvable riddle of Abraham':[35] of Abraham's impenetrable interiority. At one point, I thought that I would end up agreeing with this conclusion. Somewhat to my surprise, on rereading the text with the specific charge against Johannes in mind, I discovered considerable textual evidence that speaks against it (some of which I have just cited). At the very least, I would be intrigued to know what my opponent would say about this material. Let me make clear that I am not trying to deny the importance of 'imitation', or to downplay the potential dangers of ethically and religiously impotent 'admiration'. What I am denying is the automatic assumption that the 'reflection', if we can call it that, in which Johannes engages in relation to Abraham is sheer evasion. In *Two Ages* – a text which discusses the dangers of reflection as ethically impotent – Kierkegaard actually speaks approvingly of 'admiration', further suggesting that it is dangerous to infer, from the fact that Johannes' 'admires' Abraham, that this admiration can be condemned.[36]

My opponent seems wedded to a position analogous to that of O'Neill in her criticism of the Wittgensteinians. The plausibility of O'Neill's complaint depends upon there being a clear-cut distinction between reflecting or passing judgment on the actions of others (compare: another's interiority), and deciding what we ought to do ourselves (compare: one's own interiority). She complains: 'Typically the focus is on examples of completed action in a context that invites moral consideration or assessment, rather than on less complete examples of a situation that raises moral problems or dilemmas, as though the primary exercise of moral judgment were to *reflect* or *pass judgment* on what has been done rather than to decide among possible actions'.[37] In other words, as D. Z. Phillips puts it, 'the problems depicted in [literary examples] are not *our* problems'.[38]

The most obvious response to this charge is one made by Phillips, namely that 'a problem does not have to be ours before we can learn from it'.[39] Recognition of this point is central to any attempt to understand what is involved in relating oneself to an exemplar. The central point for which I want to argue here is that an ethical or religious outlook – and one's actions – could be radically changed by an encounter with a literary or other narrative and the exemplars they contain. (Indeed, surely this is one of the key points of religious narratives.) Contrary to O'Neill's claim that literary examples impose a spectator perspective, Noel Carroll has argued that 'narratives *involve* audiences in processes of moral reasoning and deliberation'.[40] (This seems similar to Nussbaum's line.) Moreover, they do so in a way more complex than the rather mechanistic use of examples that O'Neill would support. Rather than ethics using '"stock", schematic examples'[41] as a direct guide to action – O'Neill's explicit recommendation – Carroll suggests that learning from a narrative is not a simple *consequence* of engaging with it, but rather that 'understanding the work, enlarging one's moral understanding, and learning from the narrative are all part and parcel of the same process ... [of] comprehending or following the narrative'.[42] Thus ethics (and religion) does not have to be action-guiding in the sense that I am directly told what to do in *this* case by *that* example. What 'seeing what to do' amounts to – the development of what Aristotle calls practical wisdom – might be far less clear cut than this, and might require precisely the sort of imaginative attention and identification we have been discussing, and that I am suggesting Johannes exemplifies. Note that this is especially true if we hold, with Evans, that while in some respects Abraham is a 'guiding star', in others, the gulf between his situation and ours is enormous.[43]

Nussbaum's insistence on the importance of moral perception reserves a special role for certain novels (especially those of Henry James). But while a work with the richness and 'absorbing plottedness'[44] of a novel may be particularly well suited to the moral attention under discussion, there seems no *a priori* reason to suppose that briefer narratives making sufficient demands on our imaginative capacities could not fulfil the same role. While I am inclined to agree with Nussbaum, against O'Neill, that 'schematic philosophers' examples almost always lack the particularity, the emotive appeal, the absorbing plottedness, the variety and indeterminacy, of good fiction',[45] Nussbaum effectively acknowledges that shorter fictions than novels can have such ethical salience (for instance, her discussion of 'Learning to Fall', a twelve-page short story by Ann Beattie, in the title essay of *Love's Knowledge*). This raises the question of why an imaginative engagement with the Abraham narrative, of the kind exemplified by Johannes, cannot possess the same quality. Conway claims: 'Modernity will be redeemed not through an understanding of the interiority of Abraham or any other archaic exemplar, but through an understanding of *our own* interiority, riddled as it is with self-contempt'.[46] But why suppose that this is an either/or? Why not require both; why not suppose that our understanding of our own interiority could be greatly *aided* by the attempt to relate ourselves to exemplars (archaic or otherwise)? The fact that there are specific problems with relating oneself to Johannes' Abraham does not seem to have prevented readers of Kierkegaard from finding much of significance about faith, religious forms of life falling short of true faith, the ethical, and so on, in this text. In conclusion, is Cross' (and, it seems, Conway's) objection – that because Johannes does not directly 'imitate' Abraham, he must be engaged in a morally and religiously culpable impotent 'admiration' – dependent upon the same assumption as O'Neill, namely that imaginative identification has to be directly action-guiding if it is to be defensible?

Finally, recall Nussbaum's point that there is ethical value in engaging our emotional and imaginative faculties *outside our practical engagement in our own lives*, owing to those major 'sources of distortion' that are 'obstacles to correct vision'.[47] It is this that Johannes' emotionally and imaginatively engaged reflection on Abraham provides, and yet which Anti-Climacus' advice to 'think about myself, simply and solely to think about myself' potentially lacks. Of course excessive reflection brings with it the danger of potential evasion. But let us not lose sight of the contrary danger. The very urgency of the immediate passionate engagement which Anti-Climacus seems to demand brings with it the danger of overlooking the ethical value that can emerge from engaging our emotional and imaginative faculties outside our immediate practical engagement in our own lives. (A sort of 'more haste, less speed' of the ethical or religious life?)

We might even want to claim for Johannes something of what Nussbaum claims for Aristotle. Nussbaum suggests that

> certain forms of moral philosophy – above all Aristotle's – are equipped to form a friendship with the reader that avoids ... philosophical seductions [to excessive abstraction] and illuminates the contributions of literature. For Aristotelian moral philosophy remains close to the world of particulars, directing the reader's attention to these and to experience – including the emotions of experience – as sources of ethical insight. At the same time, this sort of moral philosophy has the dialectical power to compare alternative conceptions perspicuously, contrasting their salient features. For this reason it can be an important ally of the literary work.[48]

We have seen, first, that in his sustained focus on the Abraham narrative, Johannes too 'remains close to the world of particulars'. Second, his stress on the importance of imaginative identification with, and the 'anguish' of, Abraham, shows his recognition that 'experience – including the emotions of experience' is a source of ethical (and religious) insight. And third, the fact that he does not 'vanish' in his reflection on Abraham contributes to his ability to preserve sufficient critical distance from Abraham to 'compare alternative conceptions perspicuously, contrasting their salient features' (knight of faith from knight of infinite resignation, Abraham from 'sub-Abrahams' etc.). *Pace* Cross and Conway, we can see that Johannes' professed 'admiration' of Abraham need *not* be judged as ethically impotent. He is not the kind of poet he condemns. Indeed, we might even say that he has played a role for us, his readers, somewhat akin to that of the Aristotelian moral philosopher valorised by Nussbaum. The case against Johannes de silentio on the charge of impotent admiration is not proven.

STEPHEN MULHALL: JOHANNES AND THE LITERAL

However, there is another kind of objection that has been raised against Johannes. We return here to an issue raised towards the end of our discussion of Problema III in Chapter 5. There we pointed out how strange it might seem that Johannes, having insisted throughout upon Abraham's inability to 'speak', now not only accepts that Abraham *does* speak, but claims to understand Abraham's 'total presence' (FT 142) in what he says. Abraham, remember, says: 'My son, God will provide himself a lamb for the burnt offering' (FT 139, 142).[49] Of this 'last word', Johannes remarks: 'If it had not occurred the whole incident would lack something. If it had been a different word everything might dissolve in confusion' (FT 140).

Up to a point, Johannes seems aware of the deep water into which he seems to be getting himself here. He recognises the need to explain, given what he has been saying about Abraham's inability to speak, how he can now recognise Abraham as saying anything at all (FT 141–2). But his explanation is as follows: 'First and foremost he doesn't say anything, and that is his way of saying what he has to say. His answer to Isaac has the form of irony, for it is always irony to say something and yet not say it' (FT 142).

What is going on here? Stephen Mulhall draws attention to Johannes' related claim that 'Only one word of [Abraham's] has been preserved, his only reply to Isaac, which we can take to be sufficient evidence that he had not spoken previously' (FT 139). This seems a bizarre claim. By the same reasoning, the fact that only certain fragments of Heraclitus have been preserved would provide 'sufficient evidence' that Heraclitus never wrote anything else: absurd reasoning leading to a false conclusion. Moreover, as Mulhall points out, it is not true to the text of Genesis to say that Abraham speaks only once. According to that text, Abraham actually speaks on two occasions prior to this. When God calls his name, he answers 'Behold, here I am'.[50] And on the third day of the journey, to the young men who have accompanied him he says: 'Abide ye here with the ass; and I and the lad will go yonder and worship, and come again to you'.[51] Mulhall describes Johannes' reasoning here as 'a kind of parody of a paradox, an absurdly contradictory attempt to have his cake in one sentence only to eat it in the next'.[52]

Nevertheless there is a kind of sense to what Johannes seems to be arguing. Abraham's 'total presence' can be detected in what he says in so far as it is consistent with both his willingness to sacrifice Isaac (in which case the 'lamb' would be Isaac himself) and his belief 'on the strength of the absurd' that he will not have to sacrifice Isaac or that Isaac will be restored (in which case the 'lamb' would be something other than Isaac). However, Mulhall argues, there are problems with this. His first objection is that by characterising Abraham's reply as 'ironic', Johannes thereby associates Abraham with Socrates, whom we saw Johannes characterise as an 'intellectual tragic hero'. But we also know that one of the main contrasts Johannes makes is between the tragic hero and the knight of faith. 'Consequently, by associating Abraham with Socrates even by analogy, de silentio undercuts a central element of his own dialectical endeavour.'[53]

This objection is not really compelling. To be so, we would have to accept the automatic move from 'irony' to 'Socrates'.

While it is true that Socrates is often Kierkegaard's exemplar of irony, he is certainly not the only one. In his most sustained treatment of irony, the dissertation *The Concept of Irony*, Kierkegaard also deals in some detail with various 'romantic ironists' such as Friedrich Schlegel, Tieck and Solger.

But Mulhall's second objection seems, at least *prima facie*, much more compelling. He points out that, *pace* Johannes, Abraham's words do *not* 'say nothing'. Far from being just empty or nonsensical, these words are in fact ambiguous between two discrete possibilities: one in which the lamb is Isaac (if Abraham had to go through with the sacrifice) and one in which God provides an actual lamb (and so Isaac is spared).[54] But once we focus our attention on these two discrete possibilities, we are likely to notice something else: that neither in fact comes true. Isaac is spared, and so is not the sacrificial lamb. But neither is an actual lamb provided: the sacrificial animal is in fact a ram. In both its intended metaphorical sense and its literal sense, therefore, Abraham's utterance turns out to be inaccurate.

Mulhall anticipates but resists the possible objection that the fact that the sacrificial animal is a mature rather than a young member of the species is 'a little too pedestrian to be convincing'.[55] From a Christian perspective, the possibility that Abraham's utterance has a prophetic dimension of which he is unaware is deeply significant: the lamb that God provides will turn out to be Christ, the 'Lamb of God'. But even from Johannes' own perspective, Abraham's failure to avoid literal falsehood should be significant, since as we have seen in his discussion of the evasive preacher and the Luke passage, Johannes insists on the importance of *the literal*. A focus on this fact is, in my view, the single most important aspect of Mulhall's critique.[56]

JOHANNES AND THE LITERAL

Let us unpack the significance of this in more detail. In Mulhall's words, Johannes criticises the preacher for 'moving away ... from the concrete details of Abraham's situation by substituting more general or universal terms for the less palatable ones the biblical text actually employs'.[57] What Johannes instead implicitly recommends is 'a model of reading which reverses this process – one in which these preacherly generalities are exchanged for (translated back into) the linguistic and experiential particulars from which they originated'.[58] Instead of rushing to extract a general lesson from a biblical text ('Always give to God the best!'), we should take seriously the idea that the significance of a text might lie in its specificity. Its words may be incommensurable 'with other words, and hence with other tales that might be told by their means; we must use what we have been given rather than subjecting it to transformation'.[59] Mulhall sees this as the point of Johannes providing us with alternative figures (tragic heroes; knights of infinite resignation; sub-Abrahams) who appear superficially to be similar to Abraham but turn out on closer investigation not to be. 'These endlessly proliferating alternative narrative possibilities are designed to bring the one narrative actuality into stark and literal life – to make us, as readers and spiritual beings, refuse to trade the tale we have been given for ones of our own (and our own culture's) imagining, to recognise that its significance is not expressible in other terms.'[60]

There seems, then, to be a contradiction between Johannes' insistence that biblical texts should be taken literally, and both his claim that when Abraham speaks, he does not say anything, and his failure to notice that in fact what he says turns out to be false. Mulhall now raises the question of how we are to respond to this. Is Johannes just confused but unaware of it? Or is his confusion some kind of 'signal', a piece of indirect communication 'that he expects his readers to work a little harder to earn their bread'?[61] Mulhall sets out to reread the text with this latter possibility in mind.

I shall not attempt to give a full exegesis of this rereading, but rather to draw attention to some of its most salient features. First, recall *Fear and Trembling*'s epigraph. The ability of Tarquin's son to understand the message coded in his father's behaviour in the poppy field is an instance of what can quite literally be said without speaking. Moreover, the fact that the son understands the message not to be about literally cutting the heads off the poppies, but about putting to death or exiling Gabii's leading citizens (its 'tallest poppies'), shows that he grasps that the message needs to be understood not literally but metaphorically or allegorically.

HOW RELIABLE IS JOHANNES DE SILENTIO? 241

Mulhall makes two suggestions on the basis of this. First, that we might view Abraham as 'an oblivious messenger between God and Isaac',[62] someone who fails to see the exact sense in which the words he is constrained to use, about God himself providing the lamb, need to be understood allegorically rather than literally. That is, as we mentioned before, Abraham's words have a prophetic value – their forecasting of the coming of Christ – of which Abraham himself is unaware. Second, the utilisation of this epigraph means that the text's author wants to be interpreted allegorically: 'to think of his emphasis upon the literal as exemplary of an obliviousness to the true nature of religious uses of language, an oblivion that his readers are intended to overcome in the end, just as Abraham eventually overcomes his own misunderstandings on Mount Moriah'.[63]

Mulhall's way of putting this suggests that the author he has in mind is Johannes rather than Kierkegaard. Mulhall gives the impression that he thinks of Johannes not so much as being set up by Kierkegaard for a fall, but as himself encouraging us into certain ways of thinking and then – if we have been prepared to work hard enough for our spiritual bread – pulling the rug from under our feet. But we cannot be sure whether to credit the epigraph to Johannes or to Kierkegaard. So there remains the possibility that, as Cross and Conway think, Johannes is oblivious to his own errors, confusions and misplaced emphases. If that was the case, then we would have to see the epigraph as being in Kierkegaard's voice: as his way of signalling that Johannes is himself the messenger oblivious to key aspects of his message.

In turning to the economic imagery of the Preface and the Epilogue, Mulhall cites what we have seen Johannes describe as the 'necessary deception' of the Dutch merchants dumping spices in order to raise the price of the remainder. At the end of Chapter 5, it looked as though this was Johannes' way of ending his book by suggesting that his strategy has been to raise the price of faith. But Mulhall raises the following more complex, but intriguing, possibility:

[D]oes the deception lie rather in the fact that, by exchanging the image of a bargain for that of a luxury, de silentio hardly escapes the metaphor of economic exchange: a luxury good is still a good, still purchasable and hence still commensurable with other goods in the system. Perhaps a proper evaluation of the goods of the spirit rather requires an escape from the imagery of economic exchange altogether, and thus from the idea that every form of language use can always be evaluated in terms of a single dimension of meaning – say, the literal.[64]

Interestingly, this clearly parallels the first of the three points we saw Nussbaum use in fleshing out her account of Aristotelian moral perception. Earlier in this chapter, we touched upon the second and third of these: the priority of the particular judgements to universals, and the centrality of the emotions and imagination to ethical choice. The first point, which we did not discuss there, was Aristotle's attack on the claim that all valuable things are commensurable: his idea that there is no single scale in virtue of which they can all be compared and ranked. In response to Cross, we claimed that Johannes uses the second and third aspects of this Aristotelian picture. If Mulhall is right, he also uses the first point indirectly, by (deliberately) failing to take it on board and leaving us to see the problem with failing to do so. If, on the other hand, Johannes is Kierkegaard's fall guy, then Johannes' failure to recognise this first point is Kierkegaard's way of getting us to see its significance. Either way, we would be supposed to see that not all valuable things are commensurable, and that there is thus no ground for the claim that taking a text *seriously* necessarily means taking it *literally*.

To the extent that the Christian allegorical reading discussed in Chapter 6 is plausible, this aspect of Mulhall's reading might strike us as convincing. But there is a problem when Mulhall tries to shed further doubt on Johannes on the basis of the Attunement. He has two worries about the man – almost certainly Johannes himself – who is presented as being obsessed with the Abraham story. First, Mulhall notes Johannes' 'ironic dig at scholarship in comparison to pious simplicity'[65] in suggesting that part of the man's problem is that he 'knew no Hebrew; had he known Hebrew then perhaps it might have been easy for him to understand the story of Abraham' (FT 44). Mulhall questions whether Johannes' irony or sarcasm here does not contain a literal truth: 'if our goal is to understand the biblical text in all its concrete specificity, how could it not be relevant to understand the meanings of the words in which it was originally composed? Can the problems of translation simply be dismissed as a distraction?'[66] Second, Mulhall criticises the man's obsession with Abraham, which he takes to involve focusing exclusively on his relationship to Abraham, as opposed to his relationship with God. This must be a 'fundamental error. Attempting to make oneself present to a climactic episode in another person's relationship with God does not amount to making oneself present to God; rather, it provides a potentially inexhaustible distraction from that task, and implies not only a mistaken sense of priorities but a complete lack of clarity about the only real point of reading the Bible. Can we really expect this mode of reading to clarify the true nature of religious faith?'[67]

I have two objections to Mulhall's line here. The first is internal inconsistency, since it seems to me that these two claims are seriously in tension with each other. If focusing on Abraham provides a 'potentially inexhaustible distraction' from one's own God-relationship, why cannot the same thing be said about thinking one needs to teach oneself Hebrew (and Greek, and Aramaic) in order the understand the Bible? Whereas, all other things being equal, it would indeed appear to be an advantage to be able to understand these languages, Kierkegaard often insists that the Christian message, and an appropriate God-relationship, is available to all, regardless of levels of education.[68] (Indeed, he sometimes suggests – as does Climacus – that the well-educated intellectual is sometimes at a disadvantage, in so far as scholarly equivocation and evasion can easily get in the way of the appropriation into one's life of the Christian message, a view that would seem in line with Johannes' ironic dig about needing to learn Hebrew.) But my second objection is perhaps more important. We can draw on what we have already said in response to Cross to cast doubt upon Mulhall's assumption that a focus on Abraham necessarily amounts to an evasion of one's own God-relationship. While accepting the general point that this *could* happen – just as feeling the need to learn one more ancient language before thinking about one's relationship to God *could* happen – there is no reason to suppose that this is a necessary or even likely eventuality. Such an assumption ignores that feature we drew upon Nussbaum to see: that the way to come to better self-understanding often includes coming to a better understanding of others – especially those, such as Abraham, held to be exemplary. If Johannes is aiming to understand what is involved in having faith, and if Abraham is an exemplar of faith, then – the dangers of evasion notwithstanding – it is no crime to devote considerable energy to trying to understand Abraham. Given the interrelation between self-understanding (including the kind of self-understanding that is integral to a God-relationship) and understanding exemplary others, Mulhall has no grounds for his assumption that Johannes' Abraham-focus amounts to focusing 'exclusively' on his relation to Abraham as opposed to his relation to God. The former may be a stepping stone towards the latter. Indeed, if it were not, why would the Bible consist of narratives about religious exemplars such as Abraham at all? For instance, discussing a negative religious exemplar – the priest in the parable of the Good Samaritan who passes by on the other side[69] – Kierkegaard insists: 'when you read, "But by chance a priest came down that same road, and when he saw him, he passed by", then you shall say to yourself, "It is I ... This priest is I myself. Alas to think that I could be so callous ..."' (FSE 40). Imaginative engagement with biblical exemplars – positive and negative – is, in Kierkegaard's view, a vital part of how a God-relationship is developed and deepened.

However, let us turn to Mulhall's general point that Johannes is wrong to attach so much importance to the literal. Consider the following remarks from Johannes:

> There has been no want of sharp intellects and sound scholars who have found analogies to [the story of Abraham]. Their wisdom amounts to the splendid principle that basically everything is the same. If one looks a little closer I doubt very much whether one will find in the whole world a single analogy, except a later one that proves nothing[.]
> (FT 85)

Given what we said in Chapter 6, it would seem that the later analogy is Christ. But if so, we should doubt whether this 'proves nothing' – a phrase Johannes uses to insist on the importance of the literal. Indeed, as Mulhall points out, Christ's standard mode of discourse deals not in the literal, but in parable. 'And by definition, parables are not to be taken literally; they can be understood only by analogy, by understanding the symbolic significance of the events they literally describe.'[70] This brings us back to the issue we already addressed in Chapter 6: the need to see in the Abraham story its symbolic, anagogical significance.

JOHANNES' WRONG TURNINGS?

Mulhall claims that there are two key points at which we can see Johannes 'going off the rails'.[71] The first, of course, is to do with his over-emphasis on the literal. The problem occurs as Johannes' 'legitimate desire' to get believers to pay attention to the specifics of biblical narratives such as the Abraham story gradually gets transformed into 'the principle that the only legitimate mode of interpreting those texts is in accordance with its literal meaning'.[72] This transformation ultimately leads to 'the all but unmissable contradiction' between Johannes' 'talk of Abraham as incapable of speech and his admission of the centrality of what he does say to the import of his tale and his life'.[73] A return to the last passage from *Fear and Trembling* quoted above will shed light on how Johannes is allegedly going wrong here. Contrary to what he claims in this passage, there is no good reason to equate analogy with the principle that 'everything is the same'. On the contrary, any legitimate interpretation of a text must answer 'to the details of the text itself. Interpretation by analogy ... contends that the specificity of a text, the full depth of its distinctiveness and difference from other texts, emerges only when we move from the level of literal meaning to that of the figurative.'[74] Johannes' most glaring error, then, ultimately stems from his fixation on the literal, a fixation that Mulhall thinks shows a serious misunderstanding of the nature of religious language.

This is a very interesting objection. However, it has recently been countered by Jeffrey Hanson in an important contribution to this debate. While not referring directly to eschatological trust or hope, Hanson's overall argument supports the line for which we argued in Chapter 6. Abraham's words in Genesis 22:8, that God himself will provide a lamb for the burnt offering, 'give voice to a trust *that* God will provide while remaining completely indeterminate with respect to *how* God will provide'.[75] In this sense they are, for Hanson, 'a model of all communication about faith'.[76] This is because they are 'both true and beautiful', and yet 'gesture toward a truth that eludes his grasp'.[77]

Hanson makes this argument in such a way as to engage with the second point at which Mulhall sees Johannes going off the rails. Mulhall's objection here is that in order to preserve the distinctiveness of religion and ethics, Johannes 'applies Hegelian dialectics to Abraham's ordeal'.[78] As we have seen, the problemata pose interconnected problems for a Hegelian view of religious belief (for instance, Problema I's argument that, if the ethical is the universal, then Hegel should condemn Abraham as a murderer). Here is Mulhall's gloss on Johannes' overall strategy:

> [I]n his desire to contradict the Hegelian equation of the religious and the ethical, de silentio constructs a depiction of Abraham (and hence of faith) by simply negating the three Hegelian claims about the ethical. But he thereby leaves the accuracy of those original claims unquestioned; his rejection of Hegelian claims about the realm of faith takes for granted the truth of Hegelian claims about the ethical by asserting that they have no application to faith – that faith is the negation of the ethical (as Hegel understands that realm) ... de silentio's declared hatred of all things Hegelian leads him to characterise the religious realm as a kind of mirror-image of Hegel's view of ethics. He never stops to consider that Hegel's illicit equation of the ethical and the religious realms might be as much a consequence of his misinterpretation of the ethical realm as it is of the religious realm – that the equation depends upon a misunderstanding of both relata.[79]

My objection to this echoes an earlier objection in Chapter 6. The claim that Johannes 'never stops to consider' that there might be a problem with Hegel's characterisation of the ethical seems highly dubious. As we suggested in Chapter 6 in support of Mooney and against Green, 'the ethical is the universal' can be seen precisely as the view under scrutiny, rather than a claim Johannes is making or a view he is taking for granted.

Hanson adds something important to this objection. He argues that Mulhall too offers us a false opposition: between the literal and the figurative. Rather, the way Abraham's 'final word' should be read is 'both literally and figuratively and both at once'.[80] What does this mean?

For Hanson, Abraham's 'prophetic utterance' demonstrates 'an elasticity that is an important ingredient in Abraham's faith'.[81] What he predicts does come true, but not in the sense in which 'his words intended'.[82] But we should not read this as merely 'figurative'. Drawing on an article by David Kangas on Kierkegaard's ruminations on 'the gift' in the light of James 1:17,[83] Hanson charges Mulhall with himself leaving in place 'a bedrock Hegelian principle, namely, that the literal or conceptual and the figurative or metaphorical are insurmountably heterogeneous and prioritized, with the conceptual of course always higher than the metaphorical.'[84] Mulhall simply inverts, rather than fundamentally challenges, this opposition.

It must be admitted that Hanson's route to this position is via discussion of a veronymous discourse, so Mulhall might appeal to the pseudonymous status of *Fear and Trembling* (and the purported limits of the pseudonym) to defend his position. Nonetheless, even if Hanson's strategy does not block off such counter-objections from his opponent, it will be illuminating to consider the alternative view of the figurative and the literal that he goes on to present. He proposes that Abraham's remark in Genesis 22:8 should be read neither solely allegorically, nor solely literally, but 'with a view to uncovering a truth that is available only as a gift to the inner person, where the individual is transformed by an encounter by the truth that is irreducible to discrete orders of discourse'.[85] Through a discussion of Problema III, and of Johannes' contrast between Abraham and withholding speech 'in defiance of ethical responsibility' or 'in deference to aesthetic fittingness',[86] Hanson argues that Abraham's utterance manages to preserve both aesthetic fittingness and the ethical requirement of a kind of truth-telling (however elusive): his 'final word' is 'elegant, economical, elusive, and forecasts the happy ending for which every reader longs'.[87] Note that this reading preserves, in an important sense, the idea that the existence-spheres are cumulative.[88] Going on to compare speech – neither solely literal nor solely figurative – with proclamations of love,[89] Hanson's conclusion seems to support our Chapter 6 position rather strikingly:

> To speak out a truth that is neither literal nor figurative is to adopt a whole new mode of speech, a mode of expression that reaffirms confidences and trusts – 'The Lord will provide' – while conceding that even the speaker herself has no idea *how* the Lord will provide.[90]

He adds:

> Abraham's utterance is both in form and content the paradigmatic speech about faith. Faith trusts God will provide while remaining open to the unexpected ways in which that provision will express itself: This is both *what* Abraham says and *how* he says it. His wisdom speaks *truly* and *beautifully* about a truth that the speaker cannot claim to possess but by which he is possessed.[91]

If the above line of objection is on the mark, then Mulhall's claim about *Fear and Trembling*'s strategy is, while intriguing, not compelling.[92] He claims that since Johannes

> carefully ensures that these two fundamentally misleading interpretative presuppositions [as outlined earlier] converge upon the glaring inconsistencies of his climactic treatment of Abraham's silent speech, and since both our objections to those presuppositions and our sketch of an alternative interpretation that seems more responsive to the Genesis narrative are constructed from materials supplied by de silentio himself, I think we are justified in concluding that his strident advocacy of those presuppositions is not designed to vindicate them but rather to encourage his readers to experience their seductiveness, initially accept their veracity, and only later discover their invalidity and begin to uncover more responsive and responsible ways of approaching the Abraham story.[93]

This reading of the rats we might smell in the text is ingenious but, I think, ultimately over-elaborate, and we have suggested above some reasons why it can be resisted. I do, however, agree with Mulhall that there are limits to what Johannes can tell us about faith. But this conclusion should come as no surprise, since all along Johannes admits to being an outsider to faith. His view of faith is far from complete.[94] However, not every possible objection to Johannes' procedure can be taken as a licence to suppose there is an elaborate trick being played on us as readers. For instance, some have suggested that there is a problem with Johannes' account of the Abraham story: the fact that what obsesses him is the events on Mount Moriah, and that he has relatively little interest in the surrounding context. Johannes elsewhere manifests what such critics might see as a similar tendency to focus on the bare bones of a story. In our discussion of Problema III, we noted that in his account of the 'four poetic personages', he only needs the bare bones of each story to get going. But, such a critic might allege, a story needs to be told in fuller and richer detail than this in order to be properly understood. Could this tendency in Johannes be a clue from Kierkegaard aimed at helping us to conclude that Johannes' treatment of the Abraham story is insufficiently attentive to the surrounding context and detail to be at all reliable?

Actually, I don't think so. There is evidence in Kierkegaard's journals that suggests why *Fear and Trembling* has the focus that it does. In a note from 1840–1, Kierkegaard comments on the dangers of over-familiarity with the Abraham story: 'Perhaps it does not amaze us anymore, because we have known it from our earliest childhood, but then the fault does not really lie in the truth, in the story, but in ourselves, because we are too lukewarm genuinely to feel with Abraham and to suffer with him' (JP 5: 5485). It is not hard to see why someone who thought this would want to put the focus on the *akedah* element in the Abraham story, in the process emphasising Abraham's anguish. The full background detail of his story as told in Genesis simply would not need to be repeated to an audience for whom it was well known.

CONCLUSION

What can we say in conclusion? That Johannes is fallible, and that he should not straightforwardly be taken as the spokesman for Kierkegaard's own view of faith. Such later texts as *The Sickness unto Death*, *Works of Love* and many others will need to be studied before the reader is close to coming to terms with that.[95] But I do not think that Johannes' unreliability is either as calculated a ruse as Mulhall claims, nor as big a problem as some other critics have alleged. Johannes may be flawed, but he is honestly so.[96] Central to Kierkegaard's approach to philosophy is the idea of an interested, 'subjective' rationality, much to be preferred to a disengaged, 'pure' or 'abstract' rationality. Reasoning and inquiry is carried out by finite creatures like us: creatures with personalities, interests – and flaws. Many of Kierkegaard's pseudonyms fit this description – and Johannes de silentio is no exception.[97] His attempted imaginative identification with the Abraham he so admires is a genuine attempt to relate himself to an exemplary other – and those who judge him too negatively for his failures are perhaps overlooking the sheer difficulty of success under this aspect. Johannes' flaws should not be allowed to detract from his positive features. These include his ability to breathe fresh life into an oft-repeated story; his sustained insistence upon the anguish and pathos that must accompany a trial such as Abraham's; and his recognition that ethical and religious narratives, if they are to work at all, must have some sort of impact on their readers or hearers. Above all, nobody who has ever encountered the Abraham in whom Johannes de silentio is so interested is ever likely to forget him.

NOTES

1 In contemporary scholarship, most commentators agree that there is *some* such distance, even those relatively unsympathetic to the kind of reading I shall explore in this chapter. Evans, for instance, notes that in his journals, when Kierkegaard comments on the views expressed in *Fear and Trembling*, Kierkegaard 'is generally careful to attribute those views to Johannes', commenting upon them 'as if he were simply a reader and had no role in the creation of the work' (Evans 2004: 65). Evans cites as examples JP 3: 3030, JP 6: 6434 and JP 6: 6598 (though the last is written in the guise of Johannes Climacus).

2 Another example is Kosch 2008, to which Lippitt 2008 is a reply. See also some of Mooney's recent work (e.g., Mooney 2007: Chapter 8) on Johannes as 'voyeur'.

3 See Allison 1967; Conant 1989, 1993, 1995. For criticisms of this way of reading the *Postscript*, see Lippitt and Hutto 1998; Lippitt 2000, especially Chapter 4; Rudd 2000; and Schönbaumsfeld 2007.
4 Mulhall 2001: 321–414.
5 Conway 2002: 87.
6 Conway 2002: 88.
7 Conway 2002: 89. Conway has developed his distinctive account of Johannes as a highly slippery narrator in further articles: see especially Conway 2008, 2015.
8 Conway 2002: 101.
9 Conway 2002: 99.
10 Conway 2002: 99.
11 Conway 2002: 101.
12 Conway 2002: 101.
13 Conway 2002: 101.
14 Lippitt 2000: Chapter 3.
15 Cross 1994: 211.
16 O'Neill 1989: 170.
17 See Winch 1965.
18 O'Neill 1989: 175.
19 O'Neill 1989: 175.
20 O'Neill 1989: 175.
21 O'Neill 1989: 176.
22 See JP 3: 3130 (included in the Supplement to the Hong translation of FT: 258).
23 Nussbaum 1990.
24 Nussbaum 1990: 48.
25 Nussbaum 1990: 162.
26 Nussbaum 1990: 162.
27 Gouwens 1982: 358–9, citing M. Thust (1931) *Søren Kierkegaard: Der Dichter des Religioesen*, Munich: CH Beckshe Verlagsbuchhandlung.
28 Nussbaum 1990: 54–105.
29 Nussbaum 1990: 55.
30 Nussbaum 1990: 55.
31 Nussbaum 1990: 66.
32 Nussbaum 1990: 69.
33 Nussbaum 1990: 71.
34 Nussbaum 1990: 76.
35 Conway 2002: 102.
36 In a discussion of an age's 'joking enviously about excellence', Kierkegaard says: 'That is quite all right if, after making sport of excellence, it once again *views excellence with admiration* and is able to regard it as unaltered, for otherwise it will have lost more by joking than the joke was worth' (TA 82). Shortly afterwards, admiration is described as a 'happy infatuation', as opposed to 'the unhappy infatuation of envy': 'The man who told Aristides that he was voting to banish him, "because he was tired of hearing him everywhere called the only just

man", actually did not deny Aristides' excellence but confessed something about himself, that his relation to this excellence was not the happy infatuation of admiration but the unhappy infatuation of envy, but he did not minimize that excellence' (TA 83).

37 O'Neill 1989: 170.
38 Phillips 1992: 72.
39 Phillips 1992: 72.
40 Carroll 1998: 147, my emphasis.
41 O'Neill 1989: 176.
42 Carroll 1998: 145.
43 Recall again our discussion of this in Chapter 6.
44 Nussbaum 1990: 46.
45 Nussbaum 1990: 46.
46 Conway 2002: 102.
47 Nussbaum 1990: 162.
48 Nussbaum 1990: 238–9.
49 See Genesis 22:8.
50 Genesis 22:1. Conway 2008 also makes much of Abraham's 'Here I am'.
51 Genesis 22:5.
52 Mulhall 2001: 360.
53 Mulhall 2001: 361.
54 Mulhall 2001: 361.
55 Mulhall 2001: 363.
56 An important caveat, however: Mulhall does not note that in the Danish Bible, John 1:29 (from where we get the phrase 'Lamb of God') uses the word *Lam*, whereas Genesis 22:8 uses *Dyret* ('the beast'), so the link between the two passages is less clear than in the familiar English Bible translations. Jeffrey Hanson notes a related point but argues that the typological reading does not require this detail (2015: 231–2). More on the significance of Hanson's contribution shortly.
57 Mulhall 2001: 365.
58 Mulhall 2001: 365.
59 Mulhall 2001: 366–7.
60 Mulhall 2001: 367.
61 Mulhall 2001: 368.
62 Mulhall 2001: 371.
63 Mulhall 2001: 371–2.
64 Mulhall 2001: 372.
65 Mulhall 2001: 373.
66 Mulhall 2001: 373.
67 Mulhall 2001: 373. Note the similarities with Conway's and Cross's readings here.
68 See, for instance, JP 1: 69, 106.
69 See Luke 10:25–37.
70 Mulhall 2001: 379.

71 Mulhall 2001: 380.
72 Mulhall 2001: 381.
73 Mulhall 2001: 381.
74 Mulhall 2001: 381.
75 Hanson 2015: 229.
76 Hanson 2015: 229.
77 Hanson 2015: 229.
78 Mulhall 2001: 381.
79 Mulhall 2001: 382.
80 Hanson 2015: 229.
81 Hanson 2015: 232. This is why he agrees that the figurative-literal discussion is the most important part of Mulhall's critique (Hanson 2015: 232).
82 Hanson 2015: 232.
83 Kangas 2001. Note that James 1:17–22 (a particular favourite text of Kierkegaard's) is the catalyst for the discourse 'Every Good and Perfect Gift Is from Above' (EUD 31–48) – the discourse that accompanied 'The Expectancy of Faith' – as well as later discourses.
84 Hanson 2015: 233.
85 Hanson 2015: 236; cf. also pp. 234–5.
86 Hanson 2015: 237; for the details, see pp. 237–43.
87 Hanson 2015: 242.
88 Furthermore, this reading is also consistent with our earlier suggestion that Johannes' utterances about 'the ethical' being 'the universal' are less stipulates than 'postulates to be challenged' (Hanson's phrase, in explicit support of the first edition of the Guidebook on this idea [2015: 233n14]), in so far as 'the ethical' is transfigured in the light of faith.
89 Hanson 2015: 243–4.
90 Hanson 2015: 244.
91 Hanson 2015: 244–5. This enables us to see what is problematic about Timothy Dalrymple's objection to one aspect of the first edition of this book (2010: 66–7). Dalrymple is right, in one sense, to say that 'a specific expectation' is not the same as faith (recall especially our discussion of 'The Expectancy of Faith' in Chapter 6). But more care is needed about what it means to attribute 'a specific expectation' to Abraham. Dalrymple seems to object to my holding open the possibility of an Abraham who hopes that, in the end, he will not have to kill Isaac (this is alleged to be the 'specific expectation'). He notes the Hebrews 11 view 'that Abraham believed Isaac would be resurrected, if necessary' and asserts that 'Johannes must mean that Abraham believed God would not *ultimately* take Isaac' (Dalrymple 2010: 66). Trusting 'that in some way Isaac would be saved ... does not mean that Abraham believed that Isaac would not die', and the fact that Johannes describes Abraham as 'surprised' at God's intervention, is taken to amount to Johannes being 'clear on this point' (Dalrymple 2010: 66). The main point against Dalrymple's objection is internal inconsistency, for surely, 'God will have me kill Isaac, but then He will miraculously resurrect him' is a *more* 'specific expectation' than 'The Lord will provide

(either by calling off the sacrifice, resurrecting Isaac, or in some other way beyond my comprehension)'. It seems much more plausible to read the passage that Dalrymple finds so 'clear' (see FT 65) in quite the opposite way to the one in which he suggests. Johannes is addressing two distinct possibilities, one in which 'God does not demand Isaac of him', and one ('Let us go further. We let Isaac be sacrificed') in which Isaac is indeed killed. (Compare Problema III, where Johannes has Abraham say 'Nevertheless it won't happen, *or if it does* the Lord will give me a new Isaac' (FT 139, my emphasis).) Dalrymple only seems to notice the second possibility.

92 Note that it also gives us further reason to resist Westphal's claim, considered in Chapter 6, about the 'determinate content' of biblical faith.

93 Mulhall 2001: 382–3.

94 On this point, see, for instance, Evans 1993: 22 and Westphal 2014: 60–1.

95 Tietjen suggests that 'de Silentio's views of faith are never dismissed or canceled wholesale, nor are Climacus's. Rather, each pseudonym presents a conception of faith in light of particular misconceptions that plagued Kierkegaard's contemporaries'. Nevertheless, this is part of 'the overall movement of the authorship ... toward specifically Christian categories' (2013: 116). If Tietjen is right about this, and I suspect that he is, then this poses problems for readings of Kierkegaard (such as, perhaps, Krishek 2009), that seem to present the *Fear and Trembling* conception of faith as in some sense the high point of Kierkegaard's thought.

96 On honesty as Johannes' 'chief virtue', see Tietjen 2013: 96.

97 Anthony Rudd suggests reading *Fear and Trembling* as a 'Socratic exercise ... intended to make us realise our ignorance about faith (the sense in which we are ignorant about faith) in a way that may help us move on to acquiring a deeper, existential understanding of what it is to live the life of faith' (2015: 193).

BIBLIOGRAPHY

PRIMARY SOURCES

See Reference Key to Kierkegaard's Texts.

SECONDARY SOURCES ON *FEAR AND TREMBLING* (AND OTHER KIERKEGAARD TEXTS)

Adams, R. M. (1990) 'The Knight of Faith', *Faith and Philosophy*, 7 (4): 383–95.

Agacinski, S. (1998) 'We Are Not Sublime: Love and Sacrifice, Abraham and Ourselves', in J. Rée and J. Chamberlain (eds.), *Kierkegaard: A Critical Reader*, Oxford: Blackwell, pp. 129–50.

Allison, H. E. (1967) 'Christianity and Nonsense', *Review of Metaphysics*, 20 (3): 432–60.

Blanshard, B. (1969) 'Kierkegaard on Faith', in J. H. Gill (ed.), *Essays on Kierkegaard*, Minneapolis, Minn.: Burgess, pp. 113–26.

Buber, M. (1975) 'The Suspension of Ethics', in W. Heiberg (ed.), *Four Existentialist Theologians*, Westport, Conn.: Greenwood Press.

Carlisle, C. (2010) *Kierkegaard's Fear and Trembling: A Reader's Guide*, London: Continuum.

——(2015) 'Johannes De Silentio's Dilemma', in D. W. Conway (ed.), *Kierkegaard's Fear and Trembling: A Critical Guide*, Cambridge: Cambridge University Press, pp. 44–60.

Conant, J. (1989) 'Must We Show What We Cannot Say?', in R. Fleming and M. Payne (eds.), *The Senses of Stanley Cavell*, Lewisburg, Pa.: Bucknell University Press, pp. 242–83.

—— (1993) 'Kierkegaard, Wittgenstein and Nonsense', in T. Cohen, P. Guyer and H. Putnam (eds.), *Pursuits of Reason*, Lubbock, Tex.: Texas Tech University Press, pp. 195–224.

—— (1995) 'Putting Two and Two Together: Kierkegaard, Wittgenstein and the Point of View for Their Work as Authors', in T. Tessin and M. Von Der Ruhr (eds.), *Philosophy and the Grammar of Religious Belief*, London and New York: Macmillan and St Martin's Press, pp. 248–331.

Conway, D. W. (2002) 'The Confessional Drama of *Fear and Trembling*', in D. W. Conway (ed.), *Søren Kierkegaard: Critical Assessments*, vol. III, London: Routledge, pp. 87–103.

—— (2008) 'Abraham's Final Word', in E. F. Mooney (ed.), *Ethics, Love and Faith in Kierkegaard: Philosophical Engagements*, Bloomington, Ind.: Indiana University Press, pp. 175–95.

—— (ed.) (2015a) *Kierkegaard's Fear and Trembling: A Critical Guide*, Cambridge: Cambridge University Press.

—— (2015b) 'Particularity and Ethical Attunement: Situating Problema III', in D. W. Conway (ed.), *Kierkegaard's Fear and Trembling: A Critical Guide*, Cambridge: Cambridge University Press, pp. 205–28.

Cross, A. (1994) 'Moral Exemplars and Commitment in Kierkegaard's *Fear and Trembling*', Ph.D. Thesis, University of California, Berkeley, California.

—— (1999) '*Fear and Trembling*'s Unorthodox Ideal', *Philosophical Topics*, 27 (2): 227–53.

Dalrymple, T. (2010) 'Abraham: Framing *Fear and Trembling*', in L. C. Barrett and J. Stewart (eds.), *Kierkegaard Research: Sources, Reception and Resources*, vol. I, tome I: *The Old Testament*, London: Ashgate, pp. 43–88.

Danta, C. (2011) *Literature Suspends Death: Sacrifice and Storytelling in Kierkegaard, Kafka and Blanchot*, London: Bloomsbury.

Davenport, J. J. (2008a) 'Faith as Eschatological Trust in *Fear and Trembling*', in E. F. Mooney (ed.), *Ethics, Love and Faith in Kierkegaard: Philosophical Engagements*, Bloomington, Ind.: Indiana University Press, pp. 196–233.

—— (2008b) 'What Kierkegaardian Faith Adds to Alterity Ethics: How Levinas and Derrida Miss the Eschatological Dimension', in J. A. Simmons and D. Wood (eds.), *Kierkegaard and Levinas: Ethics, Politics and Religion*, Bloomington, Ind.: Indiana University Press, pp. 169–96.

—— (2008c) 'Kierkegaard's *Postscript* in Light of *Fear and Trembling*', *Revista Portuguesa de Filosofia*, 64 (2–4): 879–908.

—— (2012) *Narrative Identity, Autonomy and Mortality: From Frankfurt and Macintyre to Kierkegaard*, London and New York: Routledge.

—— (2015) 'Eschatological Faith and Repetition: Kierkegaard's Abraham and Job', in D. W. Conway (ed.), *Kierkegaard's Fear and Trembling: A Critical Guide*, Cambridge: Cambridge University Press, pp. 79–105.

Derrida, J. (1995) *The Gift of Death*, trans. D. Wills, Chicago, Ill.: University of Chicago Press.

Dietrichson, P. (1965) 'Kierkegaard's Concept of the Self', *Inquiry*, 8 (1): 1–31.

Duncan, E. H. (1963) 'Kierkegaard's Teleological Suspension of the Ethical: A Study of Exception Cases', *The Southern Journal of Philosophy*, 1 (4): 9–18.

Evans, C. S. (1981) 'Is the Concept of an Absolute Duty toward God Morally Unintelligible?', in R. L. Perkins (ed.), *Kierkegaard's Fear and Trembling: Critical Appraisals*, University, Ala.: University of Alabama Press, pp. 141–51.

——(1992) *Passionate Reason: Making Sense of Kierkegaard's Philosophical Fragments*, Bloomington, Ind.: Indiana University Press.

——(1993) 'Faith as the *Telos* of Morality: A Reading of *Fear and Trembling*', in R. L. Perkins (ed.), *International Kierkegaard Commentary*: Fear and Trembling and Repetition, Macon, Ga.: Mercer University Press, pp. 9–27.

——(2004) *Kierkegaard's Ethic of Love: Divine Commands and Moral Obligations*, Oxford: Oxford University Press.

——(2006) 'Introduction', in S. Kierkegaard, *Fear and Trembling*, trans. S. Walsh, Cambridge: Cambridge University Press.

——(2015) 'Can an Admirer of Silentio's Abraham Consistently Believe that Child Sacrifice Is Forbidden?', in D. W. Conway (ed.), *Kierkegaard's* Fear and Trembling: *A Critical Guide*, Cambridge: Cambridge University Press, pp. 61–78.

Furtak, R. A. (2015) 'On Being Moved and Hearing Voices: Passion and Religious Experience in *Fear and Trembling*', in D. W. Conway (ed.), *Kierkegaard's* Fear and Trembling: *A Critical Guide*, Cambridge: Cambridge University Press, pp. 142–65.

Gellman, J. I. (1990) 'Kierkegaard's *Fear and Trembling*', *Man and World*, 23 (3): 295–304.

——(2003) *Abraham! Abraham! Kierkegaard and the Hasidim on the Binding of Isaac*, London: Ashgate.

Gill, J. H. (2000) 'Faith Not Without Reason: Kant, Kierkegaard and Religious Belief', in D. Z. Phillips and T. Tessin (eds.), *Kant and Kierkegaard on Religion*, London and New York: Macmillan and St Martin's Press, pp. 55–72.

Goulet, D. A. (1957) 'Kierkegaard, Aquinas and the Dilemma of Abraham', *Thought*, 32 (2): 165–88.

Gouwens, D. J. (1982) *Kierkegaard's Dialectic of the Imagination*, Ph.D. thesis, Yale University, Connecticut.

Green, R. M. (1992) *Kierkegaard and Kant: The Hidden Debt*, Albany, NY: State University of New York Press.

——(1993) 'Enough Is Enough! *Fear and Trembling* Is *Not* about Ethics', *Journal of Religious Ethics*, 21 (2): 191–209.

——(1998) '"Developing" *Fear and Trembling*', in A. Hannay, A. and G. D. Marino (eds.), *The Cambridge Companion to Kierkegaard*, Cambridge: Cambridge University Press, pp. 257–81.

Green, R. M. and M. J. Green (2011) 'Simone de Beauvoir: A Founding Feminist's Appreciation of Kierkegaard', in J. Stewart (ed.), *Kierkegaard Research: Sources, Reception and Resources*, vol. 9: *Kierkegaard and Existentialism*, London: Ashgate, pp. 1–21.

Grelland, H. H. (2013) 'Edvard Munch: The Painter of *The Scream* and His Relation to Kierkegaard', in J. Stewart (ed.), *Kierkegaard Research: Sources, Reception and Resources*, vol. 12: *Kierkegaard's Influence on Literature, Criticism and Art*, tome III: *Sweden and Norway*, London: Ashgate.

Hackel, M. (2011) 'Jean-Paul Sartre: Kierkegaard's Influence on His Theory of Nothingness', in J. Stewart (ed.), *Kierkegaard Research: Sources, Reception and Resources*, vol. 9: *Kierkegaard and Existentialism*, London: Ashgate, pp. 323–54.

Hall, R. L. (2000) *The Human Embrace: The Love of Philosophy and the Philosophy of Love: Kierkegaard, Cavell, Nussbaum*, University Park, Pa.: Pennsylvania State University Press.

Hampson, D. (2013) *Kierkegaard: Exposition and Critique*, Oxford: Oxford University Press.

Hannay, A. (2001) *Kierkegaard: A Biography*, Cambridge: Cambridge University Press.

——(2008) 'Silence and Entering the Circle of Faith', in E. F. Mooney (ed.), *Ethics, Love and Faith in Kierkegaard: Philosophical Engagements*, Bloomington, Ind.: Indiana University Press, pp. 234–43.

——(2015) 'Homing in on *Fear and Trembling*', in D. W. Conway (ed.), *Kierkegaard's Fear and Trembling: A Critical Guide*, Cambridge: Cambridge University Press, pp. 6–25.

Hannay, A. and G. D. Marino (eds.) (1998) *The Cambridge Companion to Kierkegaard*, Cambridge: Cambridge University Press.

Hanson, J. (2012) 'Emmanuel Levinas: An Ambivalent but Decisive Reception', in J. Stewart (ed.), *Kierkegaard Research: Sources, Reception and Resources, Vol. 11: Kierkegaard's Influence on Philosophy*, tome II: *Francophone Philosophy*, London: Ashgate, pp. 173–205.

——(2015) '"He Speaks in Tongues": Hearing the Truth of Abraham's Words of Faith', in D. W. Conway (ed.), *Kierkegaard's Fear and Trembling: A Critical Guide*, Cambridge: Cambridge University Press, pp. 229–46.

Hartman, D. (1999) *A Heart of Many Rooms: Celebrating the Many Voices Within Judaism*, Woodstock, Vt.: Jewish Lights.

Hatton, N. (2011) 'Martin Luther King, Jr.: Kierkegaard's *Works of Love*, King's *Strength to Love*', in J. Stewart (ed.), *Kierkegaard Research: Sources, Reception and Resources*, vol. 14: *Kierkegaard's Influence on Social-Political Thought*, London: Ashgate, pp. 89–106.

Howland, J. (2015) '*Fear and Trembling*'s "Attunement" as Midrash', in D. W. Conway (ed.), *Kierkegaard's Fear and Trembling: A Critical Guide*, Cambridge: Cambridge University Press, pp. 26–43.

Irina, N. (2013) 'Franz Kafka: Reading Kierkegaard', in J. Stewart (ed.), *Kierkegaard Research: Sources, Reception and Resources*, vol. 12: *Kierkegaard's Influence on Literature, Criticism and Art*, tome I: *The Germanophone World*, London: Ashgate, pp. 115–40.

Jacobs, L. (1981) 'The Problem of the Akedah in Jewish Thought', in R. L. Perkins (ed.), *Kierkegaard's Fear and Trembling: Critical Appraisals*, University, Ala.: University of Alabama Press, pp. 1–9.

Kangas, D. (2001) 'The Logic of Gift in Kierkegaard's *Four Upbuilding Discourses* (1843)', *Kierkegaard Studies Yearbook 2001*, Berlin: De Gruyter.

Keeley, L. C. (1993) 'The Parables of Problem III in Kierkegaard's *Fear and Trembling*', in R. L. Perkins (ed.), *International Kierkegaard Commentary: Fear and Trembling and Repetition*, Macon, Ga.: Mercer University Press, pp. 127–54.

Kellenberger, J. (1997) *Kierkegaard and Nietzsche: Faith and Eternal Acceptance*, London and New York: Macmillan and St Martin's Press.

Kirmmse, B. H. (1996) *Encounters with Kierkegaard: A Life as Seen by His Contemporaries*, Princeton, NJ: Princeton University Press.

Kosch, M. (2008) 'What Abraham Couldn't Say', *Proceedings of the Aristotelian Society*, supplementary vol. LXXXII: 59–78.

Krishek, S. (2009) *Kierkegaard on Faith and Love*, Cambridge: Cambridge University Press.

Lee, J. H. (2000) 'Abraham in a Different Voice: Rereading *Fear and Trembling* With Care', *Religious Studies*, 36 (4): 377–400.

Lévinas, E. (1998) 'Existence and Ethics', in J. Rée and J. Chamberlain (eds.), *Kierkegaard: A Critical Reader*, Oxford: Blackwell, pp. 26–38. First published in 1963.

Lippitt, J. (2000) *Humour and Irony in Kierkegaard's Thought*, London and New York: Macmillan and St Martin's Press.

———(2008) 'What Neither Abraham Nor Johannes de Silentio Could Say', *Proceedings of the Aristotelian Society*, supplementary vol. LXXXII: 79–99.

———(2013) *Kierkegaard and the Problem of Self-Love*, Cambridge: Cambridge University Press.

———(2015a) 'Learning to Hope: The Role of Hope in *Fear and Trembling*', in D. W. Conway (ed.), *Kierkegaard's Fear and Trembling: A Critical Guide*, Cambridge: Cambridge University Press, pp. 122–41.

———(2015b) 'What Can Therapists Learn from Kierkegaard?', in M. Bazzano and J. Webb (eds.), *Psychotherapy and the Counter-Tradition*, London and New York: Routledge.

———(2015c) 'Forgiveness and the Rat Man: Kierkegaard, "Narrative Unity" and "Wholeheartedness" Revisited', in J. Lippitt and P. Stokes (eds.), *Narrative, Identity and the Kierkegaardian Self*, Edinburgh: Edinburgh University Press, pp. 126–43.

———(in press) 'Kierkegaard's Virtues: Humility and Gratitude as the Grounds of Contentment, Patience and Hope in Kierkegaard's Moral Psychology', in S. Minister, J. A. Simmons and M. Strawser (eds.), *Kierkegaard's God and the Good Life*, Bloomington: Indiana University Press

Lippitt, J. and D. Hutto (1998) 'Making Sense of Nonsense: Kierkegaard and Wittgenstein', *Proceedings of the Aristotelian Society*, 158 (3): 263–86.

Loungina, D. (2009) 'Russia: Kierkegaard's Reception through Tsarism, Communism, and Liberation', in J. Stewart (ed.), *Kierkegaard Research: Sources, Reception and Resources*, vol. 8: *Kierkegaard's International Reception*, tome II: *Southern, Central and Eastern Europe*, London: Ashgate, pp. 247–83.

Mackey, L. (1972) 'The View from Pisgah: A Reading of *Fear and Trembling*', in J. Thompson (ed.), *Kierkegaard: A Collection of Critical Essays*, Garden City, NY: Doubleday, pp. 266–88.

Malantschuk, G. (1971) *Kierkegaard's Thought*, trans. H. V. and E. H. Hong, Princeton, NJ: Princeton University Press.

Malesic, J. (2013) 'The Paralyzing Instant: Shifting Vocabularies about Time and Ethics in *Fear and Trembling*', *Journal of Religious Ethics*, 41 (2): 209–32.

Malik, H. C. (1997) *Receiving Søren Kierkegaard: The Early Impact and Transmission of His Thought*, Washington, DC: Catholic University of America Press.

Miles, T. (2011) 'Friedrich Nietzsche: Rival Visions of the Best Way of Life', in J. Stewart (ed.), *Kierkegaard Research: Sources, Reception and Resources*, vol. 9: *Kierkegaard and Existentialism*, London: Ashgate, pp. 266–98.

Mjaaland, M. T. (2012) 'Jacques Derrida: Faithful Heretics', in J. Stewart (ed.), *Kierkegaard Research: Sources, Reception and Resources*, vol. 11: *Kierkegaard's Influence on Philosophy*, tome II: *Francophone Philosophy*, London: Ashgate, pp. 111–38.

Mooney, E. F. (1991) *Knights of Faith and Resignation: Reading Kierkegaard's* Fear and Trembling, Albany, NY: State University of New York Press.

——(1996) *Selves in Discord and Resolve*, London and New York: Routledge.

——(2007) *On Søren Kierkegaard: Dialogue, Polemics, Lost Intimacy and Time*, London: Ashgate.

Mooney, E. F. and D. Lloyd (2015) 'Birth, Love and Hybridity: *Fear and Trembling* and the *Symposium*', in D. W. Conway (ed.), *Kierkegaard's* Fear and Trembling: *A Critical Guide*, Cambridge: Cambridge University Press, pp. 166–87.

Mulhall, S. (2001) *Inheritance and Originality: Wittgenstein, Heidegger, Kierkegaard*, Oxford: Oxford University Press.

Nagy, A. (1998) 'Abraham the Communist', in G. Pattison and S. Shakespeare (eds.), *Kierkegaard: The Self in Society*, Basingstoke: Macmillan, pp. 196–220.

——(2009) 'Hungary: The Hungarian Patient', in J. Stewart (ed.), *Kierkegaard Research: Sources, Reception and Resources*, vol. 8: *Kierkegaard's International Reception*, tome II: *Southern, Central and Eastern Europe*, London: Ashgate.

——(2011) 'György Lukács: From a Tragic Love Story to a Tragic Life Story', in J. Stewart (ed.), *Kierkegaard Research: Sources, Reception and Resources*, vol. 14: *Kierkegaard's Influence on Social-Political Thought*, London: Ashgate, pp. 107–35.

Nørager, T. (2008) *Taking Leave of Abraham: An Essay in Religion and Democracy*, Aarhus: Aarhus University Press.

Outka, G. (1993) 'God as the Unique Subject of Veneration: A Response to Ronald M. Green', *Journal of Religious Ethics*, 21 (2): 211–15.

Pattison, G. (1999) '*Poor Paris!*' *Kierkegaard's Critique of the Spectacular City*, Berlin and New York: Walter de Gruyter.

——(2002) *Kierkegaard's Upbuilding Discourses: Philosophy, Literature and Theology*, London and New York: Routledge.

Pattison, G. and H. M. Jensen (2012) *Kierkegaard's Pastoral Dialogues*, Eugene, Oreg.: Wipf & Stock.

Perkins, R. L. (ed.) (1981) *Kierkegaard's* Fear and Trembling: *Critical Appraisals*, University, Ala.: University of Alabama Press.

———(ed.) (1993) *International Kierkegaard Commentary: Fear and Trembling and Repetition*, Macon, Ga.: Mercer University Press.

Phillips, D. Z. (2000) 'Voices in Discussion', in D. Z. Phillips and T. Tessin (eds.), *Kant and Kierkegaard on Religion*, London and New York: Macmillan and St Martin's Press, pp. 122–28.

Phillips, D. Z. and T. Tessin (eds.) (2000) *Kant and Kierkegaard on Religion*, London and New York: Macmillan and St Martin's Press.

Qi, W. (2009) 'China: The Chinese Reception of Kierkegaard', in J. Stewart (ed.), *Kierkegaard Research: Sources, Reception and Resources*, vol. 8: *Kierkegaard's International Reception*, tome III: *The Near East, Asia, Australasia and the Americas*, London: Ashgate, pp. 103–23.

Quinn, P. (1990) 'Agamemnon and Abraham: The Tragic Dilemma of Kierkegaard's Knight of Faith', *Journal of Literature and Theology*, 4 (2): 181–93.

Rée, J. and J. Chamberlain (eds.) (1998) *Kierkegaard: A Critical Reader*, Oxford: Blackwell.

Roberts, R. C. (2003) 'The Virtue of Hope in *Eighteen Upbuilding Discourses*', in R. L. Perkins (ed.), *International Kierkegaard Commentary: Eighteen Upbuilding Discourses*, Macon, Ga.: Mercer University Press, pp. 181–203.

Rose, G. (1992) *The Broken Middle: Out of Our Ancient Society*, Oxford: Blackwell.

Rudd, A. (2000) 'On Straight and Crooked Readings: Why the *Postscript* Does Not Self-Destruct', in P. Houe, G. D. Marino and S. H. Rossel (eds.), *Authority and Anthropology: Essays on Søren Kierkegaard*, Amsterdam and Atlanta, Ga.: Rodopi, pp. 119–27.

———(2015) 'Narrative Unity and the Moment of Crisis in *Fear and Trembling*', in D. W. Conway (ed.), *Kierkegaard's* Fear and Trembling: *A Critical Guide*, Cambridge: Cambridge University Press, pp. 188–204.

Rumble, V. (2015) 'Why Moriah? Weaning and the Trauma of Transcendence in Kierkegaard's *Fear and Trembling*', in D. W. Conway (ed.), *Kierkegaard's* Fear and Trembling: *A Critical Guide*, Cambridge: Cambridge University Press, pp. 247–62.

Schönbaumsfeld, G. (2007) *A Confusion of the Spheres: Kierkegaard and Wittgenstein on Philosophy and Religion*, Oxford: Oxford University Press.

Schulz, H. (2009) 'Germany and Austria: A Modest Head Start – The German Reception of Kierkegaard', in J. Stewart (ed.), *Kierkegaard Research: Sources, Reception and Resources*, vol. 8: *Kierkegaard's International Reception*, tome I: *Northern and Western Europe*, London: Ashgate, pp. 307–419.

Sheil, P. (2010) *Kierkegaard and Levinas: The Subjunctive Mood*, London: Ashgate.

Simmons, J. A. and D. Wood (eds.) (2008) *Kierkegaard and Levinas: Ethics, Politics and Religion*, Bloomington, Ind.: Indiana University Press.

Stewart, J. (2003) *Kierkegaard's Relations to Hegel Reconsidered*, Cambridge: Cambridge University Press.

———(2009a) (ed.) *Kierkegaard Research: Sources, Reception and Resources*, vol. 8: *Kierkegaard's International Reception*, London: Ashgate.

———(2009b) 'France: Kierkegaard as Forerunner of Existentialism and Post-structuralism', in J. Stewart (ed.), *Kierkegaard Research: Sources, Reception and*

Resources, vol. 8: *Kierkegaard's International Reception*, tome I: *Northern and Western Europe*, London: Ashgate, pp. 421–74.

——(ed.) (2011a) *Kierkegaard Research: Sources, Reception and Resources*, vol. 9: *Kierkegaard and Existentialism*, London: Ashgate.

——(ed.) (2011b) *Kierkegaard Research: Sources, Reception and Resources*, vol. 14: *Kierkegaard's Influence on Social-Political Thought*, London: Ashgate.

——(ed.) (2012) *Kierkegaard Research: Sources, Reception and Resources*, vol. 11: *Kierkegaard's Influence on Philosophy*, London: Ashgate.

——(ed.) (2013) *Kierkegaard Research: Sources, Reception and Resources*, vol. 12: *Kierkegaard's Influence on Literature, Criticism and Art*, London: Ashgate.

Taylor, M. C. (1981) 'Sounds of Silence', in R. L. Perkins (ed.), *Kierkegaard's Fear and Trembling: Critical Appraisals*, University, Ala.: University of Alabama Press, pp. 165–88.

Thompson, J. (ed.) (1972) *Kierkegaard: A Collection of Critical Essays*, Garden City, NY: Doubleday.

Tietjen, M. A. (2013) *Kierkegaard, Communication and Virtue: Authorship as Edification*, Bloomington, Ind.: Indiana University Press.

Tilley, J. M. (2012) 'Rereading the Teleological Suspension: Resignation, Faith, and Teleology', *Kierkegaard Studies Yearbook 2012*, Berlin: De Gruyter, pp. 145–69.

Töpfer-Stoyanova, D. (2009) 'Bulgaria: The Long Way from Indirect Acquaintance to Original Translation', in J. Stewart (ed.), *Kierkegaard Research: Sources, Reception and Resources*, vol. 8: *Kierkegaard's International Reception*, tome II: *Southern, Central and Eastern Europe*, London: Ashgate, pp. 285–99.

Villar, E. F. (2013) 'Jorge Luis Borges: The Fear without Trembling', in J. Stewart (ed.), *Kierkegaard Research: Sources, Reception and Resources*, vol. 12: *Kierkegaard's Influence on Literature, Criticism and Art*, tome V: *The Romance Languages and Central and Eastern Europe*, London: Ashgate, pp. 21–32.

Walsh, S. (2009) *Kierkegaard: Thinking Christianly in an Existential Mode*, Oxford: Oxford University Press.

Westphal, M. (2008) *Levinas and Kierkegaard in Dialogue*, Bloomington, Ind.: Indiana University Press.

——(2014) *Kierkegaard's Concept of Faith*, Grand Rapids, Mich.: Eerdmans.

Whittaker, J. H. (2000) 'Kant and Kierkegaard on Eternal Life', in D. Z. Phillips and T. Tessin (eds.), *Kant and Kierkegaard on Religion*, London and New York: Macmillan and St Martin's Press, pp. 187–206.

Williams, L. (1998) 'Kierkegaard's Weanings', *Philosophy Today*, 42 (3): 310–18.

OTHER WORKS REFERRED TO IN THE TEXT

Baier, A. C. (1994) 'Trust and Antitrust', in *Moral Prejudices: Essays on Ethics*, Cambridge, Mass.: Harvard University Press, pp. 231–60.

Beiser, F. (ed.) (1993) *The Cambridge Companion to Hegel*, Cambridge: Cambridge University Press.

Blanchot, M. (1982) *The Space of Literature*, trans. A. Smock, Lincoln, Nebr.: University of Nebraska Press.

Caputo, J. D. (1993) *Against Ethics: Contributions to a Poetics of Obligation with Constant Reference to Deconstruction*, Bloomington, Ind.: Indiana University Press.

Carroll, N. (1998) 'Art, Narrative and Moral Understanding', in J. Levinson (ed.), *Aesthetics and Ethics: Essays at the Intersection*, Cambridge: Cambridge University Press, pp. 126–60.

Cavell, S. (1981) *Pursuits of Happiness: The Hollywood Comedy of Remarriage*, Cambridge, Mass.: Harvard University Press.

Delaney, C. (1998) *Abraham on Trial: The Social Legacy of Biblical Myth*, Princeton, NJ: Princeton University Press.

Deleuze, G. and F. Guattari (1987) *A Thousand Plateaus: Capitalism and Schizophrenia*, trans. B. Massumi, Minneapolis, Minn.: University of Minnesota Press.

Descartes, R. (1973) *The Philosophical Works of Descartes*, 2 vols., trans. E. S. Haldane and G. R. T. Ross, Cambridge: Cambridge University Press.

Dickey, L. (1993) 'Hegel on Religion and Philosophy', in F. Beiser (ed.), *The Cambridge Companion to Hegel*, Cambridge: Cambridge University Press, pp. 301–47.

Engstrom, S. and J. Whiting (eds.) (1996) *Aristotle, Kant and the Stoics*, Cambridge: Cambridge University Press.

Fekete, É. and É. Karádi (eds.) (1981) *Lukács Gyorgy Levelezése 1902–1917*, Budapest: Magvető Kiadó.

Hare, J. (1996) *The Moral Gap: Kantian Ethics and God's Assistance*, Oxford: Oxford University Press.

Hegel, G. W. F. (1971) *Early Theological Writings*, trans. T. M. Knox, Philadelphia, Pa.: University of Pennsylvania Press.

——(1977) *Phenomenology of Spirit*, trans. A. V. Miller, Oxford: Oxford University Press.

——(1996) *Philosophy of Right*, trans. S. W. Dyde, Amherst, NY: Prometheus.

Heidegger, M. (1962) *Being and Time*, trans. J. Macquarrie and E. Robinson, Oxford: Basil Blackwell.

Inwood, M. (1992) *A Hegel Dictionary*, Oxford: Blackwell.

Julian of Norwich (1996) *A Revelation of Divine Love*, trans. J. Skinner, Leominster: Gracewing.

Kafka, F. (1977) *Letters to Friends, Family and Editors*, trans. R. and C. Winston, New York: Schocken.

Kant, I. (1993) *Grounding for the Metaphysics of Morals*, trans. J. W. Ellington, Indianapolis, Ind.: Hackett.

——(1996a) *The Conflict of the Faculties in Religion and Rational Theology*, trans. and ed. A. W. Wood, Cambridge: Cambridge University Press.

——(1996b) *The Metaphysics of Morals*, trans. and ed. M. Gregor, Cambridge: Cambridge University Press.

——(1998) *Religion within the Boundaries of Mere Reason and Other Writings*, trans. and ed. A. Wood and G. Di Giovanni, Cambridge: Cambridge University Press.

Lear, J. (2006) *Radical Hope: Ethics in the Face of Cultural Devastation*, Cambridge, Mass.: Harvard University Press.

Levenson, J. (2012) *Inheriting Abraham: The Legacy of the Patriarch in Judaism, Christianity and Islam*, Princeton, NJ: Princeton University Press.

Løgstrup, K. E. (1997) *The Ethical Demand*, ed. H. Fink and A. Macintyre, trans. T. I. Jensen and G. Puckering, Notre Dame, Ind.: University of Notre Dame Press.

Lukács, G. (1982) *Curriculum Vitae*, ed. J. Ambrus, Budapest: Magvető Kiadó.

Luther, M. (1959) *The Book of Concord*, ed. T. Tappert, Philadelphia, Pa.: Mühlenberg Press.

——(1964) *Lectures on Genesis, Chapters 21 to 25*, in J. Pelikan (ed.), *Luther's Works*, vol. IV, St Louis: Concordia.

Macquarrie, J. (1978) *Christian Hope*, Oxford: Mowbray.

Moltmann, J. (1974) *The Crucified God*, trans. R. A. Wilson and J. Bowden, London: SCM Press.

Nussbaum, M. C. (1986) *The Fragility of Goodness: Luck and Ethics in Greek Tragedy and Philosophy*, Cambridge: Cambridge University Press.

——(1990) *Love's Knowledge: Essays on Philosophy and Literature*, Oxford: Oxford University Press.

O'Neill, O. (1989) *Constructions of Reason: Explorations of Kant's Practical Philosophy*, Cambridge: Cambridge University Press.

Phillips, D. Z. (1992) 'The Presumption of Theory', in *Interventions in Ethics*, London and New York: Macmillan and St Martin's Press, pp. 61–85.

Plato (1974) *The Republic*, trans. D. Lee, Harmondsworth: Penguin.

Roberts, R. C. (2007) *Spiritual Emotions: A Psychology of Christian Virtues*, Grand Rapids, Mich.: Eerdmans.

Sartre, J.-P. (1948) *Existentialism and Humanism*, trans. P. Mairet, London: Methuen.

Tertullian (1972) *Adversus Marcionem*, trans. and ed. E. Evans, Oxford: Clarendon Press.

Thust, M. (1931) *Søren Kierkegaard: Der Dichter des Religiösen*, Munich: CH Becksche Verlagsbuchhandlung.

Vlastos, G. (1991) *Socrates: Ironist and Moral Philosopher*, Cambridge: Cambridge University Press.

Williams, B. (1981) *Moral Luck*, Cambridge: Cambridge University Press.

Winch, P. (1972) 'The Universalizability of Moral Judgments', in *Ethics and Action*, London: Routledge & Kegan Paul, pp. 151–70. First published 1965.

Wood, A. (1993) 'Hegel's Ethics', in F. Beiser (ed.), *The Cambridge Companion to Hegel*, Cambridge: Cambridge University Press, pp. 211–33.

INDEX

'A' 85–6, 121
absolute, the: in Hegel 94; 'absolute relation to' 96, 99–100, 102, 103, 107, 111, 114, 131–2, 137–8, 142, 185, 201
'absolute duty to God' 110–15
absurd, the 26, 46, 49–50, 54, 58, 61–3, 71, 74–5, 86, 107, 178, 183–4, 190, 197, 217, 238
admiration 24, 32, 46, 56, 58, 108, 148, 151, 193, 223–37, 251–2
aesthetic, the 75, 85–6, 120, 139, 150
Agamemnon 104–7, 115, 122–3, 139–41, 158, 231
Agnete 124, 127–34, 135, 139, 144, 200, 205
Allison, Henry 221
anguish 9, 21, 26, 30, 34–6, 39, 40, 41, 62, 64, 76, 88, 91, 109, 113, 124, 128, 140, 143, 144, 149, 165–7, 182, 199, 230, 232, 237, 249, 250
Anti-Climacus 69, 223–9, 236
Aristotle 124, 184, 229, 235–6, 242

Auden, W. H. 147–8
Axel and Valborg 126–7

Baier, Annette 79
Blanshard, Brand 185
Boesen, Emil 5, 7
Borges, Jorge Luis 148
Brod, Max 148, 208
Brutus 105–6
Buber, Martin 149, 208

Caputo, John 32–3
Carlisle, Clare 38, 39, 82, 84, 144, 213, 216
Carroll, Noel 234–5
Christ, Jesus 76, 100, 103, 104, 109, 112, 134, 138, 198, 203–5, 219, 223, 239, 241, 244–5
Christendom, Kierkegaard's attack upon 4–5, 109, 197–8
Christian readings of *Fear and Trembling* 39, 196–207, 237–50

Climacus, Johannes 21–2, 55, 70, 127, 136, 149, 193, 197, 202, 221–2, 243, 254
Clytemnestra 117, 122
Conant, James 221
concealment 7, 11, 25, 31, 47, 79, 86, 117, 119–45, 231
Conway, Daniel W. 143–4, 145, 221–3, 233, 235, 236, 237, 241
courage 36–7, 41, 44, 45, 47, 56–7, 155, 159, 176, 179, 192–4, 195, 213, 216, 217, 231–2
Cross, Andrew 73–87, 221–37, 241, 242, 243

Davenport, John 71–3, 78, 146, 172, 174–5, 176, 178, 182, 183–7, 190, 192, 195–6, 198, 204, 206–7, 212, 215, 217
de Beauvoir, Simone 148, 149, 208
Deer Park, the 55
Deleuze, Gilles 144
Delphic bridegroom, the 124–7, 139
demonic, the 123, 129–31, 134–5, 201
Derrida, Jacques 171–3
Descartes, René 20–22
despair 39, 69–70, 71–2, 73, 80, 82, 149, 178, 180, 190, 217
disclosure *see* concealment
divine command ethics 96–7, 160–4, 175, 205–6
doubt 21–3, 36–7, 136–8
Duncan, Elmer 157–8

Eiríksson, Magnús 61–2, 83
engagement, Kierkegaard's *see* Olsen, Regine
'eschatological trust' [Davenport] 59, 72, 147, 175–96, 204
ethical, the 8, 56, chapters 4, 5 and 6, *passim*, 226, 227, 236, 246–7, 253 *see also* 'teleological suspension of the ethical'
Evans, C. Stephen 10, 61–2, 109, 117, 160–4, 174, 190, 199, 210, 216, 235, 250

exception, Abraham as 89, 90–2, 96, 109
exemplarity, Abraham's 11, 14, 15, 32, 34, 41, 43, 46, 57, 82, 102–4, 132, 133, 138, 151, 157, 158, 169, 175, 187, 189, 193–4, 216, 221, 222, 226–7, 228, 232, 235, 244

faith: contrasted with 'worldly understanding' 34; as 'double movement' 46, 47, 50, 57, 68; and infinite resignation chapter 3 *passim*; Johannes de Silentio as outside 46, 55, 58–59, 61–62, 161,198, chapter 7 *passim*; knight of 25, 34, 36, 42, 45, 47–50, 53–7, 61–5, 68, 73, 79–81, 108, 113, 160, 165, 167, 177, 187, 194, 215, 233, 238 *see also* infinite resignation; psychology of 156
Faust 136–9
Fichte, Johann Gottlieb 92–3, 95
finitude / finite, the 45, 47–50, 51–5, 57, 61, 65, 67, 72–5, 133, 178, 194
'frogs in life's swamp', the 50, 179

Gellman, Jerome 159, 161, 174, 209–10
gift, divine 45, 47, 49, 56, 83, 132–3, 169, 187, 206, 213, 227, 247
Gill, Jerry 10
Gloucester, Duke of (Richard III) 135–6
'going further' 22–3, 25, 37, 43–4, 47, 123, 142, 145, 155, 222, 232
Gouwens, David J. 228
grace 76–7, 80, 196–200, 202, 205, 218, 227
Green, Ronald M. 131–2, 153–61, 173–4, 196, 197, 200–3, 205–6, 217, 218, 246
Guattari, Félix 144

Hackel, Manuela 150
Hagar 11–12
Hall, Ronald L. 65–71
Hamann, Johann Georg 152, 220
Hannay, Alastair 6, 7, 39, 83, 101, 117, 154, 169–70, 176, 181, 182

INDEX 267

Hanson, Jeffrey 150, 245–8, 252, 253
Hebrews [biblical text] 14, 86, 165, 253
Hegel, G. W. F. / Hegelianism 6, 15, 22–3, 38, 42–4, 82, 84–5, 89, 92–6, 98–105, 108–9, 111, 115–6, 117, 121, 140, 142, 155, 157, 158–60, 168, 170, 174–5, 201, 207, 246–7
Heraclitus 145, 238
Hong, Howard V. and Edna H. 2, 145
hope, 31, 34–5, 59, 61, 63, 71–2, 76, 80, 85, 133, 143, 154, 164, 175–196, 204, 210, 212, 213, 214, 215, 216, 245
see also 'radical hope' [Lear]
Howland, Jacob 38, 175
humility 56, 82, 128, 134, 180, 192, 194–6

imaginative identification 24, 32, 35, 43, 45, 125, 228–9, 231, 236, 237, 250
imitation 157, 223–37
indirect communication 8–11, 240
individual, the 53, chapters 4 and 5 *passim*, 158–9, 186, 201
infinite resignation 16, 34–5 chapter 3 *passim*, 104, 108, 132, 156, 178, 183, 215, 231, 237; 'Beowulfian' 72, 183; 'elegaic' 72, 78
Inwood, Michael 95, 103
Iphigenia 104–6, 117, 122, 144, 158
Irina, Nicolae 148, 208
irony 10, 141, 238–9, 242
Isayev, Sergey Aleksandrovich 147
Ishmael 11, 12, 18
Islam 14, 18, 19, 164

James [biblical text] 14, 247, 253
Jephthah 105–6
joy 28, 31, 35, 45–7, 54–6, 60–3, 74, 80, 84, 133, 181, 190
Judaism 18, 19, 98, 164
Judge William 84, 85, 101, 120, 127, 131
Julian of Norwich 187, 217

Kafka, Franz 147–9, 208
Kangas, David 247

Kant, Immanuel 29, 89, 90–3, 96, 98, 110, 117, 157–8, 164, 168, 174, 218
Kierkegaard, Michael Pedersen 3
Kierkegaard, Søren: life and works 2–5; writings of: *The Concept of Anxiety* 4, 39; *The Concept of Irony* 3, 239; 'The Expectancy of Faith' 83, 145, 175, 176–82; *Concluding Unscientific Postscript* 2, 4, 9, 10, 21, 55, 68, 70, 120, 136, 202, 221, 222, 251; *Either/Or* 4, 85, 86, 101, 121, 221; *Johannes Climacus* 22, 136, 145; *Point of View, The* 8; *Practice in Christianity* 4, 223; *Sickness Unto Death, The* 2, 4, 39, 69, 178, 250; *Two Ages* 17, 228, 234; *Works of Love* 2, 4, 162, 176, 180, 181, 186, 211, 213, 250
King, Martin Luther Jr. 147
knight of infinite resignation *see* infinite resignation
knight of faith *see* faith: knight of
Krishek, Sharon 85, 132–3, 144, 145, 191, 215

lad and princess, the 50–5, chapter 3 *passim*
language 29, 89, 94–6, 114, 120, 123, 141–2, 241–5
Lear, Jonathan 72, 176, 187–8, 190, 192–3, 216
Levenson, Jon D. 18, 19, 164
Levinas, Emmanuel 150–2, 171, 208
love 13, 26, 27, 29, 30, 33, 34, 40, 42, 45, 50–4, 60–4, 70, 72, 74, 89, 91, 105, 106, 113, 116, 121, 126–7, 129–30, 132–3, 134–6, 156, 160–4, 172, 174–5, 179, 181, 183, 184, 186–7, 192, 196, 198, 199, 204–5, 212, 213, 224, 228, 248
Lukács, György 147, 150
Lund, Henrik 5
Luke, gospel of 109, 112, 114, 197, 239
Luther, Martin 39, 85, 181
Løgstrup, Knud Ejler 87

Mackey, Louis 196–7
Macquarrie, John 191–2
Malantschuk, Gregor 154, 209
Marcel, Gabriel 147
Martensen, Hans Lassen 22–3, 38, 137, 145
Mary [mother of Jesus] 109, 114
mediation 99–103
Meinung [Hegel] 94–6, 102, 111, 112, 140
merman, the *see* Agnete
Mjaaland, Marius Timmann 171, 173
Mooney, Edward F. 9, 38, 52, 59–65, 156, 159, 164–71, 174, 212, 215, 246
Moralität [Hegel] 92–5
moral perception 229, 235, 242
Mulhall, Stephen 132, 197, 203–6, 221, 237–50
Munch, Edvard 147
Mynster, Jakob Peter 5, 22

Nagy, Andras 147
Nietzsche, Friedrich 32, 151
nihilism 32, 34
Nussbaum, Martha 68, 82–3, 168, 226, 228, 229–37, 242, 244

Olsen, Regine 2, 3, 5–7, 18, 38, 67, 125, 130, 144, 153–5, 206, 212, 218
O'Neill, Onora 92, 225, 234
Outka, Gene 203

paradox, faith as 26, 43, 44, 50, 56, 67, 69, 88–9, 99–100, 102, 108–9, 111–5, 120–1, 123, 127, 131–2, 135–9, 142, 197, 201, 232
particular *see* individual
Patočka, Jan 171
Pattison, George 39, 55, 210, 212
Paul, St. 14, 39, 82, 133, 182, 200
Percy, Walker 148
Perkins, Robert L. 1
Phillips, D. Z. 117, 234
Plenty Coups, *see* 'radical hope' [Lear]

preacher 36, 37, 41–2, 112, 155, 197, 239–40
privacy *see* language
pseudonymity 8–11, 58, chapter 7 *passim*

'radical hope' [Lear] 72, 187–96, 210, 216
receptivity 165, 169–71
reliability, Johannes de Silentio's 10, 33, 58, 143, chapter 7 *passim*
repentance 98, 128–34, 201, 203, 205
resignation, infinite *see* infinite resignation
resoluteness, Abraham's 36, 73, 77–8
responsibility 171–3
Richard III *see* Gloucester
righteousness, Abraham's 14, 82, 133, 196
Romans [biblical text] 14, 82, 133, 182, 213
Rudd, Anthony 173, 254

Sarah, wife of Abraham 12–3, 25, 27–8, 34–5, 109, 119
Sarah and Tobias 124, 134–6, 139
Sartre, Jean-Paul 149, 150, 165, 208, 211
Schlegel, Fritz 5
silence 10, 11, 13, 16, 25, 31, 115, 119–42, 144, 150, 171, 180, 200, 213
sin 12, 28–30, 56, 98, 131–4, 138, 196–203, 205, 218, 232
Sittlichkeit [Hegel] 92–4, 101, 109, 116, 143, 163
Socrates 101, 140–1, 145, 238–9
Stewart, Jon 22, 38, 93
'sub-Abrahams' 24, 25–32, 38, 56, 79, 160, 166, 175, 190, 193, 230, 237, 240

Tarquin the Proud 152–3, 241
Taylor, Mark C. 120, 129–30
'teleological suspension of the ethical' 16, chapter 4 *passim*, 131, chapter 6 *passim*

temptation 29, 68–70, 82, 98, 99, 107–8, 113, 120, 122, 177
'Theophilus Nicolaus', *see* Eiríksson, Magnús
Tietjen, Mark 49, 254
tragic dilemmas 165–6
'tragic hero', the 29, 35, 36, 43, 45, 73, 83, 86, 98, 104–10, 113, 115, 120, 122–3, 127, 139–40, 158, 165–6, 173, 177, 195, 215, 231, 238, 240
trust 21, 25, 33–4, 54, 75, 78–82, 128–33, 143, 146, 161, 163–4, 167, 180–96, 204, 227, 246, 248; 'eschatological' *see* 'eschatological trust'

universal, the 30, 67, chapters 4, 5 and 6 *passim*, 246, 253

virtue(s) 94, 107, 117, 159, 165, 170–1, 193
Vlastos, Gregory 141

weaning 19, 25, 27–8, 30–1
Westphal, Merold 115, 117, 118, 142, 174, 191, 196, 213, 214, 215, 254
Whittaker, John 199
Williams, Bernard 168
Williams, Linda 27, 39
Winch, Peter 225
Wittgenstein, Ludwig 148, 225
'worldly understanding' 34–5, 74–5, 114